Redeeming the Six Arts

A Christian Approach to Chinese Classical Education

REDEEMING THE SIX ARTS

A Christian Approach to Chinese Classical Education

BRENT PINKALL

Foreword by Dr. Christopher Perrin

Redeeming the Six Arts: A Christian Approach to Chinese Classical Education
by Brent Pinkall

Published by Roman Roads Press
Moscow, Idaho
info@romanroadspress.com | romanroadspress.com

ISBN: 978-1-944482-69-5

General Editor: Daniel Foucachon
Editor: Carissa Hale
Cover Design by Joey Nance
Interior Layout by Carissa Hale

Also available in Chinese:

救赎六艺
中国古典教育向基督教古典教育的回归
〔美〕丁家威 (Brent Pinkall) 著
蔡业盛等 译

Editions Available:
ISBN: 978-1-944482-69-5 (English Edition, Paperback)
ISBN: 978-1-944482-70-1 (Chinese Edition, Paperback)

Version 1.0.0 • September 2022

ENDORSEMENTS

"Brent Pinkall's fine book marks an important step forward for the Classical and Christian education movement. We know that the gospel transformed the Greek- and Latin-speaking cultures of the Mediterranean region, giving rise to the educational tradition of the Christian West, which we celebrate. Important as this story is, it is not the only story worth telling. Christian education at its best is far greater than western Christendom, and even Homer nods. Pinkall reminds us that Chinese culture, too, bears the indelible stamp of the God in whom we live and are moved and have our being. May this book inspire a gospel transformation in the Chinese tradition of learning, a tradition that will one day fortify a Chinese Christendom with intellectual backbone. Indeed, the kingdom of God is neither Greek nor Roman; it is good news for those from every nation, from all tribes, peoples, and languages, who will stand before the throne and before the Lamb."

Christopher Schlect, Ph.D.

Fellow of History at New Saint Andrews College; contributing author of the *Omnibus* series (Veritas Press) and *Repairing the Ruins: The Classical and Christian Challenge to Modern Education* (Canon Press)

"In reading this book, I was again struck by the apt saying that 'all truth is God's truth.' In *Redeeming the Six Arts*, Brent presents a short, but helpful history of China, especially emphasizing how education was viewed and conducted in the various dynasties. Again and again, the similarity with the Western development and practice we call 'classical education' is almost startling! The essential reality is that each culture has a classical period that was uniquely formative to all that followed. Here are just a few of the common, classical aspects the East and West share:

- Wisdom and virtue are two of the highest goals for any educated person.

- There are specific, identified 'liberal arts'—six in Chinese education, seven in Greco-Roman education.

- Both base quality education on a limited number of ancient texts, written by people widely recognized across generations as great thinkers.

- Both also recognize and study their unique foundational ancient languages, from which most other dialects come.

- These ancient texts and languages form the basis of a strong and widely used curriculum which lasts for centuries in the respective cultures.

- The pedagogy of instruction, well-formulated in John Milton Gregory's 1886 book, *The Seven Laws of Teaching*, is predated by (but very similar to) the Chinese use of six 'laws' or best practices for instruction.

- Finally, for my purpose here, the frames (i.e. age-related characteristics, aptitudes, and qualities) of the students are to be carefully considered. Instruction should 'cut with the grain' of the students' natural abilities, which change as the student matures.

Brent does an excellent job pointing out how Christ and His Word fulfill the ultimate purpose of both classical traditions—that is, to make a truly wise and virtuous man. In fact, without the acknowledgment of Christ as the creator and sustainer of all that can be known, all 'education' is an exercise in futility, as Ecclesiastes points out.

This book, along with other essential books on classical Christian education (e.g. *Recovering the Lost Tools of Learning* and *The Case for Classical, Christian Education*—both written by Doug Wilson, and *The Seven Laws of Teaching*, by Gregory) have the great potential to bless and guide the formation of uniquely Chinese, classical Christian schools. May God the Father be pleased to raise up many Chinese Christians to bring this gift to generations to come!"

Tom Garfield

Logos School Superintendent, 1981–2016; founding board member of the Association of Classical and Christian Schools (ACCS) for 25 years; contributing author of *Repairing the Ruins: The Classical and Christian Challenge to Modern Education* (Canon Press)

CONTENTS

Foreword *by Christopher Perrin*   xi

Introduction   xix

PART ONE:

A BRIEF HISTORY OF
CHINESE CLASSICAL EDUCATION

The Dynasties of China   2

Chapter 1: Shang Dynasty to Eastern Zhou Dynasty
(1600–256 BC)   3

Chapter 2: Qin Dynasty to Tang Dynasty
(221 BC–907 AD)   37

Chapter 3: Song Dynasty to Qing Dynasty
(960–1912 AD)   59

PART TWO:

REDEEMING THE SIX ARTS

Chapter 4: Christian Foundations and the Western
Tradition   87

Chapter 5: The Necessity of Chinese Roots   99

Chapter 6: A Christian Approach to Chinese
Classical Education   117

Chapter 7: Rites and Music (礼乐)   143

Chapter 8: Script and Calculation (书数)   165

Chapter 9: Archery and Charioteering (射御)   203

Chapter 10: Obstacles to Classical Christian
Education in China: Pride, Paganism, and Politics   223

Chapter 11: Conclusion   261

Glossary   265

Notes   273

Bibliography   329

FOREWORD

by Christopher Perrin

I n America, we have been undergoing a renewal of classical Christian education for about the past 30 years. It can rightly be said to be a renewal, as we are not seeking to do something original that has never been done before, but rather to make present or "new" what has existed and blessed many for centuries. The traditional goal of a classical Christian education is wisdom, virtue, and eloquence formed in a soul that has been nurtured on truth, goodness, and beauty. For the last 100 years, however, modern education in America has not cultivated very much wisdom, virtue, or eloquence.

Therefore, we look to the past to revivify and bless the present. What we are doing as educators is much like what artists and musicians do. To find our own voice, we don't seek to sing or play while purposefully ignoring those who have composed and sung before us. Those who try this almost always find that either 1) their new voice turns out not to be very beautiful, or 2) if their voice is beautiful it has already been done before. In other words, it is supremely difficult, if not impossible, to compose a song that will be completely original and also beautiful.

The great musicians and artists always find their "voice" by studying the traditions that went before them. Do you want to find your own style and also be compelling and beautiful? Study the masters. As we study the masters, we don't become identical to them. We become like them, but we also bring our own temperament, gifts, background, and proclivities to our study such that by studying the masters, we find our own true self.

Jesus says as much in Luke 6:40: "A student after he has been fully-trained, will be like his master." Consider the disciples of Jesus. They had all followed Him, they had all studied with Jesus as their master—they all became like Jesus. In fact, to be called "Christian" meant to be called a "Christ-one." People saw Jesus in the disciples—they were like Him, they were Christ-ones.

Yet consider how different the disciples were from one another. Consider the difference between Peter, always speaking and acting boldly (sometimes rashly), and John, the disciple who reclines on Jesus's breast during the last supper. The disciples were all like their master and yet different from one another.

If the renewal of classical Christian education means that we study the masters that have gone before us, then it means that no matter how carefully we study them, we still do something new. This has in fact been the history of classical Christian education. It has always involved the study of some persisting themes like the study of language, art, music, beauty, mathematics, and virtue that is contained in the best literature, history, and poetry. The way these themes have been embodied, ordered, sequenced, and emphasized has varied with successive generations and centuries. In other words, these great, classical ideas have taken on new forms while retaining the same content. This has been true wherever classical Christian education has been planted—it flourishes, and as it flourishes, it diversifies.

Brent Pinkall has used the analogy of a flourishing garden to describe classical Christian education in China. He has picked a rich, traditional metaphor for describing what education should be. Yes, children are like flowers or trees that we cultivate, water, and prune so that they bear fruit—the fruit of wisdom, virtue, and eloquence. We cultivate these trees or flowers with truth, goodness, and beauty. As we all know, however, China has its own famous trees and flowers, native to its soil. China has the China fir and the Yunnan cypress; America has its redwoods and the great American oak.

There are beautiful trees in China and in America—they differ in some ways, but they are all recognized as trees and recognized as beautiful. The same will be true as China renews classical Christian education. The renewed classical Christian education in China will be similar to the renewed classical Christian education in America, but also different in some important ways. Chinese classical education will grow like a China fir; American classical education will grow as an American oak.

They will be similar because both Chinese and American classical education will be renewing and embodying the same ideas—truth, goodness, beauty. Anything that is true, good, or beautiful rightfully comes from and belongs to God, no matter who discovers it and no matter how it is discovered. Plato said many true things; Confucius said many true things—yet they all rightfully belong to God.

Another profound reason why both Chinese and American education will be similar is because both countries will be renewing classical *Christian* education. While Plato and Confucius discovered and reported much that is true, we find the fullness of truth in Jesus Christ Who is the Way, the Truth, and the Life. The incarnation of Jesus Christ, and His life, ministry, death, and resurrection, reveal to us the fullness of truth and enable us to unite and better understand all truths acknowledged before and after Him. Therefore, Plato and Confucius find their fulfillment in Jesus. Yes, Jesus will correct many of the things that Plato and Confucius said that were in error—but He will also ratify and confirm the true things they have said and unite those true things with Himself Who is the Truth and the Author of all that is true. We can say the same for whatever is good and beautiful, for He is the Author of all that is good and beautiful.

There are many great books that embody much that is true and good, and some of them were written by non-Christians. We can study these profitably though carefully. According to Basil, we should be like the honey bee who flies from flower to flower with discrimination, choosing some flowers to gather pollen from but rejecting others. Naturally, we will read generously from Christian authors from the east, west, south, and north. Of course, we study the Scriptures most amply and regularly. The collection of books that Chinese students read and that American students read will have many similarities (we will all read Augustine), but there will be differences as well. The book lists will vary (though with many shared texts), but the study of truth will be the same. Our grounding in the study of Scripture will make our reading and choice of books careful and discriminating, enabling us to discern truth from error in whatever books we study.

Let me change the analogy once more. Wherever Christ comes, He brings redemption. He takes whatever is true and good in a culture and puts them like jewels in His own crown so that the good of the culture is extolled and magnified when united to Jesus. Plato and Confucius found and saw many good things—many jewels—but these jewels were not their own. They belonged to a king they had not yet met. Some of the sayings of Plato and Confucius cannot be placed in the crown of Christ, but those sayings that are true and good should be seen as honoring Christ the King and rightly belonging to Him.

Thus, Augustine can say of Plato and other Greek philosophers:

> Moreover, if those who are called philosophers, and especially the Platonists, have said aught that is true and in harmony with our faith, we are not only not to shrink from it, but to claim it for our own use from those who have unlawful possession of it. For, as the Egyptians had not only the idols and heavy burdens which the people of Israel hated and fled from, but also vessels and ornaments of gold and silver, and garments, which the same people when going out of Egypt appropriated to themselves, designing them for

a better use, not doing this on their own authority, but by the command of God, the Egyptians themselves, in their ignorance, providing them with things which they themselves were not making a good use of; in the same way all branches of heathen learning have not only false and superstitious fancies and heavy burdens of unnecessary toil, which every one of us, when going out under the leadership of Christ from the fellowship of the heathen, ought to abhor and avoid; but they contain also liberal instruction which is better adapted to the use of the truth, and some most excellent precepts of morality; and some truths in regard even to the worship of the One God are found among them. Now these are, so to speak, their gold and silver, which they did not create themselves, but dug out of the mines of God's providence which are everywhere scattered abroad, and are perversely and unlawfully prostituting to the worship of devils. These, therefore, the Christian, when he separates himself in spirit from the miserable fellowship of these men, ought to take away from them, and to devote to their proper use in preaching the gospel. Their garments, also—that is, human institutions such as are adapted to that intercourse with men which is indispensable in this life—we must take and turn to a Christian use.[1]

Augustine's metaphor of "refashioning Egyptian gold" became the way that the church (with a few exceptions) understood how to relate to cultures not under its influence. Jesus will be glorified and exalted as He reclaims the jewels from our cultures and histories for His own crown. In so doing, the best of both Chinese and Western cultures will be lifted up and drawn together in the crown of Jesus.

The Greeks (and the Romans following them) discovered much that was true and good. They discovered the way that language was structured and the way it could be taught well (grammar); they (particularly Aristotle) observed the way that reason functions (logic); and they (particularly Aristotle, Quintilian, and Cicero) discovered how language could be used with beauty, imagination, and eloquence to delight, instruct, and move others (rhetoric). They observed that human virtue was real and desirable and that vices should be avoided. These and other discoveries of the Greeks were human discoveries, not merely Greek discoveries. The church, upon encountering these jewels, reclaimed them for the church and the glory of Christ, and they now belong to us all.

Is this not true of China as well? What of its treasure? Truth, goodness, and beauty are not unknown to Chinese culture. The Greeks helped gather the liberal arts of grammar, logic, rhetoric, arithmetic, geometry, music, and astronomy. Has not China also gathered arts that contain the true, good, and beautiful? Has it not studied music? Has it not studied mathematics and astronomy? Has it not studied the "good life"? The six arts, like the seven liberal arts, are doorways leading to truth.

A great culture like China has its own treasury of jewels to offer to Christ's crown. What's more, the world (not only China) will be blessed as these jewels are reclaimed and recovered. I note just one contemporary American example. Steve Jobs, the founder of Apple, reported that his favorite college class was calligraphy. Anyone who uses Apple products will note the way beautiful scripts and fonts (as well as beauty in general) have been woven into the design of those products. Calligraphy (part of *shu*, one of the six arts of China) has had a remarkable impact on an American technological company.

The prospect of the Chinese renewal of classical Christian education will, I believe, bless the world. China has the advantage of renewing education with the knowledge of the seven liberal arts (long known in China and being renewed today) and with the prospect of renewing its own six arts. Brent Pinkall believes the time is ripe for the blossoming of these six arts under the cultivating care of Christian educators. Would not such a blossoming bless China and the world and bring glory to God? And what might the meeting of the seven arts and the six arts mean? What might such a confluence of rivers produce? To extend our garden metaphor, what lovely tree might we see when a branch from the West and a branch from the East are grafted into the same tree? What fruit will the world then enjoy?

Christopher Perrin, M.Div., Ph.D.

Co-founder and CEO of Classical Academic Press;
vice chair of the Society for Classical Learning;
executive director of the Alcuin Fellowship; author of
An Introduction to Classical Education: A Guide for Parents
(Classical Academic Press)

INTRODUCTION

For in him all the fullness of God was pleased to dwell, and through him to reconcile to himself all things . . .

-Colossians 1:19–20

The early church faced many formidable challenges during the first and second centuries. Within the church, dangerous heretics twisted fundamental doctrines of the faith, threatening to lead astray unsuspecting believers. Outside the church, a polytheistic society accused Christians of blaspheming the gods long revered by their ancestors. Even more troubling, a hostile government accused them of treason for pledging allegiance to a Lord other than Caesar.

When we think of the trials confronting the early church, these are the ones that typically come to mind. But Christians at the time faced another challenge, one which we often overlook but which was no less formidable—namely, the problem of education. New converts were charged with raising up their children in the nurture and admonition of the Lord, but they possessed no Christian literature besides the Holy Scriptures and a few scattered writings by Christian leaders. They themselves had received an education rooted in classical literature, written by the great poets, philosophers, and historians of the past—men such as Homer and Virgil, Plato and Aristotle, Herodotus and Livy. Although these authors were widely regarded as men of great wisdom and virtue, they were still pagan. Consequently, their writings contained much that conflicted with Christian teaching. Should Christians pass on to their children this long tradition of learning that gave birth to the culture in which they lived but which contained no little error, or should they reject it outright and only teach literature written by Christians?

Some church fathers advocated for the latter. The second-century apologist Tertullian famously quipped, "What has Athens to do with Jerusalem?",[1] implying the answer: "Nothing." Others, however, argued that although pagan learning contains much error, it also contains gems of wisdom which Christians can mine and appropriate for godly purposes. Gregory likened this to the Israelites sharpening their knives in the camp of the Philistines.[2] Augustine likened it to plundering the Egyptians.[3] These men believed that all the riches of wisdom and knowledge are hidden in Christ (Col. 2:3). He is the sun in Whose light we are able to see anything. And yet pagans are not blind. Before the dawn of Christian civilization, the world sat in darkness but a moon hovered over Athens. Pagan philosophers could see, however dimly, for what is moonlight but sunlight at second hand?[4]

As Christians we have access to the infallible Word that far surpasses the speculative philosophy of the Greeks. And yet this does not render Greek philosophy useless. Pagan philosophy may be fallible, but this does not necessarily mean it is false. Greek culture was built by men made in the image of God. We should therefore expect to find traces of Him in their temples and courts, in their literature and laws. Even the Apostle enjoyed an occasional moonlit stroll through the Acropolis.[5]

The early church eventually came to a consensus on these matters and developed a tradition of learning that has come to be known in our day as "classical Christian education" or "Christian classical education." Of course, throughout most of Western history it was simply called "education." This tradition entails inquiring of both our pagan and Christian fathers, eavesdropping on the "great conversations" of men before us. It was passed down through generations of Christians for nearly two thousand years until education reforms in the nineteenth and twentieth centuries largely supplanted it with more "modern" approaches to education. As a result, few Christians in the West today have ever read Aristotle or Augustine. Few know the meaning of *Credo ut intelligam.*

Some, however, have resisted this trend. More and more Christians are beginning to rediscover their long-forgotten heritage. We are seeing in the twenty-first century the firstfruits of an undeniable renaissance of classical education. Moreover, this renaissance is not limited to the Western world. Christians in China are also beginning to look to the classical Christian tradition for an alternative to secular government schools. But as they mine the riches of this inheritance, a question naturally arises: What form should classical Christian education take in an Eastern context?

Christians in the West have almost unanimously defined classical Christian education as a Western tradition rooted in the study of Western literature and the seven liberal arts. "Classical educators take responsibility for the Western tradition."[6] "The classical method was born in ancient Greece and Rome."[7] "It is a long tradition of education that has emphasized . . . the study of the liberal arts and the great books."[8] "The Classical education movement advocates a form of education based in the traditions of Western culture."[9] If Chinese Christians inquire of contemporary resources on classical Christian education, they will inevitably conclude that faithfulness to the tradition requires them to teach Western literature and the seven liberal arts. I believe this is mistaken.

Classical Christian education *per se* is not a curriculum of specific texts, languages, or subjects. It is an *approach* that seeks wisdom by inquiring of one's own fathers. It is obedience to the Fifth Commandment: "Honor thy father and thy mother." For Christians in the West, this amounts to teaching the arts and literature emphasized by our European ancestors. Christians in China, however, come from a different bloodline. Their *Christian* fathers are the same as ours, but their *cultural* fathers are different. Their curriculum, therefore, must also be different.

Christ does not erase our cultural identities. He redeems them. The saints in Heaven are not worshiping Him only in Latin. They are singing in many tongues (Rev. 7:9).[10] While Chinese Christan schools can learn much from the classical tradition promoted by their Christian forbears in the West, they should not study this tradition in order to become Western, Jesus did not come to make the world Western. He came to make it Christian.

If the Chinese church embraces their Christian identity, then they must also embrace their ethnic identity. Jesus had strong words to say to those who renounce their earthly fathers under the pretense of serving their Heavenly Father:

> God commanded, "Honor your father and your mother," and, "Whoever reviles father or mother must surely die." But you say, "If anyone tells his father or his mother, 'What you would have gained from me is given to God,' he need not honor his father." So for the sake of your tradition you have made void the word of God. You hypocrites!" (Matt. 15:4–7)[11]

Chinese Christians must honor their Chinese fathers. They must engage with their own culture and their own past. When they do, they will discover that the moon did not only rise over Athens. It swept the skies over Chang'an. It illumined the hills of Hebei and the valleys of Sichuan. The Chinese of old saw something, and they were not silent.

PART ONE:

A BRIEF HISTORY OF CHINESE CLASSICAL EDUCATION

Hear, my son, your father's instruction, and forsake not your mother's teaching.

-Proverbs 1:8

THE DYNASTIES OF CHINA

Xia Dynasty (2070–1600 BC)

Shang Dynasty (1600–1046 BC)

Western Zhou Dynasty (1046–771 BC)

Eastern Zhou Dynasty (771–256 BC)

Qin Dynasty (221–206 BC)

Han Dynasty (206 BC–220 AD)

Period of Disunity (220–589)

Sui and Tang Dynasties (589–907)

Song Dynasty (960–1279)

Yuan Dynasty (1271–1368)

Ming Dynasty (1368–1644)

Qing Dynasty (1644–1912)

CHAPTER 1

Shang Dynasty to Eastern Zhou Dynasty
(1600–256 BC)

Shang Dynasty (1600–1046 BC)

Some of the earliest Chinese legends speak of the existence of schools. Almost nothing is known about these schools except that they were established by the government in order to raise up qualified officials. By the time of the Shang dynasty, there were two main schools located at the capital—the *youxue* (右学) or "west school" for older boys, and the *zuoxue* (左学) or "east school" for younger boys. These terms were later replaced in the Zhou dynasty with *daxue* (大学) or "upper school" and *xiaoxue* (小学) or "lower school"—terms which are still used in China today. Children typically entered the lower school at the age of eight[1] and the upper school at the age of fifteen, where they studied until their early twenties.[2]

The curriculum of these schools was based on the six arts (*liuyi* 六艺). The *Rites of Zhou* (*Zhouli* 周礼), compiled during the Han dynasty (206 BC–220 AD), contains the earliest account of the six arts curriculum. Although it describes education during the Zhou dynasty, records indicate that Shang education was based on these same arts.[3] The *Rites of Zhou* describes six arts education as follows:

> The Bao clan has the authority to advise and admonish the king and to raise up the children of officials according to the *Dao*. Therefore, the following six arts shall be taught: First, the five rites (*li* 礼); second, the six kinds of music (*yue* 乐); third, the five techniques of archery (*she* 射); fourth, the five techniques of driving (*yu* 御; i.e. charioteering); fifth, the six scripts (*shu* 书); and sixth, the nine methods of calculation (*shu* 数).[4]

This passage first tells us that six arts education was not available to all children. It was only available to *guozi* (国子) or children of aristocrats. Other statements in the same document expand this scope a bit more, granting six arts education to all children of *shi* (士), that is those in the military class.[5] *Shi* were not only soldiers but also government officials, teachers, and scholars. The military class was also the educated class and the ruling class.[6] Six arts education, therefore, was an elitist education—the education of a *junzi* (君子) or "superior man."

This passage next tells us that the six arts must be taught "according to the *Dao*." The *Dao* is the absolute principle underlying all reality, the creative power that is the source of all things and all change.[7] It is the ultimate Way or Truth toward which we all must strive. This emphasis on the *Dao* is not specific to the Shang or Zhou dynasties but characterizes the entire span of classical education in China, as we will see. The passage then goes on to list the six arts in order of priority, with the most foundational listed first. Although rites and music are given priority here, this was only the case beginning in the Zhou dynasty. In the Shang dynasty, archery and charioteering were most foundational.

The bow and arrow were not mere instruments of warfare in ancient China.[8] They were mysterious and sacred objects—even magical. One of the earliest figures in Chinese mythology is the legendary archer Hou Yi (后羿), who defeats supernatural monsters and prevents natural disasters with his bow. Hou Yi is most famously credited with shooting down nine of the ten suns, leaving us with the one sun we see today. Fu Xi (伏羲) is one of a handful of legendary figures credited with inventing the bow. He is also credited with inventing hunting and fishing, as well as the "eight trigrams" (*bagua* 八卦) that form the basis of one of the oldest and most important philosophical books in the Chinese classical tradition, the *Book of Changes* (*Zhouyi* 周易). It is significant that Fu Xi is credited with inventing the bow rather than Chi You (蚩尤), the mythical inventor of metal weapons. Fu Xi is typically associated with the interests of literati, suggesting that the bow was valued more for its intellectual and moral benefits than its military benefits. The bow also represented man's dominion over the natural environment, which we see in Hou Yi's mastery over the natural world, as well as in the popularity of ritualized hunting expeditions.

Wang Anshi of the Song dynasty explains the significance of archery in ancient times as follows:

> When members of the aristocracy were educated in ancient times, they placed top priority on archery and chariot driving ... If a man received an injury during his life, that would put an end to it; otherwise no one ever abandoned archery or the study of it. If there was entertaining to be done, they used archery; if there were religious rites to be performed, they used archery; and if they had to make a distinction between the abilities of two members of the aristocracy, they used archery to do that, too. No one was admitted to archery unless he had been tested in ritual (*li*) and music; and no one was admitted to religious observance involving music and ritual (*li*) unless they had also been tested in archery ... When resident in the administrative centers of the state, they used archery to practice music and ritual (*li*); when abroad they used it to practice military skills. As the aristocracy engaged in this pursuit incessantly, there were many who were skilled in it.[9]

Clearly, archery is inseparable from ritual and music, and therefore we cannot understand the one apart from the others. Most scholars agree that *li* was originally some type of religious observance or ceremony. The word is commonly translated into English as "rite" or "ritual," which is an appropriate description of its early manifestations. There is no doubt that rites existed in primitive societies long before the Shang and Xia dynasties, but their origin is greatly contested among scholars.[10] Generally speaking, *li* appears to originally have had a twofold purpose, namely to order society and to seek favor from ancestors and the gods.[11] It included ceremonies like weddings and funerals, as well as sacrificial rites. In the *Record of Rites*, we are told that the ancients created *li* to establish standards for marriage that would distinguish men from beasts:

> But if (men were as) beasts (*qinshou*), and without (the principle of) propriety (*li*), father and son might have the same mate. Therefore, when the sages arose, they framed the rules of propriety (*li*) in order to teach men, and cause them, by their possession of them, to make a distinction between themselves and brutes (*qinshou*).[12]

The *Zuo Tradition* (*Zuozhuan* 左传) suggests *li* originated with rules regarding filial piety.[13] These suggestions, as well as most others, all demonstrate a desire to respect some sort of cosmic order. Xu Shen (许慎, 58–149 AD), in his ancient dictionary *Shuowen Jiezi*, directly draws the connection between performing *li* and pleasing the gods: "When *li* is performed, the gods are served and blessing comes."[14] He also points out that the traditional character for *li* (禮) contains the character *li* (豊), which is a vessel used for presenting offerings to the gods.

In the Shang dynasty and the Xia dynasty before it, rites were not well-developed as an independent discipline.[15] They were usually studied as an aspect of music. The two are often considered one entity in classical Chinese writings (i.e. "*liyue*" 礼乐). Music included vocal and instrumental music, as well as dance. Poetry was also closely related. Music, like ritual, served a dual purpose. It was both an aid in religious worship as well as a tool for ordering society, particularly through shaping one's emotions and sentiments:

> The ancient kings, in their institution of rites and music, did not seek how fully they could satisfy the desires of the appetite and of the ears and eyes; but they intended to teach the people to regulate their likings and dislikings, and to bring them back to the normal course of humanity.[16]

Specific forms of music and ritual were not decided arbitrarily but were designed in imitation of nature:

> Music is (an echo of) the harmony between heaven and earth; rites reflect the orderly distinctions (in the operations of) heaven and earth. From that harmony all things receive their being; to those orderly distinctions they owe the differences between them.[17]

The relationship between the notes in their music reflected relationships between people. "They made the underlying principles of the relations between the near and distant relatives, the noble and mean, the old and young, males and females, all to appear manifestly in the music."[18] As the people performed this music and practiced these rituals, their habits and sentiments were gradually brought into conformity with natural order:

> Hence in the fine and distinct notes we have an image of heaven; in the ample and grand, an image of earth; in their beginning and ending, an image of the four seasons; in the wheelings and revolutions (of the pantomimes), an image of the wind and rain. (The five

notes, like) the five colors, form a complete and elegant whole, without any confusion. (The eight instruments of different materials, like) the eight winds, follow the musical accords, without any irregular deviation. The lengths of all the different notes have their definite measurements, without any uncertainty. The small and the great complete one another. The end leads on to the beginning, and the beginning to the end. The key notes and those harmonizing with them, the sharp and the bass, succeed one another in their regular order. Therefore, when the music has full course, the different relations are clearly defined by it; the perceptions of the ears and eyes become sharp and distinct; the action of the blood and physical energies is harmonious and calm; (bad) influences are removed, and manners changed; and all under heaven there is entire repose.[19]

Archery, as we saw, was also closely related to rites and music. Archery rites were often formalized competitions used to select individuals for office or to determine who would offer sacrifices on behalf of the kingdom. Participants were judged not only based on their shooting accuracy but on their form. The entire process was carefully choreographed to music, requiring participants to move and shoot at appropriate musical cues. Different tunes were thought to encourage different attributes in the contestants.

Charioteering was also used in rites but appears to have been studied more for its practical benefits both in war and hunting. A chariot typically held two or three soldiers— one driver and one or two archers or spearmen. As the translation above reflects, the Chinese word we translate as "charioteering" (*yu* 御) actually means "driving." Although charioteering was a team endeavor, the study of charioteering *per se* concerned only the techniques of the driver. The "five techniques of driving" cited above are *mingheluan* (鸣和鸾) or "the motion of the carriage keeping time to the bells upon the horse"; *zhushuiqu* (逐水曲) or "driving in and out of dangers like water flowing amid rocks"; *guojunbiao* (过君表) or "passing round the outside of the princes' outer gates, making a sweep or curve"; *wujiaoqu* (午交衢) or "feats of skill in turning any way on a cross road"; and *zhuqinzuo* (逐禽左) or "driving the beast or animal hunted out on the left side."[20] If archery is concerned with mastering an inanimate object, then charioteering is concerned with mastering an animate object—an animal. By taming and training a horse, man exercises dominion over the natural world, bringing himself and the horse into conformity with natural order.

These four arts—archery, charioteering, ritual, and music—made up the core of the ancient curriculum. They are sometimes referred to as the "greater arts" (*dayi* 大艺). The "lesser arts" (*xiaoyi* 小艺) played a less prominent but still important role in the ancient curriculum. Script (*shu* 书) originally referred to literacy education—both reading and writing. The term is often translated as calligraphy, but this is misleading because calligraphy suggests an aesthetic purpose. The Chinese did not begin valuing script for its aesthetic beauty until the late Han dynasty. During the Shang dynasty, script was taught entirely for its literary value, primarily to equip future rulers to fulfill their administrative duties.

Shu (数) is often translated into English as mathematics, but its scope in the six arts curriculum was traditionally much broader. It is better understood as calculation. Calculation included subjects like arithmetic, geometry, surveying, geography, and astronomy. This knowledge aided in basic administrative duties, military strategy, and calendar making. Although calculation was studied primarily for practical purposes, like the other arts it also had religious benefits. For example, the "eight trigrams" used in divination relied heavily upon mathematics and astronomy.[21]

It is not clear exactly how or at what age the six arts were taught in school during this time. The *Pattern of the Family* (*Neize* 内则) in the *Record of Rites* (*Liji* 礼记) says students began studying calculation at age six, script and rites at age ten, music at age thirteen, and archery and charioteering when they were "mature" (fifteen or older), meaning the latter two were not taught until the upper school.[22] Other sources, however, suggest that all six arts were taught in the lower school.[23] Regardless, it is clear that the lower and upper schools were one integrated curriculum. A child just beginning the lower school was receiving a "six arts" education, even if he was only studying one or two arts at the time, just as a man is said to be "building a house" even if all he has laid is one brick.

Western Zhou Dynasty (1046–771 BC)

By the Western Zhou dynasty, the six arts had developed into a relatively polished and robust curriculum. The Zhou curriculum differed from the Shang curriculum primarily in its emphasis on virtue (*de* 德). Educators believed a *junzi* should study the arts not merely for their social, religious, and administrative benefits but for their moral benefits. "When we speak of a *junzi* we intend chiefly his virtue."[24]

Virtue as an educational ideal was especially heralded by the Duke of Zhou (周公). His kingdom is described in the *Book of Documents* (*Shangshu* 尚书) as follows:

> The judicial officers ruled the people with fair punishment and taught them to reverence virtue. The glory of the king shined among all those under him, throughout the four corners of the land, and all were diligent in cultivating virtue. In this way, they enforced punishments fairly and regulated the people while encouraging them toward obedience.[25]

The Duke of Zhou believed that a *junzi* should cultivate virtue not simply for his own sake but for the sake of his people. In *Against Luxurious Ease* (*Wuyi* 无逸) and *Announcement of the Duke of Shao* (*Shaogao* 召告), the Duke of Zhou explains to King Cheng that the king's virtue determines the virtue of his people, for he is the role model that they will imitate. This emphasis can also be seen in the *Book of Poetry* (*Shijing* 诗经), the oldest collection of Chinese poems. "Follow the pattern of King Wen, and all the peoples will trust you."[26] "He secured the confidence due to a king and became a pattern of all below him."[27]

A *junzi* learns virtue primarily through music and rites. "Music cultivates one's inward being; rites cultivate one's outward being. When rites and music are combined, they manifest themselves outwardly as peacefulness and serenity, reverence and refinement."[28] We can also see music's function as cultivator of virtue in the *Canon of Shun* (*Shundian* 舜典), where the emperor describes the job of the music teacher. "The Emperor said, 'Kui, I appoint you to be in charge of music, to teach our sons, so that they may become upright and mild, generous and dignified, firm but not tyrannical, simple but not arrogant.'"[29] Poetry, which was closely related to music, had a similar function. The *Book of Poetry* contains a number of poems by the Duke of Zhou himself that admonish readers toward brotherly love and care for one's neighbor.

Whereas rites previously existed primarily as an aspect of music, in the Zhou dynasty they became a subject all their own and surpassed the other arts in importance. *Li* was now the foundation of the six arts curriculum.[30] In the Zhou dynasty, the meaning and practice of *li* extended far beyond religious ceremonies to include proper forms of behavior for nearly every domain of human life, from family to politics to education to the military. It encompassed all ethical, social, and political norms of human behavior.[31] The common English translation of "rites" is far too narrow to describe the nature of *li* from this time on. James Legge gets closest to the meaning with his translation "rules of propriety."[32] Even G. K. Chesterton is not too far off characterizing *li* as "manners."[33] For the sake of convenience, however, in this book I will continue referring to *li* as "rites." These rules of behavior were not decided arbitrarily but, like the *li* of earlier periods, attempted to imitate the cosmic order.[34] Zhou rulers viewed *li* as a kind of cultural catechism capable of instilling virtue. To give a modern-day example, a boy by nature might not be inclined to honor girls, but if he is taught from a young age to open doors for girls, this habit over time may produce in him a genuine respect for girls. Chenyang Li helpfully characterizes *li* as "cultural grammar."[35] One must study *li* in order to interact with and influence culture in a meaningful and virtuous way, just as one must study grammar in order to communicate effectively. Although *li* in itself does not constitute culture or virtue, it is the foundation of those things, just as grammar is the foundation of language. Moreover, *li* is not a static code of conduct that never changes but is rather, like grammar, a set of rules decided by society that gradually changes over time as it is passed down from generation to generation.

The more *li* was emphasized in the Zhou dynasty, the more archery was ritualized. As with rites and music, a man's archery abilities were thought to reflect his virtue. "Archery is a means to examine the extent of a person's virtue. For this reason, in ancient times the Emperor used archery to select nobles, senior officials, sheriffs, and qualified officers."[36]

Eastern Zhou Dynasty (771–256 BC)

Constant strife between rival states during the latter half of the Eastern Zhou dynasty created a fertile environment for Chinese intellectuals, who began traveling between competing states to debate the central questions of life and politics. The latter half of this dynasty, known as the Warring States Period, was arguably the most creative and intellectually diverse period of Chinese history. The many competing philosophies during this time are famously referred to as the Hundred Schools of Thought (*zhuzi baijia* 诸子百家).

As government powers eroded, states could no longer provide stable institutions of learning to their people. This led to the sudden rise of private teachers, called *ru* (儒), who began offering their services to any who wished to learn. *Ru* were usually lowly-ranked *shi*, and students would travel long distances for the opportunity to study under a master *ru*. Education became a matter of studying under a particular teacher rather than studying a particular curriculum. The most famous of these *ru* was Confucius, which is why the term later came to refer specifically to Confucian scholars.

Confucius (*Kongqiu* 孔丘 or *Kongzi* 孔子, 551–479 BC) was the first to systematically articulate the purpose and meaning of education.[37] He looked highly upon many of the educational and political ideals of the Western Zhou dynasty and described himself as a transmitter of an older tradition, "a transmitter and not a maker, believing in and loving the ancients."[38] In reality, though, he was more of a synthesizer. Occasionally he advocated for a strict return to certain early Zhou practices, but more often he expanded the original intention of Zhou philosophy and practice to include his own ideas. He did not seek to live in the past but to "study the past in order to understand the present."[39]

Confucius loved learning. He believed education was worth pursuing simply for its own sake—for the mere pleasure of knowing what is true and acting on it. "To study and at due times practice what one has studied, is this not a pleasure?"[40] He viewed learning not merely as a duty but as a delight. "Knowing something is not so good as loving it; loving it is not so good as taking joy in it."[41]

As the son of a military officer, Confucius received a six arts education.[42] But he was troubled that only children of aristocrats could experience this great pleasure. He believed all children should have access to education.[43] "In teaching there should be no distinction of classes."[44] He thought this because he believed that humans by nature are the same. "By nature, men are nearly alike; by practice, they get to be wide apart."[45] A child may be born into one class, but through education he can advance to a different class. In other words, all men should have access to education because all men have the potential to improve themselves.[*] The earlier tradition understood a *junzi* to be an ideal aristocrat, but Confucius understood a *junzi* to be an ideal human. The "superior man," he says, is not superior because

---

[*]   Immediately following this statement, however, Confucius explains that "the most intelligent (*shangzhi* 上知) and the most stupid (*xiayu* 下愚)" cannot change.

of his high social class but because he fully realizes his humanity. All men, therefore, should aspire to become a *junzi*. Confucius criticized those in his day who viewed education merely as a means of obtaining seats of power in the government. "Men of antiquity studied to improve themselves; men today study to impress others."[46] The goal of education, he says, is not to raise up qualified officials (though officials should be well-educated), but to raise up complete human beings. Teaching is not a matter of transmitting knowledge but of transforming people. "The *Dao* of Great Learning lies in making bright virtue brilliant; in making the people new; in coming to rest at the highest good."[47] As individual people are renewed, families are restored and society flourishes:

> The ancients who wished to illustrate illustrious virtue throughout the kingdom, first ordered well their own states. Wishing to order well their states, they first regulated their families. Wishing to regulate their families, they first cultivated their persons. Wishing to cultivate their persons, they first rectified their hearts. Wishing to rectify their hearts, they first sought to be sincere in their thoughts. Wishing to be sincere in their thoughts, they first extended to the utmost their knowledge. Such extension of knowledge lay in the investigation of things. Things being investigated, knowledge became complete. Their knowledge being complete, their thoughts were sincere. Their thoughts being sincere, their hearts were then rectified. Their hearts being rectified, their persons were cultivated. Their persons being cultivated, their families were regulated. Their families being regu-

lated, their states were rightly governed. Their states being rightly governed, the whole kingdom was made tranquil and happy.[48]

The final *telos* of education for Confucius is the creation of a harmonious society, but the *locus* of education is the individual. Society is transformed only through personal transformation:

> From the Son of Heaven down to the mass of the people, all must consider the cultivation of the person the root of everything besides. It cannot be, when the root is neglected, that what should spring from it will be well ordered.[49]

This focus on personal transformation has led some to suggest that Confucius was only concerned with human affairs. They call his philosophy a "secular" philosophy. This is a modern interpretation that has no basis in historical fact.[50] Although he certainly *focuses* on human affairs, his philosophy is rooted in Heaven. Confucius considers his mission of restoring culture as the will of Heaven. "With King Wen dead, is not culture (*wen*) invested here in me? . . . If Heaven does not intend this culture to be destroyed, then what can the men of Kuang do to me?"[51] Failure to accomplish this mission would displease Heaven. "Wherein I have done improperly, may Heaven reject me! may Heaven reject me!"[52] Confucius was troubled that few people had heard of him or his teachings, but he found solace in the fact that at least Heaven knew him. "The Master said, 'Alas! there is no one that knows me . . . But there is Heaven—that knows me!'"[53]

For Confucius, education is ultimately submission to the will of Heaven. "What Heaven ordains is called one's nature. To follow one's nature is called the *Dao*. Cultivating the *Dao* is called education."[54] Honoring our "Heavenly natures" (*tianxing* 天性) through personal cultivation is honoring Heaven who gave us those natures. Even though Confucius is primarily concerned with understanding people, he recognizes that we cannot understand people apart from knowing their Creator:

> Wishing to cultivate his character, [the *junzi*] may not neglect to serve his parents. In order to serve his parents, he may not neglect to acquire knowledge of men. In order to know men, he may not dispense with a knowledge of Heaven.[55]

The *Dao* of the *junzi*, therefore, begins with a proper respect both for the ancients and for Heaven. "There are three things which the *junzi* reveres. He reveres the ordinances of Heaven. He reveres great men. He reveres the words of sages."[56]

Following the *Dao* primarily entails seeking *ren* (仁). *Ren* is the all-encompassing ethical ideal that includes all desirable qualities in a man.[57] It is humanity "in its highest state of perfection."[58] In fact, it is often translated into English as "humanity." If a *junzi* is an ideal man, then *ren* is simply all the qualities that make him a *junzi*. The two words are more or less interchangeable.[59] *Ren* is primarily moral perfection involving the pursuit of virtue—an emphasis clearly based on earlier Zhou philosophy. A man of *ren* is marked by such characteristics as respectfulness, trustworthiness, and kindness,[60] but also less-obviously moral characteristics like a fondness for mountains.[61] Education for Confucius, therefore, is primarily moral education:

> If a man withdraws his mind from the love of beauty, and applies it as sincerely to the love of the virtuous; if, in serving his parents, he can exert his utmost strength; if, in serving his prince, he can devote his life; if, in his intercourse with his friends, his words are sincere—although men say that he has not learned, I will certainly say that he has.[62]

Building on a previous metaphor, if *li* is grammar then *ren* is mastery of language. Herein we see the importance of rites in the attainment of *ren*. A child who never learns grammar will never master language. "One has nothing to establish oneself on without learning *li*."[63] Virtue is impossible without it. "Respect without *li* results in futility, caution without *li* results in timidity, bravery without *li* results in disorder, and straightforwardness without *li* results in hastiness."[64] Confucius sees a society's observance of rites as an indicator of its health, just as poor grammar reflects poor language comprehension. He points to his own society's disregard of Zhou *li* as evidence of its decline and advocates for a return to Zhou *li* as the path toward restoration.

Confucius's emphasis on rites is occasionally misunderstood as a kind of blind, inflexible adherence to social rules. But in Confucian thought, *ren* is superior to *li* and restrains it. "If a man be without *ren*, what has he to do with *li*?"[65] Just as a man who has mastered a language may intentionally violate grammar rules in order to produce a desired effect on his audience, so a man of *ren* may violate *li* if righteousness (*yi* 义) requires it. Mencius gives the example of a man whose sister-in-law is drowning.[66] Although *li* prohibits him from physically touching her, in this particular case he is permitted to touch her because saving her life is more important than observing *li*. *Li* exists in order to help actualize a man's humanity—to attain *ren*, just as grammar exists in order to help a man communicate well. But when it conflicts with that end it may be violated. Shakespeare occasionally violates grammar, and a man of *ren* occasionally violates *li*. *Li* is never an end in itself.

Li is primarily learned by observing and imitating others, just as a child first learns to speak by mimicking his parents' speech. However, the fact that a child can gain a basic competence in grammar by imitating those around him does not nullify the need to teach it to him formally. Likewise, there is great benefit to formally studying *li*. Confucius recognizes that this is difficult for a child, just as the rules of grammar may seem cumbersome to a child first learning them. But once a child has mastered them, they come naturally without effort.

Having established himself on *ren*, the student may then proceed on to *wen* (文):

> A young man should be filial within his home and respectful of elders when outside, should be careful and trustworthy, broadly caring of people at large, and should cleave to *ren*. If he has energy left over, he may study *wen*.[67]

The term *wen* for Confucius has a very broad meaning, including written documents (especially the Confucian classics), cultural tradition (especially rites and music), rhetorical eloquence, and an overall love of learning.[68] It is perhaps best understood as "culture" in the sense of a "cultured" man—a well-spoken man who observes proper social etiquette and is knowledgeable in his culture's tradition, especially literature and the arts. Confucius views *wen* as a kind of ornament. In the *Analects*, one of his disciples compares wen to tiger skin, saying that the real substance (*zhi* 质) of the tiger is what is under its skin, and yet without its skin it is no longer a tiger.[69] A man without *wen* is naked in his natural "substance," and is therefore coarse and uncultured. But focusing too much on *wen* is equally dangerous:

> When natural substance prevails over wen, you get the boorishness of the rustic. When *wen* prevails over natural substance, you get the pedantry of the scribe. Only when *wen* and substance are duly blended do you get the *junzi*.[70]

A *junzi* must study *wen*, but Confucius often reminds his readers that *wen* must be subject to the restraints of *li*. Moreover, intellectual cultivation should never supersede moral cultivation. We must always prioritize moral virtue above all.

As mentioned above, *wen* for Confucius includes rites and music, but it was his emphasis on *wen* as literature that especially captured the attention of later scholars.[71] Previous formulations of the six arts did not emphasize texts.

Archery, charioteering, rites, and music were not taught with textbooks, and it is even questionable whether script and calculation relied on textbooks.[72] In the Zhou dynasty, however, texts began to assume a central role in education. About fifty years before Confucius, Shen Shushi (申叔时, 614–591 BC) listed nine books that were to be taught to the prince.[73] These texts were not part of the six arts curriculum but rather texts to be studied after mastering the six arts.[74]

As we have already seen, Confucius viewed himself as a transmitter of culture, and part of that responsibility involved compiling and editing classical texts which were based on the authority of the earlier Zhou institutions. Unlike Shen Shushi, however, Confucius believed that texts should be taught not only to aristocrats but to all people and that they should not be a mere addendum to the six arts but a central part of the six arts curriculum. Confucius's curriculum included a few of the books from Shen Shushi's suggested curriculum, namely the *The Book of Poetry* (*Shijing* 诗经), the *Book of Rites* (*Yili* 仪礼),† the *Book of Music* (*Yuejing* 乐经), and the *Spring and Autumn Annals* (*Chunqiu* 春秋), but also included other texts from the Zhou tradition like the *Book of Documents* (*Shangshu* 尚书) and the *Book of Changes* (*Zhouyi* 周易). These six books came to be known as the Six Classics (*Liujing* 六经) and are first mentioned as such in the Guodian Chu

---

† The *Book of Rites* refers to the *Yili* (仪礼), not to be confused with the *Record of Rites* (*Liji* 礼记), which was produced a few centuries later. Some translate the latter as *Book of Rites*. In this book I will be using the terms above.

bamboo slips (350 BC).[75] However, these same slips also refer to the Six Classics by another name—the Six Arts (*Liuyi* 六艺). Eventually, the term "six arts" came to refer primarily to the Six Classics and only occasionally to the original six arts.

What exactly led to this change in terminology is debated, but it is significant because it allowed later dynasties to root the teaching of classical texts in the ancient "six arts" tradition. Chinese culture traditionally viewed the distant past as a kind of golden age, and therefore people were more likely to accept new ideas and practices that were rooted in ancient tradition. The fact that these texts shared the name of the ancient curriculum certainly added to their appeal.

Some believe this change came about due to an academic trend valuing skill (*shu* 术) over study (*xue* 学), and therefore scholars preferred to speak of arts (*yi* 艺) instead of texts (*jing* 经).[76] The most likely explanation in my opinion, however, is that it was simply a marketing ploy by Confucius's disciples.[77] The term "six arts" was already laden with significant meaning because it referred to the best kind of education available at the time (but which was available only to elites). If Confucius's disciples wanted to make elitist education available to all, what better way to market their curriculum than by calling it by the same name? Moreover, because Confucius had received a traditional six arts education, many likely concluded that the Six Classics which he advocated expounded them. Therefore, when he recommended studying the Six Classics, some likely concluded that they were an extension of the traditional six arts, or even that they provided direct instruction in them.[‡]

While the Six Classics do teach aspects of the six arts, they are a far cry from a detailed compendium of the arts. The *Book of Rites* and the *Book of Music* directly correspond to two of the six arts. The *Book of Rites* at this time referred to the *Yili* (仪礼) or *Observances and Rituals*, which details various rites practiced during Zhou times. In the Han dynasty, two more rites classics appeared, namely the *Liji* (礼记) or *Record of Rites* and the *Zhouli* (周礼) or *Rites of Zhou*. These three texts together were sometimes counted as one single classic and sometimes as three separate ones. There is no extant copy of the *Book of Music*, and it is highly contested whether it even existed.[§] Because of this, the Six Classics are often referred to as the Five Classics, which is how I will be referring to them in this book.

The other four classics, though indirectly related to the six arts, do not take the arts as their primary subject matter. The *Book of Poetry* is the oldest compilation of Chinese poems, generally considered to have once been sung, though the book itself does not teach music *per se*. The *Book of Changes* is an ancient divination book based on the "eight trigrams." Although one must understand mathematics in

---

[‡] See my discussion on Lu Jia (陆贾) of the Han dynasty in Chapter 2 for one such example.

[§] Some argue that it was lost when the First Emperor of Qin ordered the burning of the books. Others argue that it existed only as a musical score to the *Book of Poetry*. Still others argue that it was incorporated into the *Liji*. See Endymion Wilkinson, *Chinese History: A New Manual*, 369.

order to use the trigrams, the book itself does not teach math. The *Spring and Autumn Annals* is an official chronicle of the state of Lu (Confucius's home state), covering events from the years 722–481 BC. The chronicles are very succinct, giving basic details about accessions, marriages, deaths, battles, and unusual natural phenomena. The *Book of Documents* is a collection of prose attributed to some of the most famous rulers and statesmen of ancient China, from the founding of the Xia dynasty to the beginning of the Eastern Zhou dynasty.

Scholars have summarized the content of the Five Classics as consisting of five categories of knowledge: poetry, politics, social science, history, and metaphysics.[78] More than these, however, Confucius recognized the Classics as sources of virtue:

> Confucius said, "When you enter any state you can know what subjects (its people) have been taught. If they show themselves men who are mild and gentle, sincere and good, they have been taught from the *Book of Poetry*. If they have a wide comprehension (of things), and know what is remote and old, they have been taught from the *Book of Documents*. If they be large-hearted and generous, bland and honest, they have been taught from the *Book of Music*. If they be pure and still, refined and subtle, they have been taught from the *Book of Changes*. If they be courteous and modest, grave and respectful, they have been taught from the *Book of Rites*. If they suitably adapt their language to the things of which they speak, they have been taught from the *Spring and Autumn Annals*."[79]

The Five Classics are not light reading. They are dense and sometimes obscure. Because of this, scholars soon began composing commentaries, the most popular of which became classics themselves. Studying the Five Classics, therefore, always meant studying both the Classics and their commentaries. Classical studies did not include only these works, however. "A *junzi* broadly studies (*boxue* 博学) all *wen*."[80] Confucius believed students should study as broadly as possible, but the Five Classics were to remain the cornerstone of the curriculum.

Confucius never indicates that he considers the Five Classics to be an exposition of the six arts. His disciples refer to the Six Classics as the "Six Arts," but he himself never does so. Nor does his emphasis on classical texts mean he desired to depart from the traditional six arts curriculum. He obviously highly valued the study of music and rites. Nothing suggests that Confucius taught script or calculation,[81] but we would not expect this, considering that these subjects were traditionally taught in the lower school. Confucius's students were of upper-school age. He obviously must have encouraged the study of script, considering his emphasis on the classics. Although Confucius was skilled in archery and charioteering, it is doubtful that he taught either of them.¶ But he did certainly encourage their study, especially as they relate to rites. Unlike the earlier tra-

---

¶   For an explanation of the passage in Sima Qian's *Historical Records* where Confucius's disciple Ran You says he learned military skills from Confucius, see Liu Zhijiu's article in Endnote 81. In short, other more reliable documents refute the claim.

dition, however, he never stresses their military benefits.[**] This is partly due to developments in military technology. By this time, chariots were being replaced with cavalry and therefore had little practical use in warfare. The development of the crossbow also rendered traditional bows and archery techniques impractical. Of course, for Confucius, the purpose of archery was never ultimately to fight enemies or even to win competitions. "Archery is not principally concerned with scoring hits."[82] Archery is principally concerned with cultivating virtue, as he indicates in *The Meaning of Archery*:

> As a father, being a good father should be your target; as a son, being a good son should be your target. As a lord, being a good lord should be your target; as an official, being a good official should be your target. So each archer shoots at his own target.[83]

Archery trains a man in virtue by allowing him to practice acting out in ritual form disciplines and attitudes that he ought to be living out day to day. "The Master said, 'In archery we have something like the way of the superior man. When the archer misses the center of the target, he turns round and seeks for the cause of his failure in himself.'"[84]

By emphasizing the Five Classics, Confucius certainly expands the traditional six arts curriculum, but his curriculum taken as a whole is clearly still rooted in the six arts. The goal of this curriculum is not primarily knowledge or

---

[**] For a detailed examination of every occurrence of archery and charioteering in the *Analects*, see pp. 69–70 of Liu Zhijiu's article in Endnote 81.

skill but virtue—specifically, *ren*. He elegantly sums up his educational philosophy in the *Analects*: "Set your heart on the *Dao*, base yourself on virtue, lean upon *ren*, and journey in the arts."[85] Even though Confucius viewed himself only as a transmitter of an older tradition, he undeniably transformed the nature of Chinese education. Six arts education now entailed mastering a canon of texts.

Even though the word "Confucianism" in English bears the name of Confucius,[86] it is not a static philosophy rooted in the teachings of only one man. Rather, it is a living tradition passed down and interpreted by a long line of disciples, the most influential of which have achieved fame similar to that of Confucius himself. Mencius is one such man.

Mencius (*Mengzi* 孟子, 372–289 BC) did not consider himself a teacher and rarely discussed education. Nevertheless, some of his ideas came to have significant influence on Chinese education. One such idea concerns the nature of man. Confucius only assumed the innate goodness of man. Mencius taught it.[87] We all have the ability to perfect ourselves, he says, not merely to become a *junzi* but to become a *shengren* (圣人) or "sage."

Mencius also greatly influenced the traditional Chinese approach to history. Although Confucius greatly admired the past, he rarely claimed to speak authoritatively on historical matters. He admitted that most information about historical events was not available to him. Mencius, on the other hand, often constructed inaccurate historical accounts that reflected the perceived character of historical figures. Even if such accounts were not accurate representations of historical fact, they sought to accurately represent the nature of moral reality. This view of history as a series of moral stories rather than factual events permeated historical studies in China for the next two millennia.

Xunzi (荀子, 313–238 BC) was another very influential Confucian. He is largely responsible for the emphasis placed on classical learning in later dynasties. Whereas Confucius made the Five Classics subordinate to other studies, Xunzi made them primary. Contrary to Mencius, Xunzi believed that human nature was innately evil. The purpose of education, according to Xunzi, is to convert this evil nature to good through moral training and rites.

Xunzi greatly influenced the rise of Legalism (*fajia* 法家) [88]—the most formidable challenger to Confucianism in history. Led by men like Han Feizi (韩非子, 279–233 BC) and Sunzi (孙子, 544–496 BC), Legalism promoted Xunzi's view of human nature. It concluded that because man is innately evil, it is impossible to order a society through morality. Order can only come through strict enforcement of laws and proper administrative structures. Legalism was an eminently pragmatic philosophy that tended to dismiss moral and cultural considerations in favor of practical, expedient ones. [89] Some have likened Legalist theories to those of Machiavelli. [90]

Chinese history can be characterized as a never-ending contest between Confucianism and Legalism, especially in the realm of politics. Both advocated for a government built on the principle of meritocracy, whereby rulers are selected based on their qualifications. Their disagreement lay in the nature of these qualifications. Confucius primarily stressed the moral qualifications of a ruler; skill and knowledge were secondary. Legalists, on the other hand, believed moral qualifications were irrelevant. The most qualified men to rule were those with the skills to do so. The implications of this on education were profound. Government schools existed primarily to raise up qualified government officials. The curricula of these schools, therefore, was shaped according to the government's definition of "qualified." If the government adopted Confucian ideals, schools necessarily focused on moral cultivation. But if it adopted Legalist ideals, schools emphasized intellectual cultivation.

This battle for ideological control of state schools had not yet materialized in Confucius's day. As we've already seen, institutional schools did not exist for the most part during the Warring States Period. Confucius never founded an institutional school, although he never opposed them. His legacy primarily lay in advocating for private education. Later Neo-Confucian scholars used him as a basis for their private "academies" or *shuyuan* (书院), which were set up in opposition to government schools. At the same time, Confucius appealed to an ancient tradition that gave the responsibility of education to the state. Later dynasties, therefore, also appealed to Confucius to justify a state-run education system.

The first significant development in the rise of state-run schools occurred in the middle of the fourth century BC. Aware that they could benefit from the counsel of scholars learned in history and religion, the rulers of the Wei and Qi states began inviting many scholars to pursue studies at their capitals. The states provided stipends so that these scholars could devote themselves fully to their intellectual pursuits.[91] Occasionally, the most respected members of the academy were also appointed to the honored position of *boshi* (博士) or "broadly-learned official-scholar," whose job it was to teach and to offer opinions on difficult issues facing the government. This courting of scholars is the first example on record of a government acting as a patron of scholarship.[92] These *boshi* were not limited to teaching only the six arts. *Boshi* appealed to Confucius on this point, pointing out that he taught more than just the six arts. They even claimed that the "hundred schools" came about as a result of Confucius opening his doors to all.[93]

The Qi state especially valued the input of *boshi* and, as a result, established the Jixia (稷下) Academy in around 360 BC in order to attract scholars. At its height, more than 10,000 scholars and students studied there.[94] Some of the most famous thinkers in Chinese history studied and taught at the school including Mencius and Xunzi, who was appointed its director.

Records indicate that the Jixia Academy had a very strong private character.[95] The government exercised little control beyond providing a physical environment in which scholars could study and exchange ideas. It was this rich intellectual environment that produced several of the most important ancient books in China, most notably the *Rites of Zhou*. Although the Academy hosted many Confucian scholars, it also recruited a number of famous Daoist thinkers.[96] Considering that Confucius supported both private and government education, the Jixia Academy is most probably the kind of institution of higher education he had in mind.

We also begin to see works addressing the topic of practical teaching methods during this fruitful time. The *Record of Learning* (*xueji* 学记) is the earliest systematic treatment of pedagogy in the world, and through it we get a glimpse of the nature of classical pedagogy in China:

> The first precept of the academy is precaution (*yu* 豫): Guard against bad habits before they become ingrained. The second is readiness and timing (*shi* 时): Choose the most efficacious time for teaching. The third is felicity and flexibility (*xun* 孙): Adjust the structure and sequence of your teaching to suit subject and student. The fourth is observation and discussion (*mo* 摩): Let students improve each other through interaction. These four precepts are the way to ensure effective instruction. If you try to prohibit bad habits after they have formed, no matter how hard you struggle with them, you will fail. If students miss the right moment to learn, it will be difficult for them to succeed regardless of how assiduously they apply themselves. If the teacher lacks structure and fails to make the necessary connections, there will not be much that learners can make of the fragments and confusion they receive. If students study alone without the company of peers and friends, they become idiosyncratic in their manner and limited in their learning. Students who always party with friends tend to turn against their teachers, and those who engage in too many frivolous activities and distractions tend to neglect their studies. These six failings will lead to ineffective teaching and learning.[97]

In this passage we see a great sensitivity to the developmental stages of children. A first-grader has natural tendencies that make learning certain subjects especially easy and other subjects especially difficult. The teacher should try to "adjust the structure and sequence of his teaching to suit" these tendencies. As the child matures, his tendencies change, and the teacher's methods should change along with them.

A student's age is not the only factor that a teacher must consider, however. He must also consider the nature of the student's "mind-heart" (*xin* 心). Students each have their own individual strengths and weaknesses, and teachers must adapt their teaching accordingly:

> Teachers must understand the four errors that students make. In their attitude to their studies, some err on the side of overextending themselves, and some in focusing too narrowly; some err on the side of thinking it is too easy, and some in giving up. These four errors arise from differences in the temperament (*xin* 心) of the learners. It is only when teachers understand the temperaments of their students that they can save them from error.[98]

The classical Chinese tradition does not view students as robots into which the teacher merely uploads information. It views them as *humans*. For many Chinese people, traditional Chinese education conjures up images of students mechanically memorizing and reciting texts. But the *Record of Learning* condemns this way of teaching:

Those who would respond to questions by the mind-less recitation of memorized texts are not worthy of becoming teachers. It is essential that teachers listen and respond to the questions that students have, and it is only when students are unable to formulate their own questions that teachers offer them instruction. When students after having been instructed still do not understand, teachers may dismiss them and wait for a more opportune time.[99]

Classical Chinese pedagogy encourages students to think critically and to ask questions. In the *Analects*, Confucius says, "To question closely and reflect on things near at hand, *ren* lies therein."[100] We are told that when Confucius entered the grand temple, "he asked about everything."[101] He even called question-asking a form of *li*.[102] Teachers must also excel at asking questions. True teaching is not simply reciting information to the class but arousing students' imaginations through thought-provoking questions:

Those who are good at asking questions approach their task as if carving hard wood. First, they chip away at the soft parts and then set to work on the knots. If they keep at it, the difficulties are gradually resolved. Those who are poor at asking questions do just the opposite.[103]

[. . .]

The role of a *junzi* as a teacher is to enlighten: to lead students forward through reasoning and inspiration rather than to drag them, to offer them encouragement rather than to hold them back, to open their minds rather than to provide them with fixed answers.[104]

Classical Chinese education was not a matter of simply memorizing "facts" about the world. It was less concerned about teaching children *what* to think than about teaching them *how* to think. It sought to develop a student's ability to think critically about the world around him so that he could apply that knowledge in virtuous and upright ways. As the *Doctrine of the Mean* admonishes us: "Study it broadly. Question it meticulously. Reflect on it carefully. Distinguish it clearly. Practice it earnestly."[105]

CHAPTER 2

Qin Dynasty to Tang Dynasty (221 BC–907 AD)

Qin Dynasty (221–206 BC)

In 221 BC, King Zheng—better known as Qin Shihuang (秦始皇) or the First Emperor of Qin—unified all of China for the first time under one ruler, ending the constant strife of the Warring States Period. The emperor was an advocate of Legalism, and as a way of silencing competing views, he officially banned private book ownership in 213 BC, giving only court-approved *boshi* the right to study books. Just one year later he supposedly ordered the infamous "burning of books and burying of scholars" (*fenshu kengru* 焚书坑儒), in which he destroyed all literature tied to the Hundred Schools of Thought and buried alive 460 Confucian scholars. Most scholars now, however, believe this to be a fabrication by later Confucian Han scholars who attempted to paint the Qin dynasty as vehemently opposed to classical learning.[1] While the emperor did likely order the destruction of certain books that he considered subversive, records indicate that he ordered two copies of each of these to be kept in imperial libraries, making the

Qin government in one sense a guardian of classical learning (though certainly not a propagator of it).

On the whole, however, Qin reforms proved detrimental to education. The government not only discouraged but outlawed private education, replacing private teachers with less-qualified government officials It also forbade commoners from studying archery in order to prevent armed uprisings. The fertile intellectual environment of the Warring States Period was almost entirely stifled.

The Qin reforms did contain one silver lining, however. In the past, each state had developed its own script, which made written communication (and therefore education) across states difficult. The Qin dynasty solved this problem by instituting a standardized script, making literature more accessible to students and to scholars. Educators published elementary primers teaching the new script, the most famous of which was Li Si's *Cangjie Pian* (仓颉篇) or *Three Chapters* (三仓). This groundbreaking text became the prototype for future Chinese dictionaries. It also became a prototype for later elementary textbooks, along with Zhao Gao's *Yuanli Pian* (爰历篇) and Hu Wujing's *Boxue Pian* (博学篇).[2] Moreover, although private book ownership was forbidden, the comprehensive, centralized library of the Qin government gave certified *boshi* access to more works than were previously available to any one scholar. Access to this amount of knowledge, exclusive as it may have been, was nevertheless unprecedented.

Han Dynasty (206 BC–220 AD)

The Qin Dynasty's reforms were short-lived. When King Zheng died, mutiny broke out and the general Liu Bang (刘邦) established what became one of China's most prosperous and formidable dynasties.

Early Han rulers believed the Qin dynasty fell largely due to its reliance on strict regulations. As a result, they adopted the Daoist principle of "ruling by doing nothing" (*wuweierzhi* 无为而治), which sought to grant as much freedom as possible, removing constricting laws and regulations. The prohibition on private learning was lifted and scholars were once again allowed to own books and study freely.

When Emperor Wu (武帝) came to power in 141 BC, however, things changed once again. He was not convinced of previous explanations for why the Qin dynasty fell. After soliciting the opinions of scholars regarding the matter, the emperor finally found answers in the Confucian Dong Zhongshu (董仲舒, 179–104 BC). Dong's application of Confucian principles not only won the approval of the emperor but succeeded in elevating Confucianism to unprecedented heights. In a move remarkably similar to that of the Qin dynasty, Dong convinced Emperor Wu that the state must adopt a single ideology and that conflicting ideologies must be banished. The emperor declared Confucianism the official state ideology, heralding the motto "dismiss the hundred schools, revere only Confucius."[3]

In order to explain the Qin dynasty's collapse, Dong searched for universal, causal principles that could both explain the past and provide direction for the future. Like a good Confucian, he did not base these principles on abstract *a prioris* but rather on tradition and classical texts. He found his most central principle in the *Spring and Autumn Annals*. By meticulously analyzing the historical events described in the *Annals*, Dong observed that Heaven directed human affairs according to predictable patterns.

Dong drew from earlier Confucians like Xunzi, who emphasized the unique roles of Heaven, Earth, and Humanity. According to Xunzi, Heaven gives birth to things and instills moral inclinations, Earth provides for material needs, and Humanity perfects all things by following patterns established by Heaven (i.e. rites and music).[4] Dong suggested that the patterns of Heaven, Earth, and Humanity correspond to the "three bonds" (*sangang* 三纲) of human relationships—namely, those between rulers and subjects, fathers and sons, and husbands and wives. By stressing the priority of the ruler-subject relationship over the others, Dong established the primacy of the state over all ethical and social affairs.

Dong went beyond the Confucian tradition by integrating these principles with Zou Yan's (邹衍) philosophies of *yinyang* (阴阳) and the "five forces" (*wuxing* 五行), essentially trying to show in more detail how man's activities relate to those of Heaven. Moreover, he suggested that Heaven does not act according to one invariable pattern but according to three sets of constantly shifting patterns, each shift being marked by irregular events in nature and history. It is the ruler's job to determine when such a shift is taking place so that he might adjust his actions accordingly. Failure to do so would result in the "Mandate of Heaven" being revoked from him and given to another. Dong believed that the emperor could only discover the patterns of Heaven by relying on the sages—Confucius in particular. Confucius understood these patterns and "hid" them within the Confucian classics.[5]

Dong's new formulation of Confucianism transformed the status of the Confucian classics and the nature of education for centuries to come. The emperor officially canonized the Five Classics, making classicist education a central priority of the state. At the same time, he minimized the importance of military education and thoroughly implemented the policy of "emphasizing *wen* over military arts" (*zhongwen qingwu* 重文轻武).

Emperor Wu dramatically reduced the number of *boshi* to only seven and limited them to teaching only the Five Classics, each *boshi* being charged with keeping the tradition of one school of interpretation of a particular classic. The number of *boshi* later increased as more schools were officially sanctioned. Although only the Five Classics were canonized, the most widely-studied works of the time were the *Classic of Filial Piety* (*Xiaojing* 孝经) and the *Analects* (*Lunyu* 论语), largely because they were easier to understand and therefore accessible to a greater number of people.

We should not think that the Han government's promotion of the Five Classics was in any way a departure from the six arts tradition of pre-Qin times. Lu Jia (陆贾, ?–170 BC), adviser to Liu Bang, was the first to refer to the Five Classics as the "Five Classics" (*wujing* 五经). In his critique of education, he describes Confucius's contribution as follows:

> Thus the later sage (Confucius) defined the Five Classics and taught the six arts (*liuyi*), following the principles of Heaven and Earth, all the while exhaustively pursuing the minutest ways of things and events . . . he edited and revised the classics to be passed on to future generations . . . This way he curbed extravagance, rectified customs, and extended true culture.[6]

Although the term "six arts" by this time usually referred to the Six (Five) Classics, we know Lu is using the term here in its original sense because he distinguishes them from the "Five Classics." The juxtaposition of these two terms is significant because it shows that people saw a direct relationship between the Five Classics and the six arts. In Chinese, the text is written in such a way as to suggest that Confucius defined the Five Classics *as a means of teaching* the six arts. In other words, instruction in the Five Classics *is* instruction in the six arts. Although, as we've seen, the Five Classics do not provide *comprehensive* instruction in the six arts, this text demonstrates that Lu (and presumably others) at least thought they presented substantial instruction in them. Later on in the same document, Lu explicitly recommends that "the six arts be established as a model"[7] for the Han education system. Thus, we can see that Dong Zhongshu and Emperor Wu considered their text-based model of education a continuation of the six arts tradition.

The Han dynasty also sowed the seeds of what would later become the imperial examination or *keju* (科举), a system that would have unparalleled influence on education in China. Han rulers adopted Confucius's idea of moral meritocracy, but the problem remained of how to select the most morally qualified candidates. In the beginning, the emperor required officials to recommend students for office. Different offices had different qualifications, usually moral in nature. The most common of these was "filially pious and uncorrupt" or *xiaolian* (孝廉). Rulers determined the moral virtue of a candidate primarily on the basis of the candidate's observance of rites. In addition to moral qualifications, some government positions also required specialized knowledge of the classics, law, or military affairs. A written exam was later added to the recommendation system, requiring students to complete a policy debate essay.* The subjects covered in the imperial examinations came to influence the curriculum of government schools, which prepared students for the exams. Therefore, by tracing the development of the imperial examinations through various dynasties we can understand how the curriculum of Chinese schools changed.

In order to prepare students for the exams and promote teaching of the classics, Emperor Wu founded the Imperial University or *Taixue* (太学) at the capital and gave *boshi* the responsibility of teaching students there. Students came primarily from families of officials, though any young man with good academic potential was eligible for admission.[8] The curriculum of the school consisted exclusively of the Five Classics; however, one should not therefore conclude that only "literature" was taught. Educators at the time did not divide the content of education into

---

* Dong Zhongshu's reforms were recommended to the emperor in one such essay.

narrowly-defined "subjects" as they do today. We've already seen that the content of the Five Classics covers a wide range of knowledge.

Because the university curriculum consisted exclusively of the Five Classics, two of the six arts were especially emphasized—namely, ritual and music.[†] Special rites and music were developed especially for use at the school. At the same time, the policy of "emphasizing literature over military arts" meant that archery and charioteering received little attention. The ritualistic archery competitions that played such an important role in previous dynasties almost entirely lost their ritualistic and moral emphases.[9] Archery was still practiced in military training, but only for its military benefits. Even so, traces of archery and charioteering were still present in certain aspects of campus culture. The top *boshi* who acted as headmaster of the university was given the title *puye* (仆射), literally "charioteer archer."[10] Exams were called *shece* (射策), literally "shoot the test question." Scholars disagree about the precise meaning of this term—whether it refers to an actual ritual in which students used a bow and arrow to shoot targets on which their test questions were posted, or whether the meaning is entirely metaphorical in which taking exams is like trying to hit a target with an arrow.[11] Neither calculation nor script were taught at the Imperial University. However, both were commonly studied privately with the aid of private book collections and were often transmitted through families.[12]

[†]   Music education, however, did not entail instruction in playing instruments or singing, as it does today. It was rather rudimentary music theory related to the practice of rites.

The Imperial University began with 50 students, but by the time of Wang Mang's (王莽) reign (90 AD) there were over 10,000.[13] Wang Mang placed an even greater emphasis on the importance of rites at the university, constructing elegant buildings on campus and orchestrating elaborate ceremonies that elevated the status of the university and its students even more. By the time of Emperor Shun (舜帝, 125 AD), the university boasted over 30,000 students.[14]

In 178 AD, the government broadened its educational interests beyond the scope of the Confucian classics by establishing the first government technical school, the Hongdu Gate Academy (*Hongdumen xue* 鸿都门学), which specialized in literature, art, and calligraphy. Whereas people in earlier dynasties had studied script solely for its linguistic value, people now began studying it for its aesthetic value (i.e. calligraphy), first through families and later through schools like the Hongdu Gate Academy. Many more such schools followed in later dynasties.

In addition to establishing the Imperial University, Han officials also enacted legislation to establish lower schools in practically all local administrative units.‡ Although the Qin dynasty was the first to charge local officials with the responsibility of educating the young, local schools were not established on a large scale until the Han.[15] Little is known about what was taught at these schools, though it is certain that the classics constituted most of the curriculum. Because the Five Classics were too difficult for younger children, lower schools generally taught the *Classic of*

---

‡   This was only an ideal. In reality, only a relatively small number of schools were actually established.

Filial Piety and the *Analects*. In 29 AD, the government for the first time decreed that local schools must observe the village libation rite, as well as the sacrifice to the Duke of Zhou and Confucius, further ritualizing primary education and exalting the status of Confucius.

Despite the prominence of government schools during the Han dynasty, private education flourished and even outperformed government schools.[16] As the quality of government schools languished toward the end of the Han dynasty, students flocked to private teachers. Even official *boshi* who taught at the Imperial University had their own private students, sometimes numbering in the thousands. Students in private lower schools continued to study the *Classic of Filial Piety* and the *Analects* as well as primers like the *Jijiu Pian* (急就篇) and the first Chinese dictionary, the *Erya* (尔雅). They also studied rudimentary calculation skills.

Period of Disunity (220–589 AD)

When the Han dynasty collapsed, China underwent a period of great political and social turmoil known as the Period of Disunity. As various dynasties vied for power, the Imperial University languished. The original intent of the university—to raise up qualified officials—was supplanted by the rise of an aristocratic social structure that guaranteed children of officials a place in office, rendering a university degree irrelevant. Therefore, in 272 the Jin dynasty established the School of National Youth or *Guozi Xue* (国子学). Only descendants of the ruling class were allowed to enroll at the university. All other students had to attend the Imperial University. The founding of the School of National Youth is significant because it officially divided students into two classes based on social status and gave the higher class access to better education. During the time of the Northern and Southern dynasties, both the North and the South had their own Imperial Universities and Schools of National Youth, maintaining the distinction between the two classes of students. Even though this distinction ran completely counter to Confucius's original project of abolishing such class distinctions in education, it persisted until the thirteenth century.

University education underwent another significant change during this period when new subjects were added to the curriculum. The first School of Law (*lüxue* 律学) was founded in 227, later followed by the first ever School of Calligraphy (*shuxue* 书学). In 420 the university curriculum was officially divided into four subjects: Confucian studies (*ruxue* 儒学), mysterious learning (*xuanxue* 玄学) (i.e. knowledge of the *Book of Changes* and the Daoist works of Laozi and Zhuangzi), historical studies (*shixue* 史学), and literary studies (*wenxue* 文学). A school of medicine (*yixue* 医学) was established in 433 with three *boshi* appointed to three different areas of expertise—medicine (*yixue* 医学), massage (*anmo* 按摩), and exorcism (*zhoujin* 咒禁). The fact that three *boshi* were appointed to the School of Medicine suggests that medical knowledge was considered as important as history and literature. Although these schools were all part of the state university system, they each had their own students, curricula, and examinations. Most of them, however, still required students to study at least some of the Confucian classics.

This new distinction between categories of knowledge—particularly historical studies and literary studies—was significant because it acknowledged that historical and literary texts besides the Confucian classics were relevant to becoming morally complete. Literary studies reached a new height in the beginning of the sixth century with the publication of Xiao Tong's (萧统) *Selections of Refined Literature* or *Wen Xuan* (文选), an anthology of more than 700 literary pieces ranging from poems to prose to funeral essays to correspondences. As one of the world's oldest literary anthologies, *Wen Xuan* reflected literature's newly exalted position in Chinese intellectual history. Language study (i.e. script), which once played a subordinate role in the earliest form of six arts education, had now become a central focus of six arts education.

We can see the development of literary theory during this time in Liu Xie's (刘勰) early sixth-century work *The Literary Mind and the Carving of Dragons* (*Wenxin Diaolong* 文心雕龙). In this work, Liu attempts to defend literature from the charge that *wen* is mere ornament. Liu roots the study of literature (*wenxue*) in the ancient concept of *wen*, viewing *wen* as a kind of pattern observable in the cosmos. The sun and moon have their own patterns or *wen*.[§] Mountains and rivers have their own *wen*. Animals have their own *wen*. Collectively, these patterns are the *wen* of Heaven and Earth. But the *wen* of man is entirely unique:

[§]   The Chinese word for astronomy (*tianwen* 天文) is literally "the *wen* of the heavens."

Only the human being, endowed with the divine spark of consciousness (*xingling* 性灵), ranks as a third with this pair. And they were called the Triad [Heaven, Earth, and human beings]. The human being is the flower of the elements: in fact, the mind (*xin* 心) of Heaven and Earth. When mind (*xin*) came into being, language was established; and with the establishment of language, pattern (*wen*) became manifest. This is the natural course of things, the *Dao*.[17]

Man is unique in that only he is capable of perceiving the *wen* of Heaven and Earth. The mountains and rivers display the *Dao*, but they are not conscious of the fact. Only man, endowed with a mind and soul, can perceive these patterns. He is the "mind of Heaven and Earth" in that he orders the cosmos and elucidates its patterns, and he does so through language. Language, therefore, is the unique pattern or *wen* of man (*renwen* 人文), and it is the primary means by which the *Dao* manifests itself. "That which stirs the world into movement is preserved in language."[18] Language functions in part as an ornament (Liu describes man as "the flower of the elements"), but language is not *merely* an ornament. It is rooted in the beginning of all things. "The origins of human pattern (*renwen* 人文) began in the Primordial."[19] Literature is important because it is the primary means by which we understand and communicate the *Dao*. "Thus we know that the *Dao* sent down its pattern (*wen*) through the Sages, and that the Sages made the *Dao* manifest in their patterns (*wen*)."[20] Although the *Dao* can be seen in many different writings, Liu says it is most fully manifest in the Five Classics. This deep reverence for language and literature foreshadowed the coming renaissance of the Tang Dynasty.

In addition to establishing technical schools in the central university system, governments in the north and south also established a number of ancillary schools (*fushe xuexiao* 附设学校) specializing in mathematics, astronomy, archery, and divination. Even though these schools were not part of the central university system, government officials were still selected from them.

Buddhism first entered China during the latter part of the Han dynasty, but it was not integrated within Chinese culture until the Period of Disunity. One of Buddhism's greatest contributions to Chinese education was its emphasis on oratory and public lectures. Before this time, Confucian teachers typically met with select advanced students in a seminar-like setting. Buddhist masters, on the other hand, typically held large public lectures where they would chant Buddhist scriptures, teach, and debate doctrine. Because these lectures were a central part of their religious lives, Buddhists highly valued oratory—something Han classical scholars had never previously emphasized. Confucian educators soon began imitating this "lecture" style of teaching.

Buddhists also helped to revive music in China. Owing in large part to the disappearance of the *Book of Music*, the Han dynasty paid little attention to music education and especially music theory.[21] The singing and chanting of Buddhist scriptures revived interest in this lost art. Although formal Chinese education at this time rarely included instruction in playing instrumental music, educated people were expected to learn an instrument on their own (the lute was especially popular). This expectation persisted throughout most of Chinese history afterward.[22] Buddhist chanting also influenced how textbooks were studied in Confucian classrooms. Students began chanting elementary primers in order to memorize them more easily. One of the most popular of such primers at this time was the *Thousand Character Classic* (千字文), which was widely used for the next one and a half millennia.

The Period of Disunity ushered in a kind of renaissance for six arts education. The government school system that once taught only the Five Classics now boasted schools specializing in calligraphy, calculation, and archery. Although music was not taught formally in schools, it was nevertheless encouraged. At the same time, the division of these arts into separate schools reflects a splintering of the curriculum. Rather than receiving a comprehensive, integrated education in all the arts, students in government schools were encouraged to specialize in certain ones, to the neglect of others. The addition of other subjects to the curriculum also challenged the assumption that the six arts alone were sufficient to educate young men.

Even though various governments throughout this period expanded education beyond the study of the Five Classics, the Classics still remained at the heart of the Imperial University. By the turn of the sixth century, however, *boshi* were no longer restricted to teaching only one classic with one particular school of interpretation. They were now free to lecture on any classic they wished, using any commentary they preferred.

Sui and Tang Dynasties (589–907 AD)

Curricula continued to expand and evolve throughout the Sui and Tang dynasties. The School of Mathematics, which was previously an ancillary school, became part of the central university system. New ancillary schools also began to appear, including schools of music and veterinary medicine. The government also began sending *boshi* to teach special classes on the classics to soldiers in the military.

One of the most important features of education during this period was the "standardization" of texts. Literary anthologies like the newly compiled *Wen Xuan* attempted to provide the best examples of Chinese literature, but these anthologies presupposed a certain standard of literary excellence. Unsurprisingly, the government made itself the arbiter of that standard and appointed a team of scholars to create "standardized" (i.e. government-sanctioned) literary anthologies (a revised version of the *Wen Xuan* made the list). Historical texts underwent a similar process, along with commentaries on the Confucian classics, which came to be called *The Standard Meanings of [the Commentaries to] the Five Classics* (*Wujing zhengyi* 五经正义).

This standardization endeavor extended to rites, as well. Confucian scholars since the Qin dynasty often asserted that the rites performed after antiquity never sufficiently embodied their original meaning and intention.[23] Confucian scholars maintained that the rites required constant revision to adapt to the times, and this was even more true in the pluralistic society of the Tang dynasty. The government, therefore, codified a number of state rites and commissioned scholars to compile a standard collection of ritual works.

As the state endeavored to standardize texts, it also increasingly relied on the imperial exam to choose officials. Although the exam existed in rudimentary form in previous dynasties, most appointments to office in those times were made on the basis of recommendation. This changed during the Tang dynasty when the exam became the primary method for selecting candidates. The imperial exam prioritized meritocracy, and to ensure that candidates were judged solely on the basis of their academic abilities, proctors covered student names with a piece of paper. They even sometimes copied the essays by hand to prevent graders from recognizing students' handwriting.

The imperial exam during this time was based solely on the newly standardized texts, which had a considerable influence on the university curriculum. If the job of the university was to prepare students for the imperial exam, then it had little choice but to teach only from the standard texts. Critics would soon come to blame the increasing centrality of the imperial examination for stifling intellectual progress and consequently diminishing China's power and influence.

The Tang dynasty is best known for its contributions to literature and poetry. Tang education greatly emphasized *wen*, which scholars at the time interpreted almost exclusively in literary terms (as opposed to the broader meaning of "culture"). Children in elementary schools were made to memorize large numbers of Chinese characters and compose essays at a very young age. The imperial exam for the subject of "advanced scholar" or *jinshi* (进士)—the most prestigious and most difficult subject—was expanded to include miscellaneous essays in addition to the standard policy debate essays. Eventually, the exam came to consist exclusively of poetic writings. The classics were still central to the Tang curriculum, but teachers primarily emphasized their literary value. In short, Tang culture considered literary prowess the distinguishing mark of an educated man.

The imperial exam saw another significant development when Wu Zetian (武则天) ascended to the throne in 690. Wu violated the long-held principle of "emphasizing literature over military arts" by instituting a military service exam (*wuju* 武举) in 702. Overseen by the Ministry of Defense, the military service exam was separate from the traditional civil service exam (*wenju* 文举), though it was still part of the imperial examination (*keju*) system. The exam tested candidates in the three styles of archery (general archery, cavalry archery, and infantry archery) and equestrianism, which replaced charioteering due to advancements in battle tactics. Although the military service exam never reached the same prominence as the civil service exam, it was implemented by all future dynasties and resulted in a renewed interest in martial arts.

Although some had attempted in previous dynasties to establish state-run elementary schools, these schools did not begin to appear in significant number until the Tang dynasty.[24] Even so, elementary education mostly remained in private hands. State-run schools provided working-class children with instruction in basic literacy and calculation skills, while private schools provided children of aristocrats with more advanced studies in the classics.[25]

One of the earliest extant records that details the daily class routine of government lower schools is a stone tablet composed in 1054 found in modern-day Xi'an. Although this tablet dates to the early Song dynasty, it describes lower schools in the late Tang. The duties of the lower school teacher are as follows:

> Each day the teachers will expound two to three pages from the Classics, explain the pronunciation and meaning of the passages assigned to the students for memorization, provide calligraphic examples for students to copy, choose topics for practice in poetic writings, decide on phrases for couplet exercises, and select passages for recitation.[26]

Students in the school were divided into three classes or grades (*deng* 等): the upper, middle, and lower class. The upper class routine is as follows:

> Each day the student will be questioned on three passages at random from the Classics already expounded by the teachers; the student should memorize passages that have more than one hundred characters, practice calligraphy for ten lines, and compose an ancient-style poem in regulated verse, with five or seven characters to each line. Every third day the student will write a rhymed-prose (*fu* 賦) with four stanzas, study a specimen of the same type of poetry, and read three to five pages of history or biography, which must contain three anecdotes for recitation.[27]

The middle class routine is similar but less intensive:

> Each day, the student should memorize a prose pas-
> sage of about one hundred characters, practice callig-
> raphy for ten lines, compose one poem of four lines,
> compose one phrase in couplet exercise, memorize
> two stanzas of a rhymed-prose, and recite one [his-
> torical] anecdote.[28]

The lower class requirements are least demanding:

> Each day, the student should memorize a prose pas-
> sage of about sixty characters, practice calligraphy for
> ten lines, and recite one poem.[29]

The curriculum described here clearly emphasizes literary skills, while entirely neglecting mathematics. But fragments from Song primers reveal that lower schools during
this time also taught mathematics. The preface to one such
primer, *Riyong Suanfa* (日用算法) or *Arithmetic for Daily
Use*, describes the content as follows: "The present book
first introduces methods of multiplication, division, addition, and subtraction. Next are problems involving measurements of all sorts. Included are also thirteen ditties
and sixty-six diagrams."[30] The primer also clarifies that it is
intended "for practical application," as can be seen by the
types of math problems it contains. The following is a typical example: "Suppose a catty (斤) of certain goods was
bought for 6,800 cash. How many would an ounce (两)
cost? Answer: 425 cash."[31] Even so, Song schools still prioritized literary education over mathematics; consequently,

a child's literary skills were considered the clearest indication of his academic potential.[32]

The daily class routine outlined above also reveals one other significant emphasis: memorization. In fact, this has characterized Chinese education from time immemorial. Students rarely studied any text without committing it to memory, and rhyme was one of the primary tools used to do so. The most popular literacy primers used rhyme, but rhyme was not limited to literacy primers. The mathematics primer mentioned above includes "thirteen ditties." Rhymed primers were also used to teach many other subjects like history (historical figures and events), science (the names of the animals and the five elements), and geography (the names of grains and seasons and the locations of famous places). Even archery and military manuals commonly relied on rhyme as a mnemonic device.[33]

By the end of the Tang dynasty, the aristocracy began to crumble and government schools languished. Consequently, education was supplied mainly through private schools, which often met in remote, scenic areas in nature. This practice began during the Period of Disunity as a result of Buddhist influences and continued throughout the Tang dynasty. Many private schools even began meeting inside of Buddhist monasteries.

Buddhism was a formidable influence in Tang culture and education. Many Confucian scholars at the time welcomed it. They saw Buddhism as an avenue for spiritual cultivation, something that Confucianism could not provide. Men often practiced both, seeking spiritual fulfillment in Buddhism and social/political/moral guidance in Confucianism. As a result, Confucianism began to develop a spiritual and religious nature. Influenced by Buddhist temples, the government soon required all local prefectural and county schools to build Confucian temples where sacrifices were regularly offered to Confucius and other sages.

CHAPTER 3

Song Dynasty to Qing Dynasty
(960–1912 AD)

Song Dynasty (960–1279 AD)

The university system of the Song dynasty continued to teach the six arts, particularly through technical schools, even though the civil service exam still tested students only in essay composition and poetry. In addition to schools of law, medicine, mathematics, and calligraphy, the government also added schools of military arts (*wuxue* 武学) and painting (*huaxue* 画学) to the university system. The Song military academy was the first of its kind in Chinese history. Although soldiers had long been trained in a kind of military training center, never before had the government established a central (*zhongyang* 中央) military academy as part of the university system. Military schools were also established at the local level.

By adding a military academy to the university system, the government clearly desired to elevate the status of martial arts education. Still, the military service exam remained separate from the civil service exam, and candidates of the latter were not tested in martial arts. This was not true in the northern Jin dynasty, however. The Jurchens[*] integrated archery completely into the university curriculum, making archery a part of the civil service exam.[1]

Archery and equestrianism remained central to the Song military curriculum, but the curriculum differed from previous dynasties in that it emphasized military strategy over technical skills—an emphasis later dynasties would retain. The military service exam reflected this emphasis.

The growing influence of Buddhism in the Tang dynasty, though welcomed by many Confucians, was not welcomed by all. Some considered it a threat to Confucianism, even suggesting that Confucianism had long ago become corrupt. Late Tang reformers Han Yu (韩愈) and Li Ao (李翱) were two such critics. On the one hand, they opposed the growing influence of Daoism and Buddhism, which they argued emphasized other-worldliness at the expense of practical affairs and human relationships. On the other hand, they opposed the high-brow culture of the literati, whom they believed had corrupted literature by promoting the extremely ornate style of writing called *pianwen* (骈文). Han Yu in particular led a movement to revive the much simpler and clearer ancient style of writing called *guwen* (古文). Echoing the literary theory of Liu Xie before him, Han Yu believed that "the purpose of writing is to manifest the Dao" (*wen yi ming dao* 文以明道),[†] not to

---

[*]   The term "Jurchens" refers to the nomadic people in northern China that founded the Jin dynasty. They were later renamed "Manchus."

[†]   A later Neo-Confucian from the Song Dynasty, Zhou Dunyi (周敦颐), coined the more popular version of this phrase—*wen yi zai dao* (文以载道), which literally means "writing (*wen*) carries the *Dao*."

display literary prowess. His essays are considered some of the most elegant prose writings in Chinese literature. The critiques of these reformers sparked a movement that came to be known as Neo-Confucianism.

Neo-Confucians claimed that classical Confucianism had never been fully implemented into society. They regarded Confucians in previous dynasties as only "pseudo-Confucians."[2] In terms of education, Neo-Confucians were most concerned that learning was being pursued for utilitarian ends—namely, to attain political office. They often cited Confucius's own rebuke in the *Analects*: "Men of antiquity studied to improve themselves; men today study to impress others."[3] Neo-Confucian sought to recover Confucius's original intent of education as a means to self-cultivation.[4] Peter Bol describes this shift as one of *wen* to *Dao*.[5]

Hu Yuan (胡瑗, 993–1059) typifies the spirit of the early Neo-Confucian revival. He describes the *Dao* as consisting of three aspects: substance (*ti* 体), function (*yong* 用), and literary expression (*wen* 文). Substance consists of the "never-changing" principles like *ren* (仁), righteousness (*yi* 义), rites (*li* 礼), music, and the bonds between ruler and subject and father and son. These principles are revealed through the literary expressions of the classics, the histories, and the writings of the philosophers, and we should study them in order to put them into practice for the good of the people and of the state.[6] This approach stands in stark contrast to the literary ideals of the Tang. According to Hu, the ancient texts were not mere repositories of ancient thought. They contained timeless principles or "substance" within them which should be applied to contemporary needs.

Neo-Confucianism has often been described as a kind of skepticism. Because the value of the classics lay not in the texts themselves but in the principles reflected within the texts, Neo-Confucian thinkers felt free to question the long-revered textual traditions associated with them. They rejected the "standard" interpretations of the Tang. They brought into question the most famous and respected commentaries on the classics and even questioned the authenticity of parts of the classics themselves. This is not to say that they looked down on the classics. On the contrary, they greatly revered them. They simply did not revere them as infallible scripture to be received by faith. Scholars were to read the texts with critical minds.

Although Neo-Confucian education was oriented primarily toward the humanities, it also emphasized the importance of natural sciences and technical studies. Hu Yuan's school consisted of two study halls—one for the classics and one for practical studies, which included government, military affairs, water control, and mathematics.[7] Later Neo-Confucians came to use his school as a model for broad learning.

The first government statesman to begin pushing for Neo-Confucian reforms at the state level was Fan Zhong-yan (范仲淹, 989–1052). Fan suggested reforming the examination for the "advanced scholar" or *jinshi* (进士) degree (the highest-level university degree) by emphasizing knowledge of the classics and political issues over poetry. He also suggested abolishing the practice of pasting a piece of paper over the examinee's name on the test paper.[8] Fan argued that the examinee's moral character was as important if not more important than his literary and intellectual abilities and that moral character could only be assessed on the basis of personal knowledge. Wang Anshi (王安石, 1021–1086) eventually implemented these reforms and eliminated all other imperial exams, leaving only the "advanced scholar" exam. He also introduced the "[exposition on] the meaning of the classics" or *jingyi* (经义) essay to the exam, which required candidates to compose a coherent essay supported by numerous and varied quotations from the classics.

Fan Zhongyan's most ambitious suggestion, however, was to establish a national school system on a scale never before seen in China. Wang Anshi eventually implemented Fan's suggestion by establishing government schools in every prefecture. The effects of such reforms, however, proved detrimental to Neo-Confucian ideals. These government schools came to be seen primarily as avenues into officialdom—the very problem Neo-Confucians were trying to combat. They also introduced other problems, such as massive debt.

Zhu Xi (朱熹, 1130–1200) saw these problems and concluded that reformers would never succeed by transforming institutions but rather by changing the way people thought about education itself. He produced a series of wildly popular commentaries on the classics and also worked tirelessly to make classical education more accessible to the common man, leading many scholars today to crown him the second-most influential thinker in Chinese history, second only to Confucius.[9]

We can see Zhu's philosophy of education most clearly in his preface and commentary to the *Great Learning* (*Daxue* 大学). Zhu begins by explaining the origin and purpose of education:

> From the time Heaven (first) sent down and gave birth to the people, it did not fail to give anyone a nature with benevolence (*ren* 仁), righteousness (*yi* 义), propriety (*li* 礼) and wisdom (*zhi* 智). Nonetheless, their endowments of innate *qi* are sometimes unequal. Consequently, some are unable to understand what their natures have and to bring them to completion. As soon as those who were intelligent and wise enough to be able to fathom their natures stood out among them, Heaven decreed that they were the rulers and teachers of countless millions, and made them rule over and educate others, so that they could revive their natures.[10]

Like Confucius, Zhu roots education not in secular principles but in transcendental ones. Teachers did not arise out of some kind of pragmatic need but because "Heaven decreed" that they should exist. When Heaven originally created man, It endowed him with a special nature. But man is ignorant of this nature, and therefore Heaven sends him teachers to teach him who he is and to help him actualize his true potential.

Zhu goes on to briefly outline the history of Chinese education. As is typical of Chinese history, it is the story of a fall from a "golden age" in the distant past. For Zhu, that golden age reached completion during the Xia, Shang, and Zhou dynasties:

> So everywhere, from the King's palace to the capitals of the states, on down to the smallest alleys there were schools. Eight years after birth, sons and younger brothers, from those of the King and Dukes on down to those of the commoners, entered the school of Lesser Learning (*xiaoxue* 小学), where they were educated about the disciplines of "sweeping and cleaning, responding and replying, entering and exiting," as well as the adornments of rites, music, archery, charioteering, calligraphy and arithmetic.[11]

Zhu emphasizes the presence of government schools during this golden age,[12] thus presenting a government school system as ideal. He describes these schools as being spread throughout the whole land, even to the "smallest alleys." Students of the schools are not limited to children of officials but include "those of commoners." The lower school curriculum consists of household etiquette and the six arts. Zhu's portrait of education during this time is not entirely accurate—schools were not nearly as prevalent as he suggests, nor were they open to commoners. Nevertheless, this is his ideal.

Zhu describes the upper school as follows:

> When they were fifteen, then from the heir apparent of the Son of Heaven and his other sons, on to the legitimate sons of dukes, ministers, chief counselors, high officials along with all who were outstanding among the people, entered the school of

Greater Learning (*daxue* 大学), where they were educated about the Way of making full use of the Pattern (*li* 理), correcting the heart, cultivating oneself, and ruling others.[13]

Zhu goes on to describe how education declined during the latter part of the Zhou dynasty. Zhu credits Confucius with attempting to restore education to its glory days but suggests that Confucius failed because he was not able to obtain a position in government office where he could implement his ideas. Instead, Confucius resorted to passing on the *Great Learning* to future generations so that they would have a record of ancient education practices that they could use as a model and standard for future schools. Zhu suggests that future educators failed to imitate this model and instead promoted "vulgar Confucian scholarship" that stressed "memorization and literary composition."[14] They also promoted "deviant doctrines" (i.e. Buddhism and Daoism), which lacked "substance" (*shi* 实), and many other teachings that obscure the *Dao*. Zhu finally ends on an optimistic note, suggesting that men in the Song dynasty have rediscovered the original Confucian understanding of education in the *Great Learning*, which Zhu goes on to expound through his commentary.

Central to Zhu's suggested reforms is the reinstitution of the six arts into the lower school curriculum. In his preface quoted above, he points to the six arts as the heart of the Zhou curriculum and suggests that Confucius passed down the record of this curriculum for their imitation. Zhu's commentary on the *Analects* reinforces this view. In the passage where Confucius makes the study of *wen* subordinate to moral education,[15] Zhu defines *wen* as "the *Book of Poetry*, the *Book of Documents*, and the six arts."[16] It is clear that the "six arts" here is not referring to the Six Classics, because two of the Six Classics are mentioned immediately before it. Zhu can only have in mind the traditional six arts. After clarifying the content of *wen*, Zhu explains its importance: "If one energetically acts but does not study the cultural arts, then one will lack the wherewithal to investigate the established paradigms of the sages and worthies, and to understand how the principle of affairs ought to be."[17] Zhu appears to emphasize the importance of *wen* (defined here as the six arts) even more than Confucius. According to Zhu, one cannot understand either ancient or contemporary issues apart from knowledge of the arts. They are not optional but essential. Of course, the six arts are only the foundation of learning for Zhu. When the student moves on to the upper school, the curriculum expands.

In his commentary on the *Great Learning*, Zhu lays out "Eight Steps" necessary to self-cultivation in the upper school. The most famous of these steps are the first two, which address the "way of making full use of the Pattern (*li* 理)" as quoted in the upper school curriculum above. These steps entail "the investigation of things" and "the extension of knowing"[18] (*gewu zhizhi* 格物致知):

> "The extension of knowing lies in the investigation of things" means that if we wish to extend our knowing it consists in fathoming the principle (*li* 理) of any thing or affair we come into contact with ... After exerting himself for a long time, one day [a man] will experience a breakthrough to integral com-

prehension (*guantong* 贯通). Then the qualities of all things, whether internal or external, refined or coarse, will all be apprehended . . .[19]

Zhu's philosophy is based on the idea of principle or *li* (理), not to be confused with the *li* (礼) of the six arts. Zhu believes there is one ultimate principle in the universe. He calls this ultimate principle the *taiji* (太极), a term appropriated from Buddhist philosophy. This ultimate principle is present in all things, "like a moon reflected on ten thousand streams" (*yueying wanchuan* 月映万川).[20] Because all things share in this ultimate principle, all knowledge is therefore interconnected. Moreover, because all things share in this ultimate principle, we can discover this principle by examining things. The "investigation of things," therefore, is the first step in learning. The principle is not apprehended by a passive, spiritual process of enlightenment, but by active investigation of the world. Eventually, this leads to "integral comprehension" (*guantong* 贯通) of all things—not because we then acquire all knowledge (which is impossible), but because we understand the common principle connecting all things. This is what it means to "extend knowing." Of course this is not the ultimate goal of learning. These are only the first two steps. The ultimate goal for Zhu is self-cultivation (i.e. moral cultivation), which in turn will lead to the restoration of the home, the state, and the world.

This new outlook on the interconnectedness of all knowledge resulted in a great interest in broad learning among Neo-Confucians. Although the Tang dynasty saw a broadening of the university curriculum, it generally encouraged specialization in one particular subject. Song education, on the other hand, encouraged individuals to pursue many areas of knowledge:

> All events under heaven are what scholars should know . . . rites, music, institutions, astronomy, geography, military strategy, and criminal justice also are all necessary for the world and are not possible to do without. All [these] must be studied.[21]

These subjects are only a sampling of the many areas of knowledge Zhu believed a scholar should study. His attitude toward books is the same: "Of the books under heaven, there is none not to be 'broadly studied' (*boxue* 博学)."[22]

Even though his proposed curriculum goes beyond the scope of the six arts, Zhu believes this is in keeping with both ancient practices and Confucius's own teaching. He points to the multiple admonitions to "study broadly" in the *Analects* to support this claim.[23] Zhu recognizes that no one man can attain mastery of every subject. The point is not mastery but general comprehension. "Although one may not be able to see through their essences and subtleties, one should nevertheless know the general outlines."[24] Zhu himself wrote treatises on astronomy, music (specifically harmonics), geography, calculation (specifically *xiangshu* 象数 or "images and numbers" used in divination), and Daosim. He also occasionally discusses medicine, mathematics, animals, and agriculture.

As can be seen in Zhu's praise of the ancient school system, he, like Fan Zhongyan, proposes a universal school system available to all. But whereas Fan's proposal was rooted primarily in a desire to raise up qualified officials, Zhu is most concerned with raising up moral individuals capable of forming a moral society. Moreover, although Zhu himself was a literatus and had much to say to other literati, he spent most of his energy trying to make education accessible to the common man, as can be seen most clearly in his works *Elementary Learning* (*Xiaoxue* 小学), *Family Ritual* (*Jiali* 家礼), and *Community Compact* (*Xiangyue* 乡约).

One way Zhu addresses the needs of the common man in these works is by reforming the system of rites. Over the past few centuries ceremonial rites had largely fallen to the wayside, due in large part to the extravagant cost required for the ruling class to conduct them, let alone the common person. Zhu adapted the traditional rites to a simpler form so that commoners could practice them in their villages and homes. Among these reforms was the re-institution of the "hospitality archery rite" from the *Rites of Zhou*. This is significant considering that the ritual aspect of archery had largely passed away by the end of the Han dynasty. Zhu revived it.

One of Zhu's most ambitious and lasting legacies, however, lay in his efforts to replace the long-revered Five Classics with a new set of works. Zhu, like other Neo-Confucians, was critical of the Five Classics. His primary concern was that they were obscure and difficult to understand. He proposed a new set of texts that communicated Confucian ideals in a clearer way for the common man. These "Four Books" (*sishu* 四书) were the *Analects*, the *Mencius*, the *Doctrine of the Mean* (*Zhongyong* 中庸), and the *Great Learning*.[25] Zhu's commentary on the four books (*Si-*

shu jizhu 四书集注) became what many have considered
to be the single most influential book in China since the
twelfth century.[26] Thanks to Zhu's tireless promotion of
these works, the Four Books were eventually canonized in
the Yuan dynasty and succeeded the Five Classics as the
most studied and revered of the Confucian classics.

Zhu never discusses curriculum in much detail, and
therefore we do not have a list of recommended texts for
each stage of learning.[27] However, based on his recommendations for works to be included in the examinations, as
well as various remarks scattered throughout his writings,
we can draw some reasonable conclusions. The first books
to be studied are the Four Books followed by the Five Classics, accompanied by their respective commentaries (almost all written by Song scholars). Several philosophical
works follow, including works by Laozi, Zhuangzi, Xunzi,
and Han Feizi. Zhu recommends a number of histories[‡] as
well as legal works. He also proposes studies in calendrical
calculation and geography. Zhu's recommendations clearly
reflect the Neo-Confucian tradition of broad learning, and
in fact he explicitly commends Hu Yuan's combination of
both classical and technical studies.

Although Zhu sought to reform the government
school system and upheld the ancient government school
system as an ideal, he appears to have had little confidence

---

‡   These include *Zuo Zhuan, The Tales of the States, Historical Records,
The Former and Later Han Histories, The History of the Three Kingdoms, Qin
History, The Southern Histories, The Northern Histories, The New* and *Old Tang
Histories, The History of the Five Dynasties,* and Sima Guang's *Comprehensive
Mirror.* This list of books is drawn from Lee.

that government schools could adequately address the educational needs in his own day. Instead, he focused his energies primarily on developing academies or *shuyuan* (书院). The word *shuyuan* originally meant a place for collecting books. It first served as a kind of private study for scholars beginning in the ninth century, but by Zhu's day academies were full-fledged schools offering quality education, often outperforming government schools. Academies were free to experiment with Neo-Confucian ideas that the government was not yet willing to adopt. This intellectual freedom attracted many of the best scholars.

Zhu was opposed to the idea of school regulations because he thought they were demeaning to students and did nothing to motivate them. Instead, he ran his academies according to moral precepts or principles taken from Confucian classics. He posted this list of precepts on the lintel of his most famous academy, the White Deer Grotto (*Bailudong shuyuan* 白鹿洞书院), with the hope that students would voluntarily live according to them. The list begins with the "Five Teachings" from *Mencius*:

> Between father and son, there should be affection.
> Between ruler and minister, there should be righteousness.
> Between husband and wife, there should be attention to their separate functions.
> Between old and young, there should be a proper order.
> Between friends, there should be faithfulness.[28]

The proper order of study follows, quoted from the Doctrine of the Mean:

> Study it broadly.
> Question it meticulously.
> Reflect on it carefully.
> Distinguish it clearly.
> Practice it earnestly.[29]

The list continues with principles for self-cultivation, for handling affairs, and for dealing with others. These precepts clearly reflect the twofold emphasis of Neo-Confucianism—moral virtue and critical thinking. This list of precepts was later adopted by nearly every academy and came to be viewed as the best summary of Confucian teachings both before and after Zhu's time.

Yuan Dynasty (1271–1368)

Zhu Xi's reforms were not generally well-received during his own time. Ironically, foreign invaders were responsible for his rise to fame. The Mongols were greatly impressed by Zhu and in 1313 officially adopted his commentaries on the Four Books and Five Classics as standard references for the imperial examinations.

They were also very impressed with the Neo-Confucian academies, which by now almost ran into the thousands.[30] The Yuan government supported their development but was not comfortable granting them complete independence–it exercised control over certain aspects of their finances and administration. As the academies became more popular, they began to bend under pressure to prepare students for the imperial examinations, sacrificing the intellectual freedom and liberal curriculum that once characterized them.

Although a number of academies adopted Zhu's proposed curriculum, the most popular curriculum was proposed by Cheng Duanli (程端礼, 1271–1345) in 1315. In his essay *Daily Schedule of Study for Different Classes in the Cheng Family School* (*Chengshi jiashu dushu fennian richeng* 程氏家塾读书分年日程), Cheng lays out a systematic reading plan for students to follow beginning at the age of eight and finishing between the ages of twenty-one and twenty-four. The student begins by reading the *Elementary Learning* followed by the Four Books (*The Great Learning, Analects, Mencius*, and *The Doctrine of the Mean*, in that order). Next is the *Classic of Filial Piety* and the Nine Classics (i.e. Five Classics),§ the order being the *Book of Changes*, the *Book of Documents*, the *Book of Poetry*, the *Book of Rites*, the *Record of Rites*, the *Rites of Zhou*, and the three commentaries on the *Spring and Autumn Annals*. Cheng also recommends a number of optional reference books written by Song authors. By this time the student is fifteen years old.

At fifteen, the student re-reads the Four Books and Five Classics with Zhu's commentaries. He then begins historical studies. First on the list are Sima Guang's *Comprehensive Mirror* (*Zizhi tongjian* 资治通鉴) and Zhu Xi's com-

---

§ The Five Classics are occasionally referred to as the Nine Classics, with the three *Rites* classics and the three commentaries on the *Spring and Autumn Annals* counted separately.

mentary on it. These are followed by *Historical Records* (*Shiji* 史记), the two *Han Histories*, and several histories by Song authors. Next, the student moves on to literary studies, beginning with the literary writings of Han Yu and *The Songs of Chu* (*Chuci* 楚辞). The student can now choose from an array of contemporary works on rites, institutions, and philological matters. At twenty years old he begins studying many of the famous policy debate essays. In his final years of study he may pursue his own interests.

As William de Bary points out, Cheng's curriculum appears to emphasize memorizing content covered in the imperial exams rather than the "studying, questioning, reflecting, and discerning" earnestly promoted by Zhu.[31] The reading list also does not include the diversity of commentaries and points of view that Zhu would have likely hoped for. Still, Cheng's goals appear to be based on those of Zhu. According to Cheng, by the age of twenty-one the student will "have established himself in reverent seriousness and righteousness, strict in his practice of mind preservation and self-examination, and firmly rooted for a lifetime of learning."[32]

Neo-Confucianism never succeeded in ridding China of the influences of Buddhism and Daoism. The three were gradually syncretized. Many academies began building Confucian temples in imitation of local schools, which by now were so ritualized that they were typically referred to as "temple schools" (*miaoxue* 庙学). Even though Buddhist influences were prevalent, Confucianism dominated Chinese culture. By the end of the Yuan dynasty, Confucianism had become a kind of national identity.[33] To be

Chinese was to be Confucian. This new identity was largely influenced by the Mongol invasion. The Chinese people had never before been completely subjugated by a foreign people. Lacking their own emperor and land, the Chinese found unity around their old Master.

Ming Dynasty (1368–1644)

After almost a century of foreign oppression, the Chinese regained independence, led by their new emperor Zhu Yuanzhang (朱元璋). The Ming government prided itself as a champion of education: "The first priority in running a country is education, and schools are the foundation of education"[34] Three years after founding the Ming dynasty, Emperor Zhu issued an edict reforming the imperial examination system and, consequently, government education. He begins by praising the education and examination system of the ancients:

> At eight years old, people in ancient times began studying rites, music, archery, charioteering, script, and calculation. At fifteen they studied how to cultivate themselves, how to regulate their families, how to govern the kingdom, and thus bring peace to all under Heaven. The official examination system of the Zhou dynasty [was based on this], namely the six virtues, the six praiseworthy actions, and the six arts. Both *wen* and martial arts (*wu*) were combined, and men were chosen based on both their virtue and ability.[35]

The emperor then critiques later dynasties for failing to live up to this ideal:

> In the Han, Tang, and up to the Song Dynasty, qualified officers were selected through the imperial examination system which varied from dynasty to dynasty: yet each set store in turning a nice literary phrase rather than seeking an all-round ability in the six arts.[36]

The emperor then praises the Yuan dynasty for attempting to return to the ancient system but explains that it was corrupted by immoral men in power. Finally, he announces that the Ming government will reinstitute the ancient system wherein students will "labor to learn from the Classics, to practice refinement, to master the things of ancient times and be conversant with current affairs, to be properly proficient in literary skills and to ensure that their ability matches their reputations."[37]

Emperor Zhu was clearly heavily influenced by Zhu Xi and other Neo-Confucians. Not since the Zhou dynasty do we see an emperor make such a determined effort to reinstitute the ancient six arts curriculum into government schools. Zhu's edict reflects a balance rarely seen in previous dynasties. He emphasizes both *wen* (literary arts) and *wu* (martial arts), both virtue and ability, both knowledge of the past and knowledge of the present. It is, indeed, an "all-around ability in the six arts."

Emperor Zhu made some strides in implementing his proposed curriculum. In addition to the Four Books and

Five Classics,¶ universities required all students to study mathematics,** calligraphy, and archery. They also revived music education, especially singing. Elementary schools implemented similar reforms, encouraging students to sing the *Books of Poetry* rather than simply reading it and incorporating archery and rites into their curricula.

The third Ming emperor, Yongle (永乐, 1360–1424), was particularly captivated by the Neo-Confucian idea of the interconnectedness of all knowledge. He issued a mandate to compile the *Yongle Dadian* (永乐大典), the largest encyclopedia in world history, containing over 11,000 volumes. It was compiled largely by university students and supposedly included all that had ever been written in the four categories of 1) the Confucian canon, 2) history, 3) philosophy, and 4) general literature, which included astronomy, geography, cosmogony, medicine, divination, Buddhism, Daoism, handicrafts, and arts.[38]

Although Zhu's educational ambitions looked promising, his despotic temperament ultimately crippled Ming education. Zhu and other Ming rulers regularly imprisoned and even executed scholars for writing material they considered offensive. Even Mencius himself could not escape the emperor's wrath. Zhu strongly opposed certain passages of the *Mencius* that challenged the abuses of a tyrannical ruler. He therefore issued an abridged version of the book

---

¶   The commentaries used for the Four Books and Five Classics during the Ming dynasty were almost exclusively by Song and Yuan authors.

**   The text studied was *Nine Chapters on the Mathematical Art* (*Jiuzhang suanshu* 九章算术).

with the offending passages removed. Zhu also forbade university students from debating sensitive political issues. Soon, teachers abandoned their duties, lectures were canceled, and students stopped living on campus.

Ming education also declined because of reforms to the imperial exam, which now required students to compose the infamous "eight-legged essay" (*baguwen* 八股文). The eight-legged essay was an evolution of the "[exposition on] the meaning of the classics" essay introduced during the Song dynasty. Like the old essay, the eight-legged essay required candidates to expound on a Confucian concept by citing multiple quotes from the Classics and weaving them together. The difference lay in the complex rules the candidate was required to follow. Each "leg" of the essay had different requirements regarding the number of sentences, number of words, format, length, style, rhyme, symmetry, tone, and so forth. At the time, eight-legged essays were heralded as brilliant displays of scholarship and literary prowess. The effect of these exams on education, however, was detrimental. The highly complex essays were impractical and did not exist outside of the exams, and yet schools were forced to spend years teaching students how to compose them. Because the essays were so difficult to compose, students spent most of their time studying and memorizing pre-written essays rather than the classics themselves, on which the essays were supposed to be based. Moreover, as the essays grew in prestige, physical (i.e. martial arts) education was marginalized.[39] Most scholars agree that these essays were a significant factor in the decline of Ming education.[40]

Classical scholarship also degenerated significantly due to the compilation of the three compendiums (*daquan* 大全) on the Four Books, Five Classics, and Neo-Confucian thought. Issued at the decree of Emperor Zhu, the compendiums have been uniformly criticized as little more than plagiarized commentaries from unreliable Song and Yuan authors.[41] Nevertheless, they were the basis of the imperial examination and exerted tremendous influence over the next 500 years.

While government schools languished, academies continued to thrive. The single-most influential figure in the development of Ming academies and Neo-Confucian thought was Wang Yangming (王阳明, 1472–1529). Wang greatly respected Zhu Xi, but he found fault with Zhu's concept of "the investigation of things." Wang famously tested Zhu's theory by staring at a bamboo plant for days on end to try to discover its inherent principle. After many days he failed to comprehend the principle. Wang concluded that the principle of things must not lie within the things themselves but in oneself—more specifically, in one's own "mind-heart" (*xin* 心). Comprehension of the Heavenly Principle was not achieved by studying the external world but by "innate knowing" or *liangzhi* (良知):

> The heart is naturally able to know. When it perceives the parents, it naturally knows that one should be filial. When it perceives the elder brother, it naturally knows that one should be respectful. And when it perceives a child fall into a well, it naturally knows that one should commiserate. This is innate knowing.[42]

Wang, therefore, interpreted the term *gewu* (格物) in the *Great Learning* not as the investigation of "things" but as the investigation of one's own mind-heart. This idea significantly impacted the future of Chinese education.

First, it inspired the rise of populist education. Since learning did not require investigating external things (like books), everyone including illiterate peasants could learn. Academies opened their doors to the public and held large open lectures, which were highly ritualized, even adorned with singers and musical instruments.

Second, Wang's philosophy promoted individualism in Chinese education. The key to knowledge no longer lay in the external world but in oneself. The phrase "learning by one's own self" (*zide zhi xue* 自得之学) became a rallying cry.[43] Related to this, "morality books" (*shanshu* 善书) encouraged critical introspection. These books contained simple phrases or sentences that admonished readers to good deeds in exchange for good retribution. The morals promoted were generally Confucian in nature, but the idea of retribution was clearly a Buddhist influence. Some of these books even functioned as moral "score cards", assigning numerical values to different acts. A person would record his daily behavior and then calculate his "moral score." Wang also promoted a system whereby local communities would publicly post the meritorious and unmeritorious deeds of its members. Local schools promoted a similar practice in which teachers would keep both an academic progress report and a moral progress report for each student.[44]

Thirdly, Wang's philosophy also precipitated a rise in anti-intellectualism. Although Wang himself promoted studying the classics and even rooted his philosophy in them, some of his disciples completely denied the need for book learning. If knowledge comes from within oneself, they argued, then books are superfluous. Some critics similarly condemned Wang's philosophy for discouraging hard work.

Unlike Yuan rulers, Ming rulers despised the academies. They saw them as subversive to government schools and a threat to the government itself. As the academies became more popular,[45] the government initiated multiple campaigns to attempt to shut them down. Occasionally, these campaigns were limited to particular academies, but sometimes they sought to eradicate them all, such as Zhang Juzheng's (张居正) edict in 1579. Promoters of the academies were sometimes arrested and even executed. The final crackdown came in 1625, when the Donglin Academy (*Donglin shuyuan* 东林书院) criticized the Ming court. All of the leading academies were demolished, bringing an end to the academy movement and marking the triumph of authoritarian control over education.

With education in rapid decline and academies demolished, some Neo-Confucian scholars began looking for new ways to recover the old learning promoted by Zhu Xi. One of the most noteworthy of these figures was Zhang Pu (张浦), leader of the Fu She (复社) movement. The Fu She was a society of scholars started in 1629 that regularly met to discuss literature, philosophy, politics, and other topics relevant to culture and society. The group sought to promote a kind of cultural renaissance and renewal of society, and they believed education reform was the key to this renewal. Zhang Pu describes the organization's purpose as follows:

> From the time education [began to] decline, scholars have not understood wisdom embodied in the Classics. Instead they plagiarize what they have heard and seen and call it their own . . . There are fewer and fewer talented men and the government gets worse every day . . . I hope to join with many scholars from all over the empire to revive the ancient teachings so that future generations will be able to provide useful service [for the country].[46]

As William Atwell points out, Zhang's call "to revive the ancient teachings" was not an arch-conservative summons to restore ancient institutions. Rather, it was a call to study lessons from the past and creatively apply those lessons to contemporary problems.[47] The Fu She was especially critical of the eight-legged essay. They argued that because students were devoting their time to studying these essays rather than studying the classics, men were being appointed to office who had no real knowledge of the Confucian tradition.

The Fu She did not limit membership to scholars. In the spirit of Wang Yangming, they welcomed and taught people from all backgrounds. Fu She members conducted research and produced writings on a number of political and social issues. Some worked to pass legislation to help the poor. Others led a number of public welfare projects including famine relief and canal maintenance. As might be expected, however, the Ming government did not take kindly to the Fu She. Fu She members were forced out of government, and the government attempted to shut down the organization altogether. When the Ming dynasty finally collapsed in 1644, the Fu She disappeared with it.

Qing Dynasty (1644–1912)

The Ming dynasty was the last to fully embrace the traditional model of Chinese education. Although the Qing dynasty implemented various aspects of the traditional model, scholars generally agree that "modern" education began with Qing reforms and the establishment of Western missionary schools.[48] The imperial exam continued to exert increasing influence on education until it was finally abolished in 1905. In 1919, the May Fourth Movement advocated for completely abandoning traditional Chinese culture, and in 1966, the Communist Party answered their call with the Cultural Revolution, which unleashed a devastating campaign against the "Four Olds"—old customs, old culture, old habits, and old ideas. China has yet to recover from this loss.

Part Two:

Redeeming the Six Arts

Now after Jesus was born in Bethlehem of Judea in the days of Herod the king, behold, wise men from the east came to Jerusalem ... Then, opening their treasures, they offered him gifts ...

-Matthew 2:1, 11

Chapter 4

Christian Foundations and the Western Tradition

A ny discussion of education must begin with Christ. We cannot understand how to teach children about this world if we do not understand who Christ is or how He relates to it. Christ is not merely one subject among many. He is the beginning and end of all of them. "All things were created through him and for him. And he is before all things, and in him all things hold together" (Col. 1:16-17). Augustine of Hippo (354–430 AD), who wrote the first treatise on Christian education, insists that the only proper object of education is God.[1] When we pursue any area of knowledge for its own sake, we commit idolatry. Ultimately, education exists not so that we can better know the world but so that we can better know and enjoy God.*

Many Christian schools have compromised the gospel by failing to understand this point. They divide their curriculum into subjects and assign the study of Christ and His

---

* In saying this, Augustine does not prohibit "enjoying" things of this world. Rather, he says that when something in this world brings us true enjoyment, it is not the thing itself that we are actually enjoying but God. Christians should not view the study of the world as opposed to the study of God, but rather as a means to studying and glorifying God.

word to only one or two of them. The rest are treated as "neutral" subjects that have no direct relationship to Christianity. This is tragic. Jesus is not Lord of only one or two subjects. He is Lord of all. Our curriculum may consist of many different subjects—literature, mathematics, natural science, music, and so forth—but in the end, they all culminate in Christ. In one sense, the Christian curriculum consists of only one subject: Jesus.[2] "For I decided to know nothing among you except Jesus Christ and him crucified" (1 Cor. 2:2).

But if we acknowledge that Christ is the source and *telos* of all things, this means we can find Him in all things. As Augustine reminds us, "Let every good and true Christian understand that wherever truth may be found, it belongs to his Master."[3] We are free to explore God's creation as long as we do it for His glory. But this still raises the question: What do we teach? God's creation is vast, and as educators we can only present a tiny sliver of it to our students.

Kevin Clark and Ravi Jain helpfully summarize the Western liberal arts tradition as consisting of six categories of study—piety, gymnastic, music, liberal arts, philosophy, and theology, in that order.[4] At the core of this curriculum are the seven liberal arts. The first three arts—grammar, logic, and rhetoric—are language arts that cultivate faculties of speech and reasoning, while the mathematical arts—arithmetic, geometry, astronomy, and music—lay the foundation for more abstract, metaphysical studies. The goal of liberal arts education is not merely to transmit knowledge. It is a holistic education that seeks to cultivate "the virtue of the student in body, heart, and mind, while nurturing a love for wisdom under the lordship of Christ."[5]

In modern times, this tradition has come to be known as "classical Christian education" or "Christian classical education." Of course, during the medieval period it was simply known as "education." This tradition was gradually snuffed out by Enlightenment-inspired education reforms during the nineteenth and twentieth centuries, but a few farsighted educators resisted these reforms and continued stoking the fading embers of classical education until it was finally fanned back into flame at the turn of the twenty-first century. At the time of the writing of this book, the classical Christian revival is still in its infancy, but the flames continue to spread.

Similarly, some Chinese Christians in the twenty-first century have begun to question contemporary models of education in China. Modern public education in China is almost entirely utilitarian. For the most part, primary and secondary education have only one goal: to prepare students for the national college entrance examination or *gaokao* (高考). The influence of the *gaokao* on modern education in China can hardly be exaggerated. In the same way that the imperial examination (*keju* 科举) stifled education in traditional China, the *gaokao* has reduced modern education to a matter of mere test preparation. The parallels between the *keju* and the *gaokao* are striking. If a student tests well enough on the *gaokao*, he then enters college where he continues to pursue equally utilitarian goals of acquiring job credentials.

Wishing to provide a more holistic and Christ-centered education for their children, more and more Chinese Christians have begun looking to the classical Christian education movement in the West for guidance and inspiration. But as they do so, an important and perplexing question arises: What form should classical Christian education take in a Chinese context?

Contemporary resources on classical Christian education almost unanimously suggest that the classical Christian tradition is by definition a Western tradition rooted in the Greco-Roman world. "Classical educators take responsibility for the Western tradition."[6] "The classical method was born in ancient Greece and Rome."[7] "It is a long tradition of education that has emphasized . . . the study of the liberal arts and the great books."[8] "The Classical education movement advocates a form of education based in the traditions of Western culture."[9] The curriculum consists of philosophers like Plato and Aristotle, poets like Homer and Virgil, historians like Herodotus and Livy, and theologians like Augustine and Calvin. It encourages the study of Latin and English. The seven liberal arts are at its core.

While this definition accurately describes the classical tradition in the *West*, is it an accurate description of the classical Christian tradition *per se*? If it is, then classical Christian schools in China must, by definition, teach a Western curriculum. Some Chinese believe this. Having a deep respect for Christian tradition, they believe imitating the church fathers in the realm of education entails teaching what they taught. The church fathers encouraged studying Cicero, so Chinese Christians should study

Cicero. The church fathers encouraged studying Latin, so Chinese Christians should study Latin. The church fathers embraced the schema of the seven liberal arts, so Chinese Christians should embrace the seven liberal arts. If the Chinese church wants to raise up its own Augustine, Boethius, Calvin, and Lewis, shouldn't it provide the same education in Western civilization that these men received? This sentiment is understandable, but I believe it is mistaken.

The classical Christian tradition *per se* is not a curriculum of specific texts, languages, or subjects. It is an *approach* that seeks wisdom by inquiring of the most respected and influential men of one's own cultural tradition. At its heart, classical Christian education is obedience to the Fifth Commandment: "Honor your father and your mother, that your days may be long in the land that the LORD your God is giving you" (Ex. 20:12). Why did early Christians respect Cicero? Why did they sit at the feet of Plato and Aristotle? Why did they listen to the stories of Virgil and Homer? Because they honored their fathers.

At this point, someone may retort, "But the church fathers were not all biologically related to Plato." Indeed, I doubt that the French theologian John Calvin can trace his bloodline back to the Greek philosopher Plato. So how can we say that Calvin studied Plato out of respect for his fathers? It is not because Plato was Calvin's ancestor but because Plato belonged to a tradition of learning that Calvin's ancestors valued.

See, for example, how Battista Guarino, an Italian Educator and contemporary of Calvin, defends his curriculum in a letter to his student: "For this is the program of teaching and the precepts of study which my father, who was learned as he was excellent—your grandfather, as it were, in literary study—used to teach his pupils."[10] Guarino promotes studying men like Plato, Virgil, and Cicero because his father did so. But notice what else he says. He identifies his father as the student's "grandfather in literary study"—in Latin, literally his "grandfather by right of teaching." In other words, the student should respect Guarino's father as his own grandfather, not because they are biologically related but because they are didactically related. As the boy's teacher, Guarino is a kind of father to him, much like the Apostle Paul considered himself a father to those he taught.[†] Throughout church history, we see Christians referring to their pagan "fathers" in both senses—sometimes as their biological ancestors and sometimes as their esteemed teachers, but in both cases they felt obligated to honor them.

But Guarino does not only appeal to the authority of his ancestors as a reason for studying these pagan authors. He continues:

> You will consider them the best precepts for this one reason in particular: that absolute princes of letters have sprung forth from his school as though from the Trojan horse. Indeed, the majority of those who have cultivated literary study both in our Italy and in the rest of the world have flowed out from his springs.[11]

---

† See 1 Cor 4:15–17, 2 Cor. 12:14–15, Phil. 1:1, 1 Tim. 1:2–5.

In other words, the student should study these authors not only because they were taught by Guarino's father but because they are *effective*. A medieval rhetorician might arrange a speech according to Cicero's framework because this is what his fathers did, but the very reason his fathers promoted Cicero's framework in the first place was because they recognized that it was *persuasive*.

God does not command us to honor our fathers and mothers merely because they gave birth to us. He also does so because our fathers and mothers are generally wiser than we are. They are older than us, and consequently they have seen and experienced more. A young man may, in his lifetime, encounter one or two wars, but his ancestors have encountered hundreds. He may have thought many years about life's big questions, but his ancestors have thought many more. As such, wisdom dictates that we heed the tradition of our ancestors—what G. K. Chesterton calls the "democracy of the dead":

> It is quite easy to see why a legend is treated, and ought to be treated, more respectfully than a book of history. The legend is generally made by the majority of people in the village who are sane. The book is generally written by the one man in the village who is mad . . . If we attach great importance to the opinion of ordinary men in great unanimity when we are dealing with daily matters, there is no reason why we should disregard it when we are dealing with history or fable. Tradition may be defined as an extension of the franchise. Tradition means giving votes to the most obscure of all classes, our ancestors. It is the democracy of the dead. Tradition refuses to submit to

the small and arrogant oligarchy of those who merely happen to be walking about. All democrats object to men being disqualified by the accident of birth; tradition objects to their being disqualified by the accident of death. Democracy tells us not to neglect a good man's opinion, even if he is our groom; tradition asks us not to neglect a good man's opinion, even if he is our father.[12]

The schema of the seven liberal arts was not devised by a group of medieval Christian educators sitting around a table at a classical Christian education forum. The Trivium and Quadrivium were inventions of Greco-Roman pagans. The church fathers believed the seven liberal arts to be the curriculum best suited for young Christians not because the Bible said so (though Cassiodorus tried to make the case)[‡] and not because a church council said so but because their *pagan fathers* said so, and they believed that these men were wise.[§]

Throughout the classical Christian tradition, therefore, we find Christians repeatedly grounding their curriculum in both of these principles: 1) this tradition was esteemed by our ancestors (and we should honor our ancestors); and 2) our ancestors esteemed this tradition because it was effective at educating children. For example, see how the

---

‡   Cassiodorus suggests that the "seven pillars" of wisdom in Proverbs 9:1 refer to the liberal arts, though his principles of exegesis are obviously questionable.

§   During the Middle Ages, the most influential text on the seven liberal arts was Martianus Capella's *The Marriage of Philology and Mercury*, a text void of any Christian teaching.

twelfth-century scholar and bishop John of Salisbury defends the liberal arts in his twelfth-century treatise on education, the *Metalogicon*:

> The liberal arts are said to have become so efficacious among our ancestors, who studied them diligently, that they enabled them to comprehend everything they read, elevated their understanding to all things, and empowered them to cut through the knots of all problems possible of solution.[13]

Another famous twelfth-century scholar and theologian, Hugh of Saint Victor, defends the liberal arts in similar terms:

> Out of all the sciences above named, however, the ancients, in their studies, especially selected seven to be mastered by those who were to be educated. These seven they considered so to excel all the rest in usefulness that anyone who had been thoroughly schooled in them might afterward come to a knowledge of the others by his own inquiry and effort rather than by listening to a teacher.[14]

The Protestant reformers also based their liberal arts curriculum both on the authority of their ancestors and on the effectiveness of the curriculum. Consider, for example, the words of Martin Luther:

> For my part, if I had children and could manage it, I would have them study not only languages and history, but also singing and music together with the whole of mathematics [i.e. the quadrivium: arithmetic, mu-

sic, geometry, astronomy]. For what is all this but mere child's play? The ancient Greeks trained their children in these disciplines; yet they grew up to be people of wondrous ability, subsequently fit for everything.[15]

Some accuse the Protestant reformers of rejecting the authority of tradition. On the contrary, they greatly respected it. They were some of the greatest proponents of classical education. Classicist Theodore Buenger describes the reformers in this way:

> We may thus say that the leaders of Protestantism were all of them well trained in the Classics, that they had in fact a knowledge of the ancient literatures which is rare nowadays even among professional classicists. They appreciated the classical authors and made them a part of their lives. That this heritage of antiquity might not be lost to their descendants they incorporated them in their schools.[16]

Some dismiss the idea of studying the ancients because "we know more now than they did." But this overlooks the nature of knowledge. The great body of knowledge that we have access to in modern books did not fall from the sky. It was *inherited*. Even truly modern discoveries were not made in a vacuum. They were made on the foundation of previous knowledge—knowledge passed down to us from our ancestors. Isaac Newton famously quipped, "If I have seen further it is by standing on the shoulders of giants,"[17] by which he meant his ancestors. We cannot properly understand modern ideas without understanding the previous ideas on which they are based. C. S. Lewis provides a helpful metaphor:

> If you join at eleven o'clock a conversation which began at eight you will often not see the real bearing of what is said. Remarks which seem to you very ordinary will produce laughter or irritation and you will not see why—the reason, of course, being that the earlier stages of the conversation have given them a special point.[18]

Lewis also makes the point that old books expose our blind spots. All of us to some extent share a contemporary worldview, and therefore we share in the same blind spots. The ancients certainly had their own blind spots, but they were not the same blind spots that we suffer from. Because of this they can help us to see more clearly in those areas where we can hardly see at all. The best remedy for this blindness, therefore, "is to keep the clean sea breeze of the centuries blowing through our minds."[19]

To summarize, classical Christian education consists of drawing from the collective wisdom of our fathers—listening to their stories, heeding their admonitions, and reflecting on their ideas. Chinese Christian educators should aim to draw their students into this "great conversation," but in order to do this, they must know who their fathers are.

CHAPTER 5

The Necessity of Chinese Roots

As Christians, we have been adopted into a spiritual family. When we believe in Jesus, we inherit a multitude of new fathers and mothers (Matt. 19:29). Moreover, this new Christian identity transcends our ethnic identity. Jesus plainly teaches that we must love Him more than our biological parents (Matt. 10:37). We are Christians first and Chinese or American or African second. Any Christian who finds his primary identity in his ethnicity or nationality has essentially denied the gospel. In Christ, "there is neither Jew nor Greek" (Gal. 3:28). Although the church fathers were willing to learn from their earthly fathers, they esteemed the words of their Heavenly Father much higher. Similarly, we should ascribe more authority to the writings of the church fathers than to those of our pagan fathers. If a Chinese Christian is asked, "Who are your ancestors?" he should think of Calvin before Confucius.

Nevertheless, Chinese Christians are still Chinese. They still belong to earthly parents whom God commands them to honor. "There is neither Jew nor Greek" does not mean that Chinese Christians are no longer Chinese. They cannot use this verse as an excuse for renouncing their Chinese heritage any more than they can use the verse "there is neither male nor female" (Gal. 3:28) as an excuse for renouncing their biological sex. We are all one in Christ, but we are still American and Chinese, male and female, and these identities come with certain obligations. There is neither male nor female in Christ, but God still requires men to "act like men" (1 Cor. 16:13). There is neither Jew nor Greek in Christ, but God still requires Chinese to act like Chinese, for that is what it means to honor their parents.

But I must clarify an important point here. When I say that the Chinese should act Chinese, I am not referring to their nationality. I do not mean that Chinese Christians must be faithful citizens of China (though they must).* The Bible generally identifies people groups based on common kinship. An Israelite is not someone who lives in a particular region in the Middle East or who lives under the authority of a particular government there. An Israelite is a descendant of Abraham who, as a result of these kindred ties, shares a common language and culture with other descendants of Abraham. Similarly, the Bible does not root Jewish education in the state. It does not view Jewish education as the teaching promoted by the state of Israel but rather as that tradition of learning passed down through generations of Israelites.

In the same way, when I speak of the "Chinese," I do not mean to identify these people on the basis of their shared *citizenship* but on the basis of their shared *kinship*. And when I speak of "Chinese education" I am not re-

---

*   See Rom. 13:1, 1 Pet. 2:13, 17, Mat. 22:21.

ferring to the education promoted by the government of China but to the tradition of learning passed down through generations of Chinese. Of course, if this is my meaning, then my use of the term "Chinese" in this book naturally invites criticism. For the "Chinese" were not traditionally one homogeneous ethnic group like the Israelites. They were made up of many different ethnic groups with different languages and cultures. If I were to be more precise, I would write separate books about "Han education," "Zhuang education," "Miao education," and so on.

But after Emperor Qin Shihuang united the country in 221 BC and instituted a common language, these ethnic groups increasingly mingled together and came to share a similar cultural and educational tradition, even as they retained certain aspects of their own unique ethnic cultures. Two Chinese people today might come from different ethnic backgrounds, but chances are their ancestors both revered Confucius. Therefore, for the sake of convenience, I speak of one common "Chinese tradition," even though the "Chinese people" are not technically one ethnic group. However, I do encourage Chinese Christians belonging to minority ethnic groups to incorporate classics from their own ethnic traditions into their curriculum, especially those groups whose culture is far removed from traditional Chinese culture, such as the Uyghurs.

I should also clarify that this view of ethnic identity does not preclude the possibility of a foreigner becoming "Chinese." The Old Testament allowed for Gentile slaves to be circumcised and to adopt Jewish culture, essentially making them "Israelites" (Ex. 12:48). Similarly, a Chinese couple may adopt an African child and become his legitimate parents. In this case, that child could rightly claim a Chinese heritage and would be just as obligated to honor his new parents and their culture as a native-born child would.

In short, when I suggest that Chinese Christians should embrace "Chinese education," I do not mean that they should embrace the education promoted by the state of China. I mean they should embrace the cultural tradition of their ancestors (which the state also often promoted). Imagine a child who refuses to listen to his father's stories, to eat the food his mother cooks him, to speak the language his parents speak, to perform the chores they assign, to heed the admonitions they give him. We would all agree that this child is not honoring his parents. In the same way, Chinese Christians who ignore the teachings and customs and values of their ancestors are not honoring them. They are disobeying the Fifth Commandment.

This command is not nullified if one's parents are pagans. We cannot refuse to honor our parents because they are not Christian any more than a Christian wife can refuse to honor her husband because he is not Christian. "Likewise, wives, be subject to your own husbands, so that even if some do not obey the word, they may be won without a word by the conduct of their wives, when they see your respectful and pure conduct" (1 Pet. 3:1–2). This command is admittedly difficult. It raises many questions: How does a Christian wife submit to a non-Christian husband who is encouraging her to sin? How does she show him respect without approving of his sin? How does she live with him without being influenced by his sin? These are difficult questions to answer, but the fact that the command is difficult to obey does not mean that she can reject it altogether. Similarly, God's command to Chinese Christians to honor their pagan ancestors raises many difficult questions: Which teachings and customs of their fathers should they teach and imitate? Which should they avoid? How do they praise their ancestors while avoiding unhealthy forms of tribalism and nationalism? How do they honor them without promoting their sin? The Fifth Commandment raises many difficult questions, but this does not mean they can opt out of obeying it.

Christians who refuse to honor their cultural heritage under the pretense of honoring their Christian heritage are like a Christian wife who refuses to honor her unbelieving husband because her "true" husband is Christ. They believe they are showing allegiance to Christ by renouncing their earthly heritage, but in reality they are dishonoring Him. When the Pharisees neglected honoring their earthly fathers under the pretense of honoring their heavenly Father, Jesus sharply rebuked them:

> God commanded, "Honor your father and your mother," and, "Whoever reviles father or mother must surely die." But you say, "If anyone tells his father or his mother, 'What you would have gained from me is given to God,' he need not honor his father." So for the sake of your tradition you have made void the word of God. You hypocrites! (Matt. 15:4–7)

Honoring our earthly ancestors is just as much a Christian duty as honoring our spiritual ancestors. It is not more

"Christian" to study Augustine than to study Mencius, just as it is not more "Christian" to talk with your pastor than with your father. God requires us to honor both men. It is not as though Augustine belongs to the category of "Christian studies" and Mencius to the category of "secular studies." In a classical Christian school, all studies are Christian studies. Chinese Christians should ascribe more authority to their Christian ancestors than to their Chinese ancestors, but they should expect God to teach them wisdom through both.

We do not dishonor our Christian ancestors by studying our pagan ancestors. On the contrary, we dishonor our Christian ancestors by *not* studying our pagan ancestors, for our Christian ancestors admonish us to study our pagan ancestors. When Chinese Christians read Calvin, they find Calvin telling them to read Confucius:

> If we reflect that the Spirit of God is the only fountain of truth, we will be careful, as we would avoid offering insult to him, not to reject or condemn truth wherever it appears. In despising the gifts, we insult the Giver. How, then, can we deny that truth must have beamed on those ancient lawgivers who arranged civil order and discipline with so much equity? Shall we say that the philosophers, in their exquisite researches and skillful description of nature, were blind? Shall we deny the possession of intellect to those who drew up rules for discourse, and taught us to speak in accordance with reason? Shall we say that those who, by the cultivation of the medical art, expended their industry in our behalf were only raving? What shall we say of the mathematical sciences? Shall we deem them

to be the dreams of madmen? Nay, we cannot read the writings of the ancients . . . without the highest admiration; an admiration which their excellence will not allow us to withhold. But shall we deem anything to be noble and praiseworthy, without tracing it to the hand of God? Far from us be such ingratitude.[1]

To refuse on principle to study the Confucian tradition is to "insult" the Spirit of God, Calvin says, because the wisdom contained in the tradition is a gift of God. Of course, wisdom is not contained only in the Confucian tradition. There is wisdom in the Mohist tradition, wisdom in the Daoist tradition—even wisdom in the Legalist tradition. Chinese Christians should be willing to learn from them all. But if we polled the dead and asked where the waters of wisdom flowed most abundantly, the majority would point to the Confucian tradition.

Calvin never visited China, so we do not have an example of him applying this teaching in a Chinese context. But a contemporary of Calvin's did visit China, and we can see how he approached Confucian culture. Matteo Ricci is one of the most well-known missionaries to China. Although he was not a Protestant like Calvin (he was a Jesuit), he believed very strongly in the idea of redeeming classical Chinese culture for the glory of God. Ricci believed that God had given much wisdom to the ancient Chinese, and he spent his life studying the Confucian classics so that he might better communicate the gospel to the Chinese and help them to see God's glory in their own cultural tradition. Although Ricci was sometimes too accommodating to Chinese culture (he attempted to reconcile ancestor worship with Christianity, for example), his general approach was adopted by many later Protestant missionaries. While these missionaries were more willing than Ricci to rebuke certain aspects of Chinese culture, they nevertheless founded schools that taught both Christian literature and the Chinese classics.

Many Christians in China are hesitant to engage with the Chinese classical tradition because they feel that to do so would be to stray from the Christian tradition which historically favored Western culture. But this is to overlook the history of the Chinese church. There were Christians in China at least as far back as the eighth century, and by the end of the sixteenth century they were eagerly engaging with the Chinese classical tradition. This continued up until the early twentieth century. If the Chinese church today decides to redeem their classical tradition, they will not be doing anything new. They will be following in the footsteps of their church fathers who began this work many centuries ago. Engaging with classical Chinese culture is not to stray from the tradition of the church. It *is* the tradition of the church. The Cultural Revolution abruptly ended this tradition, but it is the tradition of the Chinese church nonetheless. No Chinese classical Christian school can say it is committed to the Christian tradition while simultaneously refusing to learn from the Confucian tradition.

Chinese Christians are right to want to imitate their Christian ancestors who promoted Western classical education, but they must understand what true imitation entails. If we want to imitate a man who honors his parents, we do not do so by honoring *his* parents. We imitate him by honoring our own parents. If Chinese Christians desire to imitate the church fathers, they cannot simply study Plato, for the reason the church fathers studied Plato was because they respected the tradition of their ancestors. To truly imitate the church fathers, Chinese Christians must study the men whom their own ancestors revered, for if the church fathers had been born into Chinese culture, they would not have studied Plato and Aristotle—they would have studied Confucius and Mencius.

Some Chinese Christians feel especially obligated to study Western civilization because Christianity arose in the West. Jesus died at the hands of *Romans*. The New Testament epistles were written in *Greek*. Church history is woven into the fabric of Western culture, but this does not mean that Christianity is more authentic when it adopts Western cultural forms. Christianity has no ethnic identity. There is neither Jew nor Greek in Christ.

The first major debate in the early church concerned whether Gentiles had to adopt Jewish culture in order to become Christian. Those who believed that Gentiles ought to adopt Jewish culture argued that Christianity was born out of Jewish culture (and it was). They argued that Jesus viewed their classics as authoritative (and He did). They argued that the fathers of the faith were all Jews (and they were—at least most of them). And yet God said that their conclusion was wrong. "We should not trouble those of the Gentiles who turn to God" (Acts 15:19). The Judaizers were right that Christianity arose out of Jewish culture, but they were wrong that Gentiles must adopt this culture to be truly Christian. "For in Christ Jesus neither circumcision nor uncircumcision counts for anything, but only faith working through love" (Gal. 5:6). Jewish culture promotes certain dietary practices, but Christianity does not. "For the kingdom of God is not a matter of eating and drinking but of righteousness and peace and joy in the Holy Spirit" (Rom. 14:17). The Apostle Paul specifically warns us of mistaking human tradition for Christianity. "See to it that no one takes you captive by philosophy and empty deceit, according to human tradition . . . and not according to Christ" (Col. 2:8). Chinese Christian educators who advocate for Western education make the same kinds of arguments as the Judaizers: "The church arose out of Western culture." "The church fathers revered the Western classics." "The church fathers were European." But Christianity itself is not Western. Chinese Christians are not being more "Christian" by speaking Western languages or studying Western literature or singing Western music.

It is true that Christianity has historically influenced Western culture to a greater degree than it has Chinese culture, and insofar as a culture believes in and obeys Christ, it will display more Christian characteristics than those cultures that don't honor Him. We need not fall into the error of so-called "multiculturalism" and pretend that Chinese culture during the Ming Dynasty was in every respect equally superior to Western culture at the time. But the reason Christianity historically thrived in Western culture is not because Christianity is biased toward any one particular culture. The church did not flourish in the West because people there were *Western*. The church flourished in the West because people there were *Christian*. Therefore, if

Chinese Christians want to see the church thrive in China, they should not focus on teaching Western culture—they should focus on teaching Christ.

D. Z. Sheffield, a Protestant missionary who helped establish the first generation of Protestant schools in China during the nineteenth century, warns Chinese Christian educators of seeking salvation in Western civilization:

> If the old Confucian culture is simply to be adorned with a few additional trappings, borrowed from Western lands, then it is to be feared that the second estate will be worse than the first; that selfishness will only find more abundant nourishment and will produce more luxuriant fruitage. If we be asked, What is the most urgent present need of China? The answer must be, Not Western philosophy, and science, and art, but an essentially new life, in which love, and not selfishness, shall be the motive power of action . . . Western education, apart from Christianity, has no higher end to propose in life than has been presented by Confucianism.[2]

Sheffield even suggests that Christianity is needed in China "to protect China against the evils of Western civilization."[3]

Chinese Christians who adopt Western cultural forms do so because they want to express that they are part of a tradition that transcends their own cultural tradition. They sing Latin hymns because they want to acknowledge that they are Christians and not just Chinese. This is admirable, especially in a country that incessantly promotes extreme nationalism, but Chinese believers should not think that singing Latin hymns is more in keeping with the Christian tradition than singing Chinese ones. Martin Luther caused an uproar by insisting that German Christians worship in German instead of the conventional Latin. This emphasis on worshiping in one's native tongue was one of the greatest contributions of the Protestant Reformation. If the Chinese church wants to confess their protestant identity, they can certainly do it in Latin, but they can do it best in Chinese.

Unlike Islam, Christianity does not prescribe one particular cultural form—it adapts to all of them. To the Jews it becomes Jewish, to the Greeks it becomes Greek, to the Chinese it becomes Chinese. It becomes "all things to all people" (1 Cor. 9:22). The fact that the New Testament is written in Greek does not mean that God has a special affinity for Greek culture. God did not write the New Testament in Greek because He wanted to promote Greek culture. He wrote it in Greek because His audience spoke Greek. When His audience changed, so did His language. When the Spirit fell upon the disciples at Pentecost, they did not all begin speaking in Greek. They began speaking in the tongues of "every nation under heaven" (Acts 2:6). When God eventually brought the Gospel to China, He spoke in Chinese. He no longer spoke of Christ as the *Logos* but as the *Dao*. The fact that God adapted His word to a Greek context does not mean that He desires Chinese Christians to embrace Greek culture. If anything, it means that He wants them to embrace Chinese culture, for He wants them to *imitate* Him. Just as He became Greek to win the Greeks, He wants Christians in China to become Chinese to win the Chinese.

In his treatise on Christian education, Augustine tells us that love requires us to "pay special regard to those who, by accidents of time, or place, or circumstances, are brought into closer connection with us."[4] Christians in China have a greater obligation to love their Chinese neighbors than they do their European neighbors halfway around the globe. This principle should influence what they study. A chef in China can serve those around him best if he studies Chinese cuisine. If he studies Western cuisine, he may be able to cook many delicious dishes, but most of them will not be received well by the people he is serving. God has called the Chinese church to serve the Chinese people. Chinese Christians, therefore, should make it their aim to understand the palate of the Chinese mind.

Consider the Chinese language, for example. On the one hand, language provides us with a means of communicating our thoughts with our neighbor. If a Chinese Christian does not understand the language his neighbor speaks, he cannot communicate with his neighbor, and consequently he cannot Christianize his culture. But language is not only how we communicate. It is how we *think*. We process and order our thoughts by means of language, which is why the medieval Trivium views logic as inseparable from grammar and rhetoric. The words we've inherited from our fathers provide us with categories of thought by which we interpret the world. Chinese children, therefore, must study the words of their fathers in order to think and communicate clearly with their own people.

But Christians must study more than language if they want to love their neighbors. Our imaginations have been shaped by many different cultural influences, all of which must be studied. If we want to capture the imagination of our neighbors through story and art, we must understand the cultural tradition that has shaped their imaginations. Why are *The Lord of the Rings* and *The Chronicles of Narnia* so compelling to Western audiences? How were Tolkien and Lewis able to capture the Western imagination so well? Not only were they steeped in theology and church history, they were also steeped in the ancient myths and languages that shaped and formed the Western imagination. Chinese Christians who desire to write similar stories that capture the Chinese imagination must also be steeped in the ancient languages and lore of their own people. Confucius recognized long ago this connection between loving our neighbors and learning about them: "Fan Chi asked about *ren*. The Master said, 'It is to love men.' He asked about knowledge. The Master said, 'It is to know men.'"[5]

Classical education not only helps us to understand our neighbors, it also helps us to understand ourselves. Hugh of Saint Victor identifies this as one of the primary goals of classical Christian education: "Of all things to be sought, the first is that Wisdom in which the Form of the Perfect Good stands fixed. Wisdom illuminates man so that he may recognize himself."[6] Calvin makes a similar point in the beginning of his *Institutes*: "Our wisdom, in so far as it ought to be deemed true and solid Wisdom, consists almost entirely of two parts: the knowledge of God and of ourselves."[7] Understanding who we are helps us to understand who God is, for we are made in His image. Moreover, we cannot obey God if we do not understand who we are and what kind of person He wants us to become. This is not just a Christian emphasis. Mencius recognized this almost two millennia before Calvin: "A man who knows his own nature will know Heaven. By retaining his heart and nurturing his nature he is serving Heaven."[8]

The Bible gives us the clearest picture of ourselves, and therefore we should devote most of our time to studying it. But the Bible is not our only source of revelation. God also provides us with general revelation through our consciences, our reason, and the world around us. Our pagan ancestors did not have access to special revelation, but they did have access to general revelation, and they spent much time thinking and writing about the nature of man and the importance of self-cultivation. These questions are at the heart of Confucianism: *What is a* junzi, *and how do I become one?*† Confucianism cannot provide a complete answer to this question—apart from Christ, no philosophy can—but it can still tell us many truths about ourselves and the way we should live. We should not dismiss the Confucian classics simply because the Bible is more accurate and complete. The Bible tells us the most fundamental truths about ourselves and the world in which we live, but it does not tell us everything about ourselves and the world. That is why we teach books other than the Bible in classical Christian schools. The Bible tells us that God made all trees, but it does not tell us the difference between an evergreen and an aspen. The Bible tells us that God made all nations, but it does not tell us the difference between an American

---

† A *junzi* is the ideal or "superior" man, the kind of person all of us should strive to become.

man and a Chinese man. Chinese children cannot come to a complete understanding of themselves by only studying the Bible. That is why God gave them fathers.

Not everything the Chinese classics teach is correct. We listen to our fathers in order to learn wisdom, but our fathers are not all-wise. We should not listen to them as we listen to God. Our fathers are fallible; God is not. Therefore, Chinese Christians must not accept everything written in the classics without question. They should take to heart what is true and reject what is false, but even what is rejected should be studied. We are shaped both by the wisdom and folly of our fathers. A girl whose father has a low view of women will inevitably grow up with certain ideas and attitudes about herself and others that are a direct result of her father's corrupt worldview. Understanding her father's beliefs will help her better understand why she thinks and feels the way she does. When Chinese Christians understand the errors of their ancestors, they can better understand their own flaws, and as they critique the folly of ancient culture under the guidance of Christian teachers, they become better equipped to critique and correct their own culture.

Saint Basil (239–379), when admonishing young Christians to study pagan literature, emphasizes this two-fold benefit:

> If, then, there is any affinity between the two literatures (i.e. the Bible and pagan literature), a knowledge of them should be useful to us in our search for truth; if not, the comparison, by emphasizing the

contrast, will be of no small service in strengthening our regard for the better one.[9]

In other words, wherein pagan literature echoes the teachings of Scripture, it supports us in our search for truth; and wherein pagan literature contradicts Scripture, it highlights the superiority of Scripture. In both cases, the study of pagan literature benefits Christians.

But studying our own cultural tradition does not only help us to understand ourselves and our neighbors, it also helps us to recognize the beauty of the home God has given us. That is, it makes us *grateful*. N. D. Wilson, a popular American children's author and Christian, once said that he longed to live in England as a child because the magical stories he read always took place in England. He read C. S. Lewis and believed that only English wardrobes were magical. He read J. R. R. Tolkien and felt that only English trees could talk. His own American home seemed boring and lifeless, but through the help of his classical Christian school, he slowly began to recognize the unique magic of his own home. He later resolved to write stories that would make American children long to travel not to England but to their own backyards, to discover God's glory hidden inside their own wardrobes and among their own trees. If Chinese children are raised only on Western stories, they will experience the same fate as young Wilson—they will come to despise their own home and long for somebody else's; they will feel envy instead of gratitude; they will come to believe that magic exists only in the West.

The Western classical tradition has one great advantage over the Chinese classical tradition—it is largely a Christian tradition. The Gospel was sown in Western soil long before it came to China, and as a result it has had much more time to transform Western culture than it has Chinese culture. When we compare medieval Western culture with medieval Chinese culture, we can easily find aspects of Western culture that are superior to Chinese culture, but this is not a good reason to reject Chinese culture. If we discover that no one in our family believes in Christ, the proper Christian response is not to crucify them, it is to *convert* them. At one point, Western culture was even more pagan than Chinese culture. The only reason it became Christian is because the church in the West redeemed it. The Chinese church should have similar ambitions for their own culture. Jesus did not come only to redeem Western philosophy or Western literature or Western art; He came "to reconcile to himself *all things*" (Col. 1:20).

When the wise men from the East came to Jesus, they did not come empty-handed. They came bearing gifts. They laid at His feet the greatest treasures their culture had to offer. Jesus is once again calling wise men from the East to Himself, but this time He is not calling them from a manger. He is calling them from a throne. May they not come empty-handed.

CHAPTER 6

A Christian Approach to
Chinese Classical Education

T he church fathers did not despise their own classical, pagan tradition. On the contrary, they greatly respected it because they understood that the wisdom hidden in the tradition was a gift of God. In the same way, Chinese Christians must not despise their own classical, pagan tradition. For God gave wisdom to their ancestors just as He did to the ancient Greeks. At the same time, they should not be content merely to recover the old Chinese tradition, for Christianity gives us a clearer, more accurate perspective of the world. We do not want to reject Chinese classical education, nor do we merely want to recover it. We want to *redeem* it. Like the paralytic at the Pool of Bethesda, the Chinese classical tradition has spent its entire life on its back. It aspires to the towering peaks of wisdom, it thirsts for the vibrant waters of virtue, it longs for the lush-green pastures of *ren*—but it cannot move. It smells the fresh mountain air, it hears the trickling of the streams, it sees the sun-kissed horizon—and yet it is confined to a mat.

We cannot read the classics without feeling a sort of quiet dejection. The ancients describe in breathtaking detail the glories of *ren*, and occasionally they even speak as though someone might possibly attain it. But in the midst of their impressive, high-minded rhetoric, they betray an unsettling conviction that no one will actually succeed. "Long has the attainment of *ren* been difficult among men!"[1] "I have never seen one who loves *ren* and hates what is not *ren*."[2] "'Practice righteousness to attain the *Dao*'—I have heard these words, but I have not seen such men."[3] "I have no hopes of meeting a good man."[4] "It is all over! I have not seen one who loves virtue as he loves sex."[5] Confucius is not only talking about other people in these passages—he includes himself in these indictments: "The Master said, 'The way of the *junzi* is threefold, but I cannot attain it—virtuous (*ren*), he is free from anxieties; wise, he is free from perplexities; bold, he is free from fear.'"[6] He is deeply aware of his own inability:

> The Master said: ". . . In the *Dao* of the *junzi* there are four duties, not one of which I am yet able to perform: To serve my father, as I would require my son to serve me—this I am not yet able to do; to serve my prince as I would require my minister to serve me—this I am not yet able to do; to serve my elder brother as I would require my younger brother to serve me—this I am not yet able to do; to set the example in behaving to a friend, as I would require him to behave to me—this I am not yet able to do."[7]

The Chinese classical tradition is rich, but it is lame. It can teach us many things—not just about morality but about politics, philosophy, mathematics, and art—but apart from Christ, these arts are like legs that we cannot use. The tradition is remarkable, but it is maimed by sin. When Christ confronts it, however, everything changes. He looks down upon this ancient tradition long paralyzed by sin and with divine authority says, "Stand up! Pick up your mat and walk."

In Christ, all that the wise men of old longed for is fulfilled. All of their frayed philosophies are mended. The ancients could intuit much truth about God and His creation. "He did not leave himself without witness" (Acts 14:17). They could hear the song that He was composing, but they could only hear the rhythm. When we read their writings, we can sense the steady pulse of divine order and meaning echoing through the cosmos, but only in the crucified and risen Christ do we hear the melody.

As Christians, we cannot be content merely recovering the Chinese classical Christian tradition, for we do not want our students simply tapping their feet to the rhythm of the divine song—we want them to *sing*. We want them to know the entirety of the gospel song, and this can only happen if the risen Christ is at the heart of our curriculum. At the same time, we cannot dismiss the Chinese classical tradition, for it is the rhythm over which the melody is played. It is part of the song. We cannot understand the gospel of Christ without understanding the world He came to redeem. The history of China's redemption does not begin with Tang-dynasty missionaries, for God began composing this song long before any missionary stepped foot in China. He created this land. He created these people. He created this culture. He has been among the Chinese people ever since there have been Chinese people. He revealed himself first through the philosophers and the poets and the historians. "They knew God," says the Scriptures (Rom. 1:21). His law was "written on their hearts" (Rom. 2:15). They knew they had an obligation to honor Him, but they also knew they had not done so. The beating of God's law in their hearts was not to them the beating of a drum but the pounding of nails into a coffin. No matter how hard they tried, they could not live up to the impossible standards of *ren*. To them, life was little more than the incessant drilling of moral law, but when the fullness of time had come, Heaven sang the melody. Law turned into gospel; rhythm turned into song. And this time, it did not come through the mouths of the poets and philosophers, but through the prophets and evangelists. This is the same story the Apostle Paul tells the Athenians:

> And he made from one man every nation of mankind to live on all the face of the earth…that they should seek God, in the hope that they might feel their way towards him and find him. Yet he is actually not far from each one of us, for "In him we live and move and have our being" as even some of your own poets have said, "For we are indeed his offspring." . . . But now he commands all people everywhere to repent, because he has fixed a day on which he will judge the world in righteousness by a man whom he has appointed; and of this he has given assurance to all by raising him from the dead" (Acts 17:26–28, 30–31).

Paul does not say that God was absent from ancient Greek culture. On the contrary, he says that God was with them from the beginning, and moreover, He intended that they should not only "seek" and "feel their way" towards Him but "find" Him. Paul quotes pagan classics to prove that even the ancient Greeks knew of Him. Nevertheless, their knowledge of God was very limited. They knew *of* God but they did not *know* Him. He was worshiped but "unknown" (Acts 17:23).* But in Christ this God is finally and fully revealed. Through repentance and faith in Christ we can finally *know* Him. Chinese Christian educators must seek to tell this story, to sing this song. How do we redeem the Chinese classical tradition? How do we help Chinese children to see the history of Chinese culture as the history of God's redemption? We must listen. God was not silent in ancient China, and He is not silent now. May He give us ears to hear.

Before considering the content of Chinese classical education, we must first consider what the tradition says about the nature of education itself. The *Record of Rites* contains the earliest systematic treatment of education in the world—the *Record of Learning* (*Xueji* 学记). In the *Record of Learning*, we find a striking critique of "modern" education:

> Nowadays, teachers drone on as they read through their texts, making them ever more opaque. They continue to convey information, but as they move forward, they pay no heed to conveying what is meant or whether it is understood. They are unable to help students develop into virtuous and honest persons. In their teaching, they fail to guide their students to

---

* See the section on Paganism in Chapter 10: Obstacles to Classical Christian Education in China for a more detailed explanation of this theological point.

grow to their full potential. What they provide is perverse, and what they demand is absurd. Such being the case, this is why students learn to detest their studies and come to resent their teachers. They have suffered the pains of trying without realizing the benefits of learning. The moment that students complete their course of study they abandon any further interest in learning. Is this not why such ineffective teaching is a waste of time?[8]

We can hardly believe that this passage was written over two millennia ago. It is a stunningly accurate description of modern Chinese education (which just goes to show that "modern" education is nothing new). The *Record of Learning* refutes the pragmatism that characterizes much of modern education: "The Great Virtue is not limited to government office, the Great *Dao* is not a tool."[9] The *Great Learning* ends on a similar point: "In a state, gain is not to be considered prosperity, but its prosperity will be found in righteousness."[10] Many self-professed Confucians strayed from their master's teaching on this point. They pursued learning simply to impress those around them and to attain high seats of power in the government. "Men of antiquity studied to improve themselves; men today study to impress others."[11] Christian schools should recover the original Confucian emphasis of learning as pursuit of the *Dao*.

Confucius elegantly sums up his educational philosophy as follows: "Set your heart on the *Dao*, base yourself on virtue, lean upon *ren*, and journey in the arts."[12] First and foremost, learning is the pursuit of the *Dao*. The ancients understood the *Dao* as that creative Force or Principle underlying all reality and the ultimate Way or Truth toward which we all must strive. It is the very *telos* of education. In Christ, however, we learn that the *Dao* is not just a force or principle, it is a person:

> In the beginning was the *Dao*, and the *Dao* was with God, and the *Dao* was God. He was in the beginning with God. All things were made through him, and without him was not any thing made that was made. In him was life, and the life was the light of men . . . And the *Dao* became flesh and dwelt among us, and we have seen his glory, glory as of the only Son from the Father, full of grace and truth (Jn. 1:1–4, 14).†

In Christ, Confucius's call to "set your heart on the *Dao*" takes on a deeper meaning. All learning becomes a striving after knowing and enjoying Christ. In the words of Augustine:

> You are to concentrate all your thoughts, your whole life and your whole intelligence upon Him from whom you derive all that you bring. For when He says, "With all thy heart, and with all thy soul, and with all thy mind," He means that no part of our life is to be unoccupied, and to afford room, as it were, for the wish to enjoy some other object, but that whatever else may suggest itself to us as an object worthy of love is to be borne into the same channel in which the whole current of our affections flows.[13]

---

† The Chinese Bible translates Word (*Logos*) as *Dao*.

But how do we pursue this *Dao*? The first step, of course, is to believe the gospel. We are united with Christ by faith alone in His death and resurrection for us. But the Christian life does not stop there. We continue pursuing Christ by pursuing holiness. The Bible describes this process of sanctification in many ways, but in short it entails being transformed by conforming our thoughts and actions to those consistent with Christ (Eph. 4:17–23).

The ancient Chinese similarly viewed pursuit of the *Dao* as a process of becoming a "sage" (literally "holy man," *shengren* 圣人), or the more easily attainable "gentleman" (*junzi* 君子), through self-cultivation. "The *Dao* of Great Learning lies in making bright virtue brilliant; in making the people new; in coming to rest at the highest good."[14] Education is not merely about transmitting knowledge but transforming people. "From the Son of Heaven down to the mass of the people, all must consider the cultivation of the person the root of everything besides. It cannot be, when the root is neglected, that what should spring from it will be well ordered."[15]

As Christians, we understand that personal transformation ultimately only comes through a knowledge of God. Many suggest that Confucianism entirely lacks this emphasis. They paint Confucianism as a secular philosophy that is only concerned with human affairs, but this is simply not true.[16] Confucianism certainly *focuses* on human affairs, but it nevertheless acknowledges the importance of knowing and honoring Heaven. "In order to know men, [a ruler] must know Heaven."[17] "Unable to rejoice in Heaven, [a ruler] cannot perfect himself."[18] Although the duty of praying and sacrificing to Heaven was primarily laid on the shoulders of the emperor who acted as a mediator between Heaven and the people, the common man still had an obligation to honor Heaven with his life. Daily observance of rites was submission to the moral order established by Heaven. Mencius says that the common man worships Heaven through seeking personal cultivation: "By retaining his heart and nurturing his nature he is serving Heaven."[19] Confucius warns us of sinning against Heaven: "He who offends against Heaven has none to whom he can pray."[20] We find this same emphasis in other schools of thought, such as that of Mozi: "If the rulers and the gentlemen of the world really desire to follow the *Dao* and benefit the people they have only to obey the will of Heaven, the origin of magnanimity and righteousness. Obedience to the will of Heaven is the standard of righteousness."[21]

Chinese classical education, therefore, is not secular education as many claim. It is rooted in Heaven: "What Heaven ordains is called one's nature. To follow one's nature is called the *Dao*. Cultivating the *Dao* is called education."[22] Education is understanding the nature that Heaven has given us and seeking to live in accordance with it. Zhu Xi expounds on this idea in his preface to the *Great Learning*:

> From the time Heaven (first) sent down and gave birth to the people, it did not fail to give anyone a nature with benevolence (*ren* 仁), righteousness (*yi* 义), propriety (*li* 礼), and wisdom (*zhi* 智). Nonetheless, their endowments of innate *qi* (气) are sometimes unequal. Consequently, some are unable to understand what their natures have and to bring them to com-

pletion. As soon as those who were intelligent and wise enough to be able to fathom their natures stood out among them, Heaven decreed that they were the rulers and teachers of countless millions, and made them rule over and educate others, so that they could revive their natures.[23]

The purpose of education is to restore the natures given us by Heaven—our "heavenly natures" (*tianxing* 天性). This process is not something that man discovered but that Heaven "decreed." Heaven decided of Its own volition to appoint men and women to teach us so that we might restore our God-given natures.

Zhu's understanding of education is not entirely consistent with Christianity. For example, we know that our problem is not an imbalance of *qi*—it is sin. But we clearly see God's fingerprints in these passages. Heaven *did* create us; we *are* ignorant of our true identities; our natures *do* need to be restored; and they *are* restored through teachers which Heaven has appointed. Compare Zhu's words to those of Hugh of Saint Victor in the early twelfth century:

This, then, is that dignity of our nature which all naturally possess in equal measure, but which all do not equally understand. For the mind, stupefied by bodily sensations and enticed out of itself by sensuous forms, has forgotten what it was, and, because it does not remember that it was anything different, believes that it is nothing except what is seen. But we are restored through instruction, so that we may recognize our nature ... This, then, is what the arts are concerned with, this is what they intend, namely, to restore within us the divine likeness.[24]

Chinese Classical Christian schools are not promoting a form of education opposed to Zhu's. On the contrary, we are perfecting it. In Christ, the Confucian program of education finds completion. The Confucian tradition says, "In order to know men, [a ruler] must know Heaven."[25] In Christ, we know the true nature of Heaven and, consequently, ourselves.‡ The Confucian tradition says, "Unable to rejoice in Heaven, [a ruler] cannot perfect himself."[26] In Christ, we are enabled to truly rejoice in Heaven and consequently perfect ourselves. In Christ, our sins are forgiven, our knowledge is renewed, and our natures are restored. In conclusion, then, we may summarize the goal of the Christian six arts curriculum as "self-cultivation through pursuit of the *Dao* (Christ)."

Having established the goal of learning, we must now consider with what attitude to approach it. The Chinese classical tradition stresses the importance of studying with a correct frame of mind. It is not enough for a student merely to show up to class and complete his assignments. If he does not do these things with a proper attitude, then his studies will prove fruitless. Specifically, the ancients emphasized three frames of mind with which a student should approach his studies: joy, reverence, and humility.

---

‡ Some argue that the "Heaven" of ancient China was not the God of Christianity. I refute this objection in the section on Paganism in Chapter 10: Obstacles to Classical Christian Education in China.

The *Analects* of Confucius begins, "To study and at due times practice what one has studied, is this not a pleasure?"[27] Joy is the motivating force behind proper learning. When learning is motivated only by duty, not only will students fail to remember what they have learned, they will also fail to understand the material as they ought. In order to properly understand a thing, we must engage it not only with our intellect but also with our affections. "Knowing something is not so good as loving it; loving it is not so good as taking joy in it."[28] This attitude should permeate Christian classrooms, for God does not want our students merely to know about the world He has created—He wants them to delight in it. "For you, O LORD, have made me glad by your work; at the works of your hands I sing for joy" (Ps. 92:4). "Great are the works of the LORD, studied by all who delight in them" (Ps. 111:2). We might successfully teach our students all about elephants—where they live, how long they live, what special traits and abilities they possess—but if our students do not come away *loving* elephants, then we have failed them.

But approaching our studies with joy does not mean treating them flippantly like a party game. We must treat them with proper reverence. Confucius identifies three things especially worthy of our respect: "There are three things which the *junzi* reveres. He reveres the ordinances of Heaven. He reveres great men. He reveres the words of sages."[29] For the ancients, the ordinances of Heaven (what we call the "will of God") were not perspicuous, for they did not come in the form of human language. When Confucius was asked why he spoke so little, he replied, "Does Heaven speak?"[30] Heaven's ordinances were not revealed through words but through history, tradition, and conscience. Of course, Confucius was right. At that time, God had not spoken to the Chinese through words. But eventually He did reveal His will to them through words. Now, "revering the ordinances of Heaven" primarily means honoring and studying Scripture, for it is there where we most clearly see the will of God. At the same time, we must continue listening to God through general revelation, for "the heavens declare the glory of God, and the sky above proclaims his handiwork. Day to day pours out speech, and night to night reveals knowledge" (Ps. 19:1–2).

Secondly, students should revere "great men." For Confucius, this primarily means great political and military leaders. The Apostle Peter similarly instructs us, "Fear God. Honor the emperor" (1 Pet. 2:17). This principle should influence what we study. Time does not allow us to study the words and deeds of every human in history— we must pick and choose. "Revering great men" means we should favor studying influential leaders, for God frequently directs the course of society and culture through people whom He has placed in special positions of authority. For Christians, this also includes great leaders of the church.

Finally, students should also revere "the words of sages." In His grace, God bestows a special measure of wisdom on a select few throughout history, and He calls us to seek this wisdom like gold (Prv. 2:4). Frequently, this wisdom is located in great thinkers who died long ago, which is why the classical tradition especially stresses studying the ancients. "The Master said, 'I am not one who was born in the possession of knowledge; I am one who is fond of antiquity, and earnest in seeking it there."[31] Confucius identified himself as "a transmitter and not a maker, believing in and loving the ancients."[32] However, this aspect of the Chinese classical tradition still needs to be redeemed by Christ, for in the past, it often veered off into ancestor worship. We ought to honor the ancients, but, as Augustine says, our love for them must be properly ordered. Our love for our ancestors must not exceed our love for God. Moreover, we must not treat the Bible as just another "classic" among many. The Bible is our ultimate standard to which all the words of the sages must submit.

Christianity also brings new meaning to the word "sage" or "holy man" (*shengren* 圣人), for according to Scripture, the holiest of men are not those endowed with much knowledge according to worldly standards but those who are indwelt by the Holy Spirit:

> For consider your calling, brothers: not many of you were wise according to worldly standards . . . But God chose what is foolish in the world to shame the wise . . . Now we have received not the spirit of the world, but the Spirit who is from God, that we might understand the things freely given us by God. And we impart this in words not taught by human wisdom but taught by the Spirit (1 Cor. 1:26–27, 2:12–13).

Therefore, "revering the words of sages" especially means revering the words of great Christian thinkers throughout history.

To summarize, the "three reverences" orient our hearts by instilling in us a proper respect toward our studies. They also provide guidance regarding what kinds of knowledge we should prioritize. We should revere the ordinances of God: "He who reveres the commandment will be rewarded" (Prv. 13:13). We should revere great men: "They stood in awe of the king, because they perceived that the wisdom of God was in him" (1 Kg. 3:28). And we should revere the words of the sages: "Incline your ear, and hear the words of the wise" (Prv. 22:17).

Finally, besides joy and reverence, we must also approach our studies with humility. The Bible tells us, "When pride comes, then comes disgrace, but with the humble is wisdom" (Prv. 11:2). Learning requires humility because to learn something new we must first confess that we do not know it. The man who refuses to admit his ignorance cannot learn anything. "The Master said, 'Yu, shall I tell you what it is to know? To say you know when you know, and to say you do not when you do not, that is knowledge.'"[33] In fact, the more we learn, the more we recognize just how ignorant we truly are. As the *Record of Rites* says, "When he learns, one knows his own deficiencies."[34] Humility also exposes us to a greater abundance of knowledge because the proud man refuses to learn from anyone he considers inferior to himself. Sometimes Christians fall into this trap when confronted with scholarship written by non-Christians. We do not want to admit that a non-Christian might actually have something valuable to teach us, so we refuse to study it and remain ignorant. Our pride prevents us from growing in knowledge. But Confucius reminds us that a true *junzi* "loves learning and is not ashamed to ask and learn of his inferiors."[35]

Having acquired a proper frame of mind, students can then begin their studies. Chinese classical education promotes three kinds of self-cultivation—moral, intellectual, and physical, but it prioritizes moral cultivation:

> A young man should be filial within his home and respectful of elders when outside, should be careful and trustworthy, broadly caring of people at large, and should cleave to *ren*. If he has energy left over, he may study *wen*.[36]

Christians should retain this emphasis, but in praising the Confucian pursuit of moral virtue, Christians must be careful to avoid moralism and legalism. We must stress that God himself is our ultimate aim, that we pursue virtue as a means of glorifying Him, and that we live up to His moral law only by resting in His grace through Christ. Nevertheless, God *does* call us to live upright lives. The pursuit of moral virtue is an honorable thing, and the specific virtues that Confucianism promotes are worthy of our admiration and pursuit.

As for intellectual cultivation, Christian schools should promote critical thinking as vigorously as Confucius. "There may be those who act without knowing why. I do not do so."[37] "Learning without thought is labor lost."[38] This is entirely in keeping with the teaching of Scripture. "The simple believes everything, but the prudent gives thought to his steps (Prv. 14:15)." "Test everything; hold fast what is good (1 Thess. 5:21)." The *Doctrine of the Mean* helpfully summarizes the most effective method of study: "Study it broadly. Question it meticulously. Reflect on it carefully. Distinguish it clearly. Practice it earnestly."[39] Christian teachers may imitate Zhu Xi by hanging this passage above their classroom door.

Another valuable inheritance from the Confucian tradition—particularly the Neo-Confucian tradition—concerns the pursuit of *li* (理) (not to be confused with "rites" (*li* 礼)). In his commentary on the *Great Learning*, Zhu Xi explains "the investigation of things" (*gewu* 格物):

> "The extension of knowing lies in the investigation of things" means that if we wish to extend our knowing it consists in fathoming the principle (*li* 理) of any thing or affair we come into contact with . . . After exerting himself for a long time, one day [a man] will experience a breakthrough to integral comprehension (*guantong* 贯通). Then the qualities of all things, whether internal or external, refined or coarse, will all be apprehended . . ."[40]

For Zhu, properly knowing a thing does not entail simply understanding its material cause—an emphasis of modern education. We can only truly know a thing when we understand its *li*, the mysterious "principle" that gives it form and order. All things share in one ultimate *li*, the *taiji* (太极), and when we comprehend that principle (*qiongli* 穷理) we can understand the true nature of all things and how they are interrelated. For Zhu, this principle was a mystery, but God has made this mystery known in Christ. "All things were created through him and for him. And he is before all things, and in him all things hold together (Col. 1:16–17)." Like Zhu, we should not be satisfied with teaching mere "facts" about the world. The ultimate goal of Christian educators is to help students to see Christ in all things—to see "the moon reflected on ten thousand streams"[41]—and through Him to understand how all knowledge is interconnected. In his treatise on Christian education, Hugh of Saint Victor uses very similar language as Zhu to describe Christ, calling Him "the primordial Idea or Pattern of things" in whose "likeness all things have been formed."[42] Hugh says that philosophy is essentially a love for and a pursuit of this Idea or Pattern.

Chinese classical education does not promote "specialization" like much of modern education, which compartmentalizes knowledge and leads students to believe that literature has no relation to biology or that history has no relation to mathematics. The ancient Chinese recognized the unity of the cosmos. Rather than promoting "majors," they promoted "broad learning" (*boxue* 博学): "By extensively studying all learning (*boxue*), and keeping himself under the restraint of the rules of propriety (*li*), one may thus likewise not err from what is right."[43] Zhu Xi particularly emphasized this point. "Of the books under heaven, there is none not to be 'broadly studied' (*boxue*)."[44] "Scholars should know about all things under heaven."[45] This does not mean that students must have a thorough understanding of each subject they study (something no one can attain). The goal, rather, is to get a general sense of each subject and how it is related to the others. "Although one may not be able to see through their essences and subtleties, one should nevertheless know the general outlines."[46] This is the same principle that underlies the liberal arts tradition in the West.

The Chinese classical tradition also provides us with a number of very practical principles regarding the art of teaching:

> The first precept of the academy is precaution (*yu* 豫): Guard against bad habits before they become ingrained. The second is readiness and timing (*shi* 时): Choose the most efficacious time for teaching. The third is felicity and flexibility (*xun* 孙): Adjust the structure and sequence of your teaching to suit subject and student. The fourth is observation and discussion (*mo* 摩): Let students improve each other through interaction. These four precepts are the way to ensure effective instruction. If you try to prohibit bad habits after they have formed, no matter how hard you struggle with them, you will fail. If students miss the right moment to learn, it will be difficult for them to succeed regardless of how assiduously they apply themselves. If the teacher lacks structure and fails to make the necessary connections, there will not be much that learners can make of the fragments and confusion they receive. If students study alone without the company of peers and friends, they become idiosyncratic in their manner and limited in their learning. Students who always party with friends tend to turn against their teachers, and those who engage in too many frivolous activities and distractions tend to neglect their studies. These six failings will lead to ineffective teaching and learning.[47]

Many classical Christian schools in America have designed their schools according to the blueprint laid out by Dorothy Sayers in her essay "The Lost Tools of Learning." Sayers divides the classical Trivium (grammar, logic, and rhetoric) into three "stages" with each stage corresponding to the developmental stages of the child. As a child progresses through each stage, he is particularly receptive to certain kinds of knowledge and unreceptive to others. The key lies in teaching the appropriate subject matter at the most opportune time. And yet, two thousand years before Sayers, the Chinese were already stressing the importance of "choosing the most efficacious time for teaching" and "adjusting the structure and sequence of your teaching to suit subject and student."

This does not simply mean teaching age-appropriate content or using age-appropriate methods. The teacher must consider more than the students' ages. She must consider their individual personalities and tendencies:

> Teachers must understand the four errors that students make. In their attitude to their studies, some err on the side of overextending themselves, and some in focusing too narrowly; some err on the side of thinking it is too easy, and some in giving up. These four errors arise from differences in the temperament of the learners. It is only when teachers understand the temperaments of their students that they can save them from error.[48]

The classical Chinese tradition does not view students as robots into which the teacher uploads information. It views them as *people*, and so should Christians. We are not training test-taking machines. We are raising up young men and women made in the image of God. As such, we should strive to know each student, to understand his God-given personality, to realize his individual strengths and weaknesses, and to adapt our teaching accordingly.

The *Record of Learning* also provides us with many other practical teaching tips. For example:

> The role of a *junzi* as a teacher is to enlighten: to lead students forward through reasoning and inspiration rather than to drag them, to offer them encouragement rather than to hold them back, to open their minds rather than to provide them with fixed answers.[49]

[. . .]

> Those who would respond to questions by the mindless recitation of memorized texts are not worthy of becoming teachers. It is essential that teachers listen and respond to the questions that students have, and it is only when students are unable to formulate their own questions that teachers offer them instruction. When students after having been instructed still do not understand, teachers may dismiss them and wait for a more opportune time.[50]

[. . .]

> Those who are good at asking questions approach their task as if carving hard wood. First, they chip away at the soft parts and then set to work on the knots. If they keep at it, the difficulties are gradually resolved. Those who are poor at asking questions do just the opposite.[51]

Chinese readers will notice a stark contrast between these teaching methods and those employed in most modern public schools. They may even find these descriptions at odds with their understanding of ancient Chinese education. Many assume that traditional Chinese education emphasizes learning by rote with little emphasis on critical thinking. This is not true. Chinese classical education did eventually become corrupt, but this is not because teachers faithfully imitated the classical tradition. It is because they strayed from the tradition. The ancients criticized "mindless recitation of memorized texts" and "providing fixed answers." Education was not a passive experience in which the teacher lectured and the students mindlessly absorbed the teacher's words. It was a dynamic interaction between teacher and student. "To open their minds rather than to provide them with fixed answers" (*kai er fu da* 开而弗达) can be translated more literally as "he opens the way but does not conduct to the end (without the learner's own efforts)."[52] In classical Chinese pedagogy, the teacher's goal is not simply to get the student from point A to point B. It is to help the student get from point A to point B *by himself.* The teacher does not drag him. She "opens the way" to point B by asking questions that require him to use his own ingenuity and critical thinking skills to walk there by himself.

We understand a truth best when we discover it ourselves. We can tell a child that three times three equals nine, and he might memorize the formula after much practice. But he will not understand *why* three times three equals nine. He will know the "answer" but he will not understand the concept. But if we give him three pieces of candy and ask him how many pieces he would have if we did this two more times, then he will discover both the answer and the concept. The next time he is asked what four times four equals, he will be able to reason his way to the answer, even if he has never memorized the formula 4×4=16. This is what it means "to lead students forward through reasoning and inspiration rather than to drag them" (*dao er fu qian* 道而弗牽). The student who simply memorizes multiplication tables will only be able to answer the question if he has previously memorized the formula 4×4=16, and even then he still will not be able to explain why four times four equals sixteen. The classical tradition does not discourage memorizing multiplication tables or other facts. What it discourages is *mindlessly* memorizing them.

So far, we have only discussed the basic principles of Chinese classical Christian education. In short, it is the pursuit of the *Dao*. It seeks wisdom primarily through the testimony of God and our ancestors. The goal of Chinese classical education is to restore our natures, which we attain through moral, intellectual, and physical cultivation, and this comes through broad study. But we are still left with a problem. We've discussed *why* to teach and *how* to teach, but we do not yet know *what* to teach. The classical tradition encourages us to seek to understand all areas of knowledge, but our time and abilities are limited. We cannot teach fifty different subjects on the first day of elementary school. We must discriminate between them and decide which subjects are most worth teaching. Our goal is not to turn our students into world-class scholars by the time they graduate high school. Rather, we want to lay a foundation upon which students will continue to build after they graduate. As Dorothy Sayers says of the classical tradition in the West, our primary goal is to equip our students with the "tools" of learning so that when they leave high school they will be able and eager to study on their own without the need of a teacher. It is after they leave high school when their true life of study begins. So how should we build this foundation? What subjects can best prepare a child for a life of learning? The ancient Chinese were unanimous: the six arts.

For the ancients, six arts education is simply an extension of the *Dao*. "The Bao clan has the authority . . . to raise up the children of officials according to the *Dao*. Therefore, the following six arts shall be taught . . ."[53] These arts are at the very heart of Chinese classical education. They encompass everything we have discussed above. In the same way that the seven liberal arts embody the Western classical tradition, the six arts embody the Chinese classical tradition. Rites (*li* 礼) instruct a man in the formal principles of the universe established by Heaven, teaching him proper behavior and etiquette that are in keeping with these principles. It concerns every realm of human life from family to society to politics to religion. Music cultivates him inwardly, ordering his emotions and inspiring virtue. Script teaches language skills while instilling a love for beauty. Calculation trains him in mathematics and natural science, teaching him to think critically about the world around him and the sky above. Archery strengthens him physically while fostering mental acuity and moral resolve. Charioteering trains him in horsemanship, simultaneously sharpening his coordination and agility.

Confucius further enriched six arts education by emphasizing the study of *wen* (文) or classical literature, which culminates in the Five Classics, consisting of the *Book of Poetry*, the *Book of Documents*, the *Book(s) of Rites*, the *Book of Changes*, and the *Spring and Autumn Annals*. Although the Five Classics were sometimes thought to expound on the six arts, even sharing their name, in reality they significantly broadened the scope of six arts education, introducing the study of poetry, politics, social science, history, and metaphysics. Thanks to the tireless promotion of Zhu Xi during the Song Dynasty, four more books were added to the official canon, namely the *Analects*, the *Mencius*, the *Doctrine of the Mean*, and the *Great Learning*.

If Chinese classical Christian schools want to redeem the Chinese classical tradition, the six arts and the Confucian classics must hold a central place in the curriculum. Chinese civilization was built around these studies. The emperors, philosophers, poets, and historians of the past who shaped the Chinese psyche all drank from this fount. Chinese Christians cannot understand who they are and who God wants them to be without drinking from the same waters.

What might a contemporary Christian curriculum designed around the six arts look like? Only the Chinese church can fully answer that question. I am not Chinese, and my knowledge of Chinese culture and society are very limited. My goal here, therefore, is only to present a general outline and then invite to Chinese Christians to flesh out the details.

CHAPTER 7

Rites and Music (礼乐)

According to the ancients, the two most important of the six arts are rites (*li* 礼) and music (*yue* 乐). *Li* refers to formal patterns of human conduct that reflect the natural order of the world. It is a kind of "cultural liturgy." It concerns everything from participating in elaborate religious ceremonies to observing proper social etiquette. Music is closely related to *li*. It is not just technical instruction in a musical instrument, nor is it merely harmonic theory. While it includes these things, it is primarily concerned with understanding and reflecting the created order through sound. "The Great Music is in harmony with heaven and earth . . . displaying the Principle of all things."[1] The ancient Chinese understanding of music is very similar to that of the ancient Greeks. It does not merely please the ear but stirs the soul, inspiring moral virtue and worship.

Confucius identifies three virtues as the main focus of the *junzi*: "The way of the *junzi* is threefold, but I cannot attain it—*ren*, he is free from anxieties; wise, he is free from perplexities; courageous, he is free from fear."[2] Rites and music primarily cultivate the first of the three. *Ren* is the sum of all human virtue. The man of *ren* delights in what is good and hates what is evil. He treats others with kindness, respect, and goodwill. To be *ren* is to be fully human (sometimes *ren* is translated into English as "humanity").*

Rites and music help to cultivate *ren* by instilling in us proper values and sentiments toward "Heaven" (*tian* 天), "earth" (*di* 地), and "man" (*ren* 人). In the realm of human society, rites and music take on different forms within the context of the "five relationships" (*wulun* 五伦) between people: ruler-subject, father-son, elder brother-younger brother, husband-wife, friend-friend. The ancients understood that when our affections are left unregulated, they corrupt us:

> Now there is no end of the things by which man is affected; and when his likings and dislikings are not subject to regulation, he is changed into the nature of things as they come before him; that is, he stifles the voice of Heavenly principle within, and gives the utmost indulgence to the desires by which men may be possessed.[3]

Ritual and music regulate these desires:

> The ancient kings, in their institution of rites and music, did not seek how fully they could satisfy the desires of the appetite and of the ears and eyes; but they intended to teach the people to regulate their likings and dislikings, and to bring them back to the normal course of humanity.[4]

---

* The Chinese word for *ren* (仁) is homophonous with the word for "human" (*ren* 人), and the character for the latter is contained in the radical of the former.

Rites and music precede intellectual cultivation (though we continue practicing them even after our intellects mature). Before a child can rationally contemplate moral philosophy, he has already begun to imbibe certain moral and aesthetic values through daily rituals like washing his hands before a meal or kissing his parents goodnight. Proper rituals and music instill in him a love for the good, the true, and the beautiful, even before he can explain why he loves these things.

The ancient Greeks had a similar view. Although they stressed the value of story more than rites, this "music education" produced the same effect, which they called "piety." In the words of Socrates:

> A proper music education would enable a person to be very quick at noticing defects and flaws in the construction or nature of things. In other words, he'd find offensive the things he ought to find offensive. Fine things would be appreciated and enjoyed by him, and he'd accept them into his mind as nourishment and would therefore become truly good; even when young, however, and still incapable of rationally understanding why. He would rightly condemn and loath contemptible things. And then the rational mind would be greeted like an old friend when it did arrive.[5]

Whereas the Chinese classical tradition describes our problem as one of "unregulated likings and dislikings" (好恶无节), the Christian tradition describes our problem as one of "disordered loves." According to Augustine, our problem is that we love things that we should not love and do not love things that we should love, or that we love them too much or too little. Therefore, the purpose of Christian education is to "reorder" our loves—to come to love and hate the right things to the appropriate degree.[6]

Although Augustine uses different terminology than the Chinese or the Greeks, he is still expressing the same truth. He articulates our problem as one of disordered "loves" because this is how the Bible articulates it. Much like the Chinese concept of *ren*, love in the Bible is the embodiment of all virtue: "You shall love the Lord your God with all your heart and with all your soul and with all your mind. This is the great and first commandment. And a second is like it: You shall love your neighbor as yourself. On these two commandments depend all the Law and the Prophets" (Matt. 22:37–40). "Love does no wrong to a neighbor; therefore love is the fulfilling of the law" (Rom. 13:10). The Confucian idea of *ren* is actually sometimes equated with love (*ai* 爱). "Fan Chi asked about *ren*. The Master said, 'It is to love all men.'"[7] The famous Confucian philosopher Xunzi agrees: "*Ren* is love."[8] In fact, the most widely used Chinese Bible today (the Chinese Union Version) occasionally translates "love" (*agape*) by combining the two words: *ren-ai* (仁爱).[†] The word "love" (*ai*) in the Chinese classical tradition is usually confined to human relationships, but because the Christian tradition expands and enriches love to include our affection for God and His creation, I suggest modifying the traditional threefold "way" of the *junzi* from "*ren*, wisdom, and courage" to "love, wisdom, and courage."

[†]   cf. Gal. 5:6, 5:22; Eph. 6:23; 1 Tim. 1:7.

To bring this full circle then, rites and music help to order our loves by instilling in us proper values and sentiments toward God ("Heaven"), nature ("earth"), and man. I can think of nothing in the classical Chinese tradition that is more necessary or beneficial for Christian appropriation in our day than rites and music. Most Christians acknowledge that rites and music are essential aspects of Christian worship, but few recognize the importance of rites and music outside of worshiping God. Modern man scoffs at the idea that an object in the material world might require from him a certain emotional response, and that this emotional response might be "proper" or "improper." C. S. Lewis discusses this problem in his famous critique of modern education, *The Abolition of Man*:

> Until quite modern times all teachers and even all men believed the universe to be such that certain emotional reactions on our part could be either congruous or incongruous to it—believed, in fact, that objects did not merely receive, but could merit, our approval or disapproval, our reverence or our contempt.[9]

Modern man rejects this view, for to him, the universe has no meaning. It is only matter. Man is not the image of God but merely a collection of cells, and therefore we are not obligated to feel any certain way toward him. We do not have to respect him. We do not have to shake his hand. We do not even have to let him live. We can kill him in the womb. This kind of materialistic education produces what Lewis calls "men without chests"—men who can think with their heads but who are incapable of feeling appropriate affections for the world with their hearts.

But the ancients had chests. They recognized that the universe is full of meaning and order and that we are obligated to bring ourselves into conformity to this order. Rites and music help us to do this. "Rites and music resemble the nature of Heaven and Earth."[10] The word translated here as "nature" (*qing* 情) also means affection. For the Chinese, heaven and earth had *feelings*. The universe was *alive*. The Bible speaks about creation in the same way. "The mountains and the hills before you shall break forth into singing, and all the trees of the field shall clap their hands" (Is. 55:12). "Then the moon will be confounded and the sun ashamed" (Is. 24:23). "When the waters saw you, they were afraid; indeed, the deep trembled" (Ps. 77:16). This belief is at the center of the medieval Christian worldview which understands the entire universe to be moving out of love for God. Rites and music attempt to reflect this cosmic zeal through appropriate forms. As we imitate the affections of the cosmos through rites and music, our own affections become properly ordered.

Rites and music are not substitutes for genuine affection, however. This was the mistake of the Pharisees. They thought performing the appropriate rites *was* love for God. Confucius denies this: "If a man be without *ren*, what has he to do with rites? If a man be without *ren*, what has he to do with music?"[11] Although rites and music are not substitutes for genuine affection, they do promote genuine affection. When we teach boys to open the door for their female classmates, we are teaching them that women should be respected. By constantly opening the door for girls, boys develop a conviction in their hearts that women are worthy of honor and that men should sacrifice for them. It is possible that a boy might open the door for his classmate while still hating her in his heart, but even then, he will at least recognize that this hatred he feels in his heart is inappropriate. He will feel the incongruity between opening the door for her and hating her. In this way, the outward habits of ritual "restrain"[12] him and teach him how he ought to feel about his classmate, even if he doesn't feel that way at the moment. A boy who is not in the habit of opening doors for girls, however, will not feel this incongruity. The hatred he feels for his classmate will only complement his selfish habit of cutting in line and beating her out the door.

The "restraint" of rites is not like the restraint of shackles on a prisoner but rather like the restraint of form on a dancer. The dancer is not allowed to flail around in whatever manner she wishes. There are proper ways of standing and walking and jumping. At first, she may feel constrained by these forms, but after practicing for many months, she will begin to discover that she can actually jump higher by following the correct form than by using her own method. And after even more practice, she will discover that her dancing appears more elegant than before. Eventually, she will no longer even have to think about following the correct form, for she will have completely imbibed it. She will still dance with proper form, but she will not feel constrained. In reality, these "restraints" will have set her free, allowing her to dance unbidden. When we read the many "rules of propriety" in the Chinese classics, we can easily see only empty observances, in the same way that an untrained dancer reading dance steps can only see mechanical movements. But for the ancients, these "rules" were far more than mere observances. "Music cultivates one's inward being; rites cultivate one's outward being. When rites and music are combined, they manifest themselves outwardly as peacefulness and serenity, reverence and refinement."[13]

Music works in much the same way. When Christians nowadays talk about "good" and "bad" music, they are usually referring only to the lyrics of the music. "Good" songs are those with no profane lyrics, and "bad" songs are those with profane lyrics. But the ancients had a far more holistic understanding of music. A song "teaches" not only through lyrics but through the music itself. The harmony, melody, and tempo all shape our thoughts and desires:

> Now, in the nature of men there are both the energy of their physical powers and the intelligence of the mind; but for their (affections of) grief, pleasure, joy, and anger there are no invariable rules. They are moved according to the external objects which excite them, and then there ensues the manifestation of the various faculties of the mind. Hence, when a (ruler) . . . is magnanimous, placid, and kind, the notes are natural, full, and harmonious, and the people are affectionate and loving; when he is careless, disorderly, perverse, and dissipated, the notes are tedious and ill-regulated, and the people proceed to excesses and disorder.[14]

Upon reflection, we understand this to be true. Even if we do not understand the lyrics of a song, the music itself still inspires joy or fear or lust or rebellion in our hearts. There is a reason no one listens to Bach at a night club or Aerosmith at a funeral.

We do not determine the forms of rites and music arbitrarily but through careful meditation on the order of the universe as established by Heaven. "Music is (an echo of) the harmony between heaven and earth; rites reflect the orderly distinctions (in the operations of) heaven and earth. From that harmony all things receive their being; to those orderly distinctions they owe the differences between them."[15] "They made the underlying principles of the relations between the near and distant relatives, the noble and mean, the old and young, males and females, all to appear manifestly in the music."[16] When we listen to good music, we participate in nature. We hear and feel the harmony and order of God's creation and come away edified:

> Hence in the fine and distinct notes we have an image of heaven; in the ample and grand, an image of earth; in their beginning and ending, an image of the four seasons; in the wheelings and revolutions (of the pantomimes), an image of the wind and rain. (The five notes, like) the five colors, form a complete and elegant whole, without any confusion. (The eight instruments of different materials, like) the eight winds, follow the musical accords, without any irregular deviation. The lengths of all the different notes have their definite measurements, without any uncertainty. The small and the great complete one another. The end leads on to the beginning, and the beginning to

the end. The key notes and those harmonizing with them, the sharp and the bass, succeed one another in their regular order. Therefore, when the music has full course, the different relations are clearly defined by it; the perceptions of the ears and eyes become sharp and distinct; the action of the blood and physical energies is harmonious and calm; (bad) influences are removed, and manners changed; and all under heaven there is entire repose.[17]

At their heart, rites and music are submission to natural law. Materialism teaches us that this world is nothing but time acting on matter. As a result, nothing has real meaning. A girl can dye her hair green because hair is "just" hair. A man can marry a man because homosexuality is "just" love. The clothes we wear, the music we listen to, the way we sit or stand or speak—none of these things are ever "right" or "wrong" in a materialistic universe, for everything is just matter in motion. But rites and music remind us that this is a world of order and meaning. Our hair is not "just" hair. Our hair *means* something. "Does not nature itself teach you that if a man wears long hair it is a disgrace for him, but if a woman has long hair, it is her glory (1 Cor. 11:14–15)?" We are not free to dress however we want or to play whatever music we like. Some clothes are in accordance with natural law and some aren't. Some music reflects the order of the universe and some doesn't. When we properly observe rites and music, we willingly submit ourselves to a law that is higher than us, and over time our souls are nourished and our affections refined.

Confucius describes the collapse of a society as the "ruin of rites and music" (*libeng yuehuai* 礼崩乐坏). A people who refuse to observe rites and music have rebelled against natural order, and as a result there is nothing left to restrain them. In a world that has begun denying even the most basic natural distinctions like that of a man and a woman, Christian schools today must diligently work to recover rites and music.

Some may oppose the presence of rites in the Christian curriculum, calling it a philosophy of "works righteousness." They are right to worry about this. By the time of the Ming and Qing dynasties, the institution of rites had turned into a rigid, lifeless set of mere "rules" (largely due to the influence of Buddhism). But the original Confucian understanding of rites is something much different from this kind of empty observance. Confucius denounced those who performed rites outwardly without considering the state of their heart: "Rites performed without reverence, the forms of mourning observed without grief—these are things I cannot bear to see."[18] Those who see rites as merely wearing the "right" clothes or music as merely playing the "right" notes do not understand the first thing about either of them. "'It is according to rites,' they say. 'It is according to rites,' they say. Are gems and silk all that is meant by rites? 'It is music,' they say. 'It is music,' they say. Are bells and drums all that is meant by music?"[19] Christian teachers must continually stress that works without faith in Christ are dead. If we require our students to observe rites without teaching them the gospel of grace and forgiveness, we will only produce little Pharisees. But James also reminds us that faith without works is dead. Rites and music are not substitutes for faith in Christ, but they are a necessary outworking of faith in Christ. They are both a *sign* and a *means* of grace.

On the one hand, rites demonstrate the presence of grace in a person's heart. We can see this clearly in the medieval understanding of sacraments:

> Pupil: Why is a sacrament called a sign of something sacred?
> Master: Because through that which one sees outwardly, something inward and invisible is signified.[20]

Christians in the Middle Ages believed this was true not only for holy rites like sacraments but also for more ordinary forms of rites (what they called "manners" or *mores*). Consider, for example, Bernard of Clairvaux's (1090–1153) praise of St. Malachy:

> What was there in his way of walking, in his appearance, in his posture, in his facial expression, that was not edifying? Finally the serene good cheer of his face was not obscured by sadness, nor pushed to levity by laughter. Everything in him was disciplined, everything was a sign of virtue, an exemplar of perfection, grave but not austere in all things, occasionally relaxed, but never lax.[21]

We find very similar descriptions of Confucius in the *Analects*.[22] These descriptions strike the modern reader as trivial, but that is because we have lost the art of manners. The ancients describe Confucius's clothing and countenance and gait as a way of demonstrating the order of his soul. They describe the length of his sleeves, not because the sleeves are important in themselves but because they reflect the state of his heart.

But rites are not merely a sign of grace—they are also a *means* of grace. How does the Bible instruct believers to grow in love for God and each other? Through the rite of prayer (1 Thess. 5:17). How do we conform our hearts to the will of God? Through the rites of meditating on God's Word and singing hymns (Col. 3:16). The Lord's Supper is not just a sign of Christ's presence with us—by eating the bread and drinking the wine we actively "participate" in Him (1 Cor. 10:16). Again, this does not mean that rites are a mechanical process, as though we obtain grace by merely "going through the motions." God only bestows grace through these rites if they are performed in genuine faith; nevertheless, He does bestow grace through them. They really do "order our loves" and transform us.

Our manners also influence our hearts. Hugh of Saint Victor explains:

> Just as inconstancy of mind brings forth irregular motions of the body, so also the mind is strengthened and made constant when the body is restrained through the process of discipline ... Little by little, as it becomes habitual, that same image of virtue is impressed on the mind which is maintained through outward discipline in the disposition of the body.[23]

Hugh says this discipline of manners concerns four areas: dress, gestures (including walking), speech, and table manners. He provides specific instructions regarding each of these. Consider, for example, his comments on walking:

> There are six kinds of reprehensible gesture and movement, namely, an effeminate glide, a swagger, a listless shuffle, a hasty stride, a wanton strut, and a turbulent dash. The effeminate step indicates lasciviousness; the swagger, slovenliness; the shuffle, laziness; the stride, inconstancy; the strut, pride; the dash, wrathfulness.[24]

Far from viewing rites as being in conflict with Christian education, the church has long considered them an essential aspect of Christian education. The curriculum of cathedral schools during the Middle Ages was often referred to as "manners and letters."[25]

Our goal in teaching rites and music is not simply to get our students to conform to natural law outwardly but to get them to conform to it inwardly. To borrow a phrase from Pastor Doug Wilson, a prominent leader of the classical Christian education movement in America, we do not want our students merely to obey the standard but to love it. We want our boys opening doors for girls not because they have to but because they want to. This does not mean that we tell them that they only have to open the door if they feel like it. They must open the door even if they don't feel like it. *Li* is a discipline. Our ultimate goal is for children to observe rites out of genuine desire, but even when they do not want to—in fact, *especially* when they do not want to—we still enforce it, for this habit is a means of changing their desires. For children, learning new *li* is like learning new dance steps—it feels uncomfortable and unnatural in the beginning. We do not naturally prefer chewing with our mouths closed, but when our parents continually require us to chew with our mouths closed, our habits begin to change. Soon, we feel uncomfortable *not* chewing with our mouths closed.

Christians should promote rites and music for another important reason—they are incarnational. As we have already discussed, modern man believes the only world that exists is this material world, but the ancients often veered off into another extreme. Plato, for example, believed that the material world was simply a shadow or illusion and that the "real" world existed in the immaterial realm of the "forms." The goal of education for him, therefore, was to escape from the shackles of this material world and to enter the world of the forms. Many religions adopt a similar view, calling man to escape from the corruption of the material world.

Christianity, however, is very different. When God makes the material world, He calls it "very good" (Gen. 1:31). Even more remarkable, when this material world becomes corrupt through sin, God does not cast it away. He *enters* it. He becomes a *man*. The gospel is not the story of God rescuing men out of a corrupt material world. It is the story of God entering into this material world to redeem it, to make "all things new" (Rev. 21:5). We see this most clearly in Christ's resurrection. When Jesus died, He did not leave His body to rot in a tomb. He brought it back from the dead and united His spirit with it forever. The incarnation of Christ was not a momentary event, it was eternal.

Jesus will forever exist in a material body, and so will we. Just as Jesus was raised from the dead, so we will be raised from the dead. Our eternal home is not in an immaterial Heaven; it is on a material earth. Heaven is only where our souls wait to be reunited with our bodies in the resurrection. The final chapters of Revelation do not describe man leaving earth and ascending to Heaven but rather Heaven coming down to earth. "And I saw the holy city, new Jerusalem, coming down out of heaven from God, prepared as a bride adorned for her husband" (Rev. 21:2). According to Scripture, man is not just a material body, but neither is he just a soul. He is a unity of body and soul. A man without a body is an incomplete man. And this is why rites and music are so crucial for cultivating the complete man.

Although philosophy can be a great help to Christians, it also poses a great danger. When we study philosophy, we are tempted to live only in the realm of "ideas" and to forget that we are also material beings. Historically, the Christian church has often fallen into this error. Platonism has greatly influenced our attitudes about the human body and the material world. Many Christians believe their eternal home will be in some kind of immaterial realm. This is tragic. Our ultimate hope is not Heaven but the resurrection. God wants us to embrace our humanity and the material world He created. We can see this in the way He commands us to worship Him. Jesus does not require us only to believe in Him. He says we must be *baptized*. That is, we must cover our material bodies with water. He does not tell us to remember Him by only thinking high thoughts about Him. We must *eat bread* and *drink wine*. When we gather together for worship, God does not call us only to philosophize but to *sing*—to stimulate each other's ear drums with sounds from our vocal cords. In short, true worship requires us not only to think but to touch and taste and see and hear. God does not want us to worship Him only with our intellects but also with our bodies. That is, He wants us to worship Him as *humans*. He wants us to translate spiritual truths into material reality, for we are both spiritual and material beings.

Rites and music are the primary means by which we do this. They are the *Dao* made flesh. They are the *Dao* expressed through clothing and food and movement and song. Every time we participate in rites and music, we express our humanity in its fullness. Rites and music remind us that we are not only material bodies—for rites and music point to transcendent realities—and at the same time they remind us that we are not only immaterial souls—for they anchor us to earth through material forms. In this way, rites and music guard us from the errors of both materialism and spiritualism.

The most difficult part of teaching rites and music is not understanding natural law, which is clearly seen through general and special revelation, but rather understanding how to translate these truths into cultural expressions. Although these expressions are rooted in objective truth, their forms change according to culture. Nature teaches that we should respect others' property, but in one culture that might mean taking off your shoes when you enter their house, and in another culture that might mean *not* taking off your shoes when you enter their house. Rites and music are like languages that vary according to culture. Chinese Christians must determine what forms of *li* and music best reflect natural law in Chinese culture. They cannot do this by simply imitating the specific *li* described in the Chinese classics. For although these forms of *li* were carefully catered to Chinese culture, Chinese culture at that time was very different from Chinese culture today. Just as certain words used at that time might mean something very different if spoken today, so certain forms of etiquette might convey something very different in Chinese culture today than they did during the Han Dynasty. But for this same reason, Christians should not mockingly dismiss the *li* described in the classics as eccentric. These practices only seem eccentric because we are viewing them through the eyes of modern culture. In order to properly understand them, we must view them through the eyes of ancient culture.

At the same time, Christians should not affirm all forms of traditional *li*, even when considered in their appropriate cultural context, for some forms of ancient *li* are sin. The ancients did not have the benefit of the Holy Spirit or Scripture to guide them while translating natural law into ritual form, and therefore they occasionally erred. We cannot analyze *li* only through the lens of culture. We must also analyze it through the lens of Scripture. One of the greatest controversies in the early Chinese church concerned whether certain forms of traditional *li*, especially ancestor worship, are consistent with the teachings of Scripture. The "Rites Controversy" of the seventeenth and eighteenth centuries led some Christians to overstep the bounds of Scripture in the name of contextualization, dismissing certain sinful practices as mere "cultural differences." Chinese Christians must be willing to denounce the traditions of their fathers if those traditions violate the word of God. Culture and tradition are not absolute authorities. Only Scripture is absolute. The Chinese church can successfully redeem rites and music only if they have a deep understanding of the Bible, natural law, and Chinese culture.

Even though Confucius encourages formal study of *li*, he acknowledges that it is primarily learned through imitation, especially at a young age. Regular classes on rites in Christian schools would be pedantic and, for many students, unbearable. Instead, Chinese classical Christian schools should incorporate *li* into the culture of their schools primarily through routine and only occasionally through direct instruction. Many American classical Christian schools already teach *li*, referring to it as "protocol." Some even hold formal "protocol" dinners focusing on table manners and proper etiquette between the sexes. Chinese Christians, with their rich tradition of *li*, are in a position to significantly develop this study.

In addition to etiquette, *li* also includes formal ceremonies. Chinese Christian schools should give much thought to the ceremonies they hold, whether they be general school assemblies, graduation ceremonies, performances, or sports competitions. Christians should not view ceremony through materialistic, pragmatic lenses. Many modern schools hold ceremonies merely to convey information. People attend them simply to hear about plans for the next year or to see who won an award. The classical Chinese view of ceremony is much richer. Ceremony, like etiquette, transforms us. It shapes our affections and instills values.

To give only one example, ceremony reminds us that we are not only individuals but are members of a body. When students sit together and collectively focus their attention on a common object, they imbibe a sense of belonging to a greater whole. They recognize that in their everyday lives they do not only represent themselves but also their classmates and teachers. They feel a desire not just to work hard for their own good but for the good of the school. Schools should carefully consider what their ceremonies are communicating to students about God and His world. In the way we conduct ceremonies, what are we teaching students about honor and praise, authority and obedience, hard work and gratitude?

Of course, the most important forms of *li* are expressed in church where we sing, pray, hear the word preached, and partake of the sacraments. Moreover, the authority to practice these most holy forms of *li* is ultimately given to the church. Therefore, we cannot submit to the restraints of rites and music without submitting to the church. Christian schools should instill in their students a love for the local church, encouraging active participation in church activities and Sunday worship. In order to foster a life of Christian piety and worship, schools should teach Scripture, theology, and church history. Teachers should regularly pray and sing with their students. Teachers and students should feel a continuity between their worship at church on Sunday and their studies at school on Monday. Ancient Chinese schools may have erred in conducting religious ceremonies in honor of Confucius, but at least they recognized the centrality of worship in education. The "temple schools" of the Yuan dynasty were in many ways precursors to church schools. Christians today should view themselves as redeeming this important tradition by redirecting worship from Confucius to Christ.

As for music education, classical Christian schools should seek to recover the holistic Confucian understanding of music, for in most respects it is the Christian understanding. We do not simply want to teach our children songs with theologically accurate lyrics. We want the *music* to be theologically accurate. That is, we want the music to be beautiful and to reflect the glory of the Triune God. Students must be able to distinguish between good and bad music, and this cannot be achieved through simple "music appreciation" classes. Music is a language, and students can only understand what a given piece of music is "saying" if they are able to read and speak it. Therefore, students should study music theory and composition, as well as vocal and instrumental technique. God does not only want our students to be able to sing and play instruments but to do so "skillfully" (Ps. 33:3).

Much of the music in the Christian tradition is Western; moreover, the most commonly-used forms of musical notation and music theory worldwide are Western forms. Therefore, Chinese students should study the Western musical tradition. At the same time, Chinese classical schools should not limit music education to the Western tradition for the same reason that they should not teach only Western languages. God calls Chinese Christians to redeem Chinese culture, and they cannot do this if they do not understand their own musical heritage. The Chinese musical tradition also provides us with different ways of thinking about music. By studying this tradition, students can learn to create music that is unique from Western music. "Sing to the LORD a *new* song," says the Scriptures (Ps. 96:1). Diversity in music glorifies God, for it displays new aspects of His glory.

In addition to music, Christian schools may also teach dance, which was traditionally a part of music education in China. Dance combines the external movements of *li* with the internal influence of music. However, in keeping with *li*, dance should promote the natural distinctions between men and women. Dance is often taught in a way that encourages boys to move in an effeminate manner. When taught properly, however, dance can reinforce Biblical gender roles, encouraging boys to lead with strength and decisiveness while encouraging girls to follow their lead with grace and elegance.

CHAPTER 8

Script and Calculation (书数)

Whereas rites and music primarily served to cultivate *ren* (or love), script (*shu* 书) and calculation (*shu* 数) primarily served to cultivate wisdom (*zhi* 智)—the second virtue of the threefold "way" of the *junzi* (*ren*, wisdom, courage). Wisdom in the Chinese classical tradition is synonymous with knowledge (*zhi* 知). The words are often used interchangeably.* Script and calculation enable students to access the vast wealth of knowledge available to them in the world. The former cultivates language skills, enabling students to communicate and analyze human thought. The latter cultivates computational skills, enabling students to quantify and measure the natural world.

During the Shang and Western Zhou dynasties, the art of script was overshadowed by martial arts. But when the Five Classics were introduced to the six arts curriculum during the Eastern Zhou dynasty, script assumed a prominent role. Later, when the Han government began promoting the policy of "emphasizing literature over mil-

---

* Besides sharing the same pronunciation as "knowledge," the character for "wisdom" (智) also contains the character for "knowledge" (知).

itary arts" (*zhongwen qingwu* 重文轻武), script rose in importance even more.†

At its most basic level, script is the study of language. The ancients considered language study essential because language is the primary means by which man communicates. It is the window into his heart. "Without knowing language, it is impossible to know men."[1] But language does not only help us to know men. In his early sixth-century work *The Literary Mind and the Carving of Dragons* (*Wenxin Diaolong* 文心雕龙), famed literary critic Liu Xie (刘勰) roots literature (*wen xue*) in the study of pattern or *wen*. Everything has its own *wen*. The sun and moon have their own *wen*. Mountains and rivers have their own *wen*. Even animals have their own *wen*. *Wen* are the essential characteristics of a thing. Collectively, these patterns make up the wen of the *Dao*. It is the special privilege of man, "endowed with the divine spark of consciousness (*xingling* 性灵)," to observe and elucidate these patterns, which he accomplishes through the unique power of language:

> The human being is the flower of the elements: in fact, the mind (*xin* 心) of Heaven and Earth. When mind (*xin*) came into being, language was established; and with the establishment of language, pattern (*wen*) became manifest. This is the natural course of things, the *Dao*.[2]

---

† Strictly speaking, script and *wen* (literature) are not the same thing. Script is the art of reading and writing, which allows one to understand and produce *wen*. Script or *shu* (书) in modern Chinese literally means "book."

Language, therefore, is the unique *wen* of man (*renwen* 人文) by which the *Dao* manifests itself.‡ "Thus we know that the *Dao* sent down its pattern (*wen*) through the Sages, and that the Sages made the *Dao* manifest in their patterns (*wen*)."[3] This is why the study of language and literature are so important. Through them, we can know not only man but the *Dao*. "That which stirs the world into movement is preserved in language."[4] In the words of the Song Neo-Confucian Zhou Dunyi (周敦颐), "*wen* carries the *Dao*" (*wen yi zai dao* 文以载道).

The Bible has a very similar view of language. The first task that God gave Adam was that of naming the animals. "Now out of the ground the LORD God had formed every beast of the field and every bird of the heavens and brought them to the man to see what he would call them. And whatever the man called every living creature, that was its name" (Gen. 2:19). A "name" in Scripture is not an arbitrary word created to signify a thing. The Bible understands a name to be an embodiment of the person or object it signifies. When Adam named an animal, he did not think up a word at random. He studied the animal, he contemplated its nature, and in the end he gave it a name fitting to its nature. He did the same thing when he named Eve: "This at last is bone of my bones and flesh of my flesh; she shall be called Woman (*ishshah*), because she was taken out of Man (*ish*)" (Gen. 2:23). This is the same process that Liu describes. As a man created in the image of God

---

‡ The modern Chinese word for the "humanities" is literally "the study of human *wen*" (*renwenxue* 人文学).

and uniquely gifted with a "mind" (*xin*) and "personality" (*xingling*), Adam studied the unique "*wen*" of each animal and elucidated these patterns through language. Each name "manifested the *wen*" of each animal and codified it. In this way, Adam brought order to the world through language, and in doing so he imitated God, Who created the world through language and "upholds it by the word of His power" (Heb. 1:3). We speak because God speaks. Liu is not far off when he says, "The origins of human pattern (*ren wen* 人文) begin in the Primordial."[5]

As Christians, therefore, we do not only study language in order to communicate with each other. We study it in order to continue our father Adam's work of taking dominion of the earth. Language is one of the primary means by which we bring order to the cosmos. The study of language is not merely the study of words and grammar. It is the study of *wen*—the patterns of heaven and earth. We cannot write or speak about a thing unless we understand what that thing is. Only when we understand its true nature can we determine appropriate words to describe it. The ancient Chinese understanding of language is holistic. Literature is not isolated from other subjects but is intricately related to music and astronomy and mathematics and natural history, for it is only through these studies that we can understand the *wen* of the cosmos.[§]

Although we can see the patterns of the cosmos with our own eyes, our vision is often impaired. This is why we

---

§   The Chinese word for "astronomy" (*tianwen* 天文) and "topology" (*diwen* 地文) literally mean "the *wen* of the heavens" and "the *wen* of earth."

read books—to see the cosmos through the eyes of those who see more clearly than we do. For Liu Xie, these are primarily the sages. For Christians, they are primarily the saints—especially the authors of Scripture. As Christians, we do not reject the teachings of non-Christians simply because they are spoken by non-Christians. We believe that God gives wisdom even to those who do not worship Him. Therefore, we study pagan authors in addition to Christian ones. At the same time, however, we recognize that these men are fallible. Their ideas are products of human inference. God reveals truth to them through general revelation, but they still must interpret this revelation using their reason, which is impaired by sin and limited by human finitude. Special revelation, however, is communicated through very different means. When God speaks to the prophets, He does so through a process of "inspiration," communicating His will directly through their reason. This process is entirely directed by His Spirit, so that the words spoken by the prophets are the very words of God. Therefore, the church fathers believed the Bible to far surpass all other books in importance, for Scripture is not only inerrant but also answers the most important questions about God, man, and salvation. As Augustine says:

> But just as poor as the store of gold and silver and garments which the people of Israel brought with them out of Egypt was in comparison with the riches which they afterwards attained at Jerusalem, and which reached their height in the reign of King Solomon, so poor is all the useful knowledge which is gathered

from the books of the heathen when compared with the knowledge of Holy Scripture.[6]

The primary reason why Christian education has traditionally placed so much emphasis on language study is not because men write books but because God does. He reveals Himself to us through human authors, and therefore we cannot know Him without understanding human language. Martin Luther clarifies:

> Although the gospel came and still comes to us through the Holy Spirit alone, we cannot deny that it came through the medium of languages, was spread abroad by that means, and must be preserved by the same means. For just when God wanted to spread the gospel throughout the world by means of the apostles he gave the tongues for that purpose . . . In proportion then as we value the gospel, let us zealously hold to the languages.[7]

Liu Xie bases language study on the same principle. "The *Dao* sent down its *wen* through the Sages, and the Sages made the *Dao* manifest in their *wen*."[8] It is just that the *Dao* has revealed himself to the authors of Scripture in a much more direct and perspicuous way than he did the ancient sages. Nevertheless, the principle is the same—"*wen* carries the *Dao*":

> The languages are the sheath in which this sword of the Spirit is contained; they are the casket in which this jewel is enshrined; they are the vessel in which this wine is held; they are the larder in which this food is stored; and, as the gospel itself paints out,

they are the baskets in which are kept these loaves and fishes and fragments. If through our neglect we let the languages go (which God forbid!), we shall not only lose the gospel, but the time will come when we shall be unable either to speak or write a correct Latin or German.[9]

We know that language study is essential, but it is less obvious what specific languages we should study. Classical Christian educators in the West have long emphasized Latin. Many today consider it one of the primary distinctives of classical Christian education. As a result, Chinese Christians might assume that classical Christian schools in China should also promote Latin. As we've already discussed above, however, Chinese Christian schools must not think that being faithful to the classical Christian tradition means teaching the same knowledge our Christian fathers taught. We must understand *why* they taught this knowledge. We are called to imitate the *principles* they applied to education and not merely the subject matter.

We can find two such principles about language study in the following passage by the Roman orator and educator Quintilian, who greatly influenced the medieval Christian curriculum:

I prefer a boy to begin by speaking Greek, because he will imbibe Latin, which more people speak, whether we will or no; and also because he will need to be taught Greek learning first, it being the source of ours too.[10]

Quintilian promoted the study of Latin because Latin was the mother tongue of the Romans. It was the primary language people used in everyday life. Applying this same principle, we can safely assume that if Quintilian lived in China, he would emphasize the study of Mandarin, for Mandarin is the mother tongue of the Chinese people.

Unlike Latin, Greek was a second language for the Romans. Although Greek was not their mother tongue, it was still widely spoken, which is one reason Quintilian promoted it. But Quintilian also promoted Greek for another reason, namely because Greek learning was the "source" of Roman learning. Roman culture was built on the foundation of Greek culture, and therefore Roman children could not properly understand their own culture without understanding Greek culture. They could not understand Roman philosophy without studying Greek philosophy or Roman art without studying Greek art. Knowledge of the Greek language gave them access to this rich inheritance. If we apply this same principle to modern-day China, what culture is the source of modern Chinese culture? It is not Latin culture but ancient Chinese culture. Chinese children cannot understand modern China without understanding ancient China. Therefore, in addition to Mandarin they must also study classical Chinese (*wenyanwen* 文言文) in order to access this cultural heritage. On the other hand, modern-day China has also been significantly influenced by the English-speaking West. When we roam the streets of Beijing or peruse the libraries of Shanghai, we do not see any signs of Latin, but we do see English everywhere. Therefore, I think we can safely say that if Quintilian started a school in China and could only teach two languages, he would not teach Latin and Greek but rather Chinese and English.

Christians in the Middle Ages applied these same principles to their schools. They taught Latin because it was one of the most common languages at the time. It was the primary language used in theological and academic writings (which now happens to be English), and it was the language of the most widely-used translation of the Bible, the Vulgate. Latin education was later revived during the Renaissance, when Christian humanists promoted the study of classical antiquity and called for a return "to the sources" (*ad fontes*). By studying Latin and Greek, students could read classical Greco-Roman literature without having to rely on translations. More importantly, by studying Greek and Hebrew they could access the Bible in its original languages. The reason they studied Latin literature was essentially the same reason Quintilian promoted the study of Greek, namely to understand the "source" of their own culture. They wanted to discover the rich heritage passed down to them by their Greco-Roman fathers.

Therefore, it is reasonable for Western classical schools today to study Latin. On the one hand, Latin is still very much present in their students' daily lives as much of the English language is rooted in Latin. Moreover, Latin phrases can still be seen in many places in the West, from literature to court houses to colleges to coins. More importantly, American and European cultures were significantly influenced by Latin culture. By studying classical Latin literature, American and European children can better understand their cultural roots. It is less reasonable, however, for Chinese primary and secondary schools to teach Latin. Latin has basically no relation to Mandarin, nor has Latin culture significantly influenced Chinese culture. When children in the West study Latin in school, they feel like they are meeting an old relative. Latin feels familiar to them because they have unknowingly lived under its influence all their lives. But when Chinese children study Latin, they feel like they are meeting a complete stranger. It feels utterly foreign to them because it *is* foreign to them.

Some may argue that Chinese Christian children should study Latin because of its Christian roots. Many of the greatest Christian classics were written in Latin. But Chinese children do not need to know Latin in order to read them. Most of these classics are already translated into English, many even into Chinese. Even students in America who study Latin generally prefer reading the classics in English. Knowledge of Latin is helpful for Chinese scholars who want to translate classical texts, but the majority of Chinese students will not become Latin scholars. Therefore, we should not force them to study Latin in their early years. They can easily navigate the wealth of Christian literature with a knowledge of English.

I am not suggesting that Chinese Christians should never study Latin. I am simply concerned here with what subjects should form the foundations of the primary and secondary school curriculum. The purpose of primary and secondary school is to equip children with the "tools of learning," so that after graduating students can continue learning on their own without the aid of a teacher. As far as languages go, I believe Chinese and English are sufficient for this task. With a solid foundation in English, those students who want to study Latin may easily do so as an elective in high school or in college.

Some Chinese advocate for teaching Latin in elementary school because children at that age can imbibe new languages very easily. Those who wait until high school or college will find the task much more difficult. Therefore, we should "strike while the iron is hot." But if this is the case, then why don't we also teach Russian and French and Japanese? If young children are so adept at studying languages, then why stop at four? Why not five or six or seven? The reason is obvious. A child's school day only contains a limited amount of time. Every hour a child spends learning Latin is an hour that he cannot spend learning some other subject. If we teach our fourth-graders seven languages, we will have no time to teach them anything else.

In considering the question of Latin, we should not imagine two potential students—one who only speaks Chinese and English and one who speaks Chinese, English, and Latin—and then ask which one we would prefer. Of course we would all prefer the child who speaks three languages to the one who only speaks two. The question is *at what cost?* The child who studies Latin has less time to study Chinese and English, and therefore his Chinese and English skills will be weaker than the student who only studies Chinese and English. Or if his Latin studies do not supplant his Chinese and English studies, they will supplant other studies like math or music or history. Studying more Latin necessarily means studying less of something else.

Suppose we want to teach a child music, and we only have three hours every week to do so. The best way to teach him music is not to buy him six different musical instruments and require him to practice each one for thirty minutes a week. The best way to teach him music is to buy him one musical instrument and require him to practice that one instrument three hours every week. By practicing only one instrument rather than six, he will have ample opportunity to discover the intricacies of music theory and technique. After mastering that one instrument, he can then easily pick up a new instrument and learn it quickly, for he understands the essence of music theory and technique. But the child who divides his time between six different instruments every week will learn none of them well. Even after many years of study, he will have only a superficial knowledge of music. He will be able to boast to his friends that he can play six instruments, but in reality he will not be able to play any of them well. In the same way, if we want our students to master the art of language, we should not teach them many different languages superficially but one or two languages thoroughly.

Some promote studying Latin because of its inflected nature. They argue that inflected languages better exercise students' linguistic faculties than uninflected languages by requiring them to observe the grammatical function of a word in relation to others and to transform it accordingly. But English can also provide these benefits to Chinese children because it, too, is an inflected language. English is less beneficial to Western children, however, simply because it is their mother tongue. They do not need to think critically about most English grammar because it comes naturally. This is why they study Latin. But Chinese children, whose mother tongue is not English, must think much more critically about English grammar than American children do. Therefore, in many respects, English can provide for Chinese children what Latin provides for Western children. With a solid foundation in English, students can then proceed to Latin or Greek or Hebrew studies in their later years.

In deciding which languages to teach, we also must be sensitive to our students' temperaments. Their memory might be very strong when they are young, but if we use this as an excuse for cramming endless amounts of knowledge into their heads, they will eventually come to despise it. It is possible to teach them too much, as those who have attended Chinese public schools can attest. Consider this warning from Quintilian:

> I am not so careless of age differences as to think that the very young should be forced on prematurely, and that set tasks should be demanded of them. For one of the first things to take care of is that the child, who is not yet able to love study, should not come to hate it and retain his fear of the bitter taste.[11]

We should not forget that students in American classical Christian schools generally only study two languages before they graduate high school, namely English and Latin.¶ Those who want to introduce Latin to the Chinese curricu-

---

¶ Some may begin studying a third language in their final year or two of high school.

lum, however, are suggesting three languages—four if you count classical Chinese. Such a heavy course load will likely result in students coming to despise Latin, as Quintilian warns. The fact that they do not encounter Latin outside of the classroom will only add to their frustration, because they will have little opportunity to apply this knowledge in their daily lives. Moreover, American children begin studying Latin with a proficient knowledge of English, which helps them to learn Latin much more quickly. Chinese children, however, have no such foundation. As a result, they progress much more slowly in Latin than American children do. This, in addition to the fact that teachers must divide their class time thinly between four languages, means children will not be able to study Latin in any depth. By the time they graduate from high school, they will have gained only a very superficial knowledge of Latin, being able to read little more than their Latin textbooks. Therefore, as far as script is concerned, I believe Chinese classical Christian schools should focus on modern Chinese, classical Chinese, and English.

Unlike the Western classical tradition, the Chinese classical tradition did not consider grammar an essential aspect of language study. The Chinese taught script using dictionaries like the famous *Erya* (尔雅), which discussed the form, meaning, and pronunciation of Chinese characters, but they never used grammar textbooks. Some have suggested that this is because the Chinese language has no grammar, but any foreign language student of Chinese knows that this is not true. All languages have their own grammar, including classical and modern Chinese, but an-

cient Chinese educators did not devote time to systematically analyzing these rules. Students simply imbibed Chinese
grammar by studying classical literature. Educators in the
West also used classical literature to teach grammar (these
books served as models of proper grammar), but they sup-
plemented these texts with systematic discussion of grammar rules using grammar textbooks. Most modern Chinese
schools do systematically teach English grammar, but they
do not provide similar instruction when teaching Chinese.
I believe modern Chinese educators can learn from their
Western counterparts here. The Western tradition proves
that teaching children the grammar of their mother tongue
improves their ability to communicate effectively.

The ancient Chinese art of script has one significant
advantage over traditional Western language education,
however. In the Han Dynasty, the Chinese began studying
script not only for its linguistic value but for its aesthetic
value. Calligraphy taught students to compose written characters that communicated the *Dao* not only through their
meaning but through their form. This required paying attention both to the appearance of the character and to the
process by which it was produced. Each character required
a series of movements (i.e. brush strokes) that had to be
performed in a precise order, making calligraphy a kind of
li. Schools in the West also occasionally taught calligraphy,
but it was not emphasized or developed there to the degree
that it was in China. Schools devoted entirely to calligraphy
began appearing in China as early as the fourth century.

Chinese classical Christian schools today should embrace this rich tradition. God does not only care about

truth and goodness. When He created the world, He also made it *beautiful*. The garden of Eden was "pleasant to the sight" (Gen. 2:9). Students should strive for the same goal in writing. Calligraphy instills in children a proper aesthetic sense. A child who comes to appreciate a beautifully-written Chinese character will also come to appreciate a beautifully-sewn dress or a beautifully-crafted table or a beautifully-decorated home.

Chinese calligraphy schools also taught Chinese painting, which was considered an extension of calligraphy. Chinese painting employs the same techniques as calligraphy, using the same brushes, inks, and strokes. Paintings generally depict natural landscapes and are often accompanied with poems that capture in words the essence of the scenes depicted. In one sense, Chinese painting is the pinnacle of the art of *wen* (*wenxue*), for it weds together the *wen* of man and the *wen* of heaven and earth. Modern classical schools in China should retain this valuable tradition.

The Chinese classical tradition emphasized the written word but not the spoken word. In contrast, the Trivium of the Western classical tradition emphasized the study of rhetoric, which the ancients primarily understood as the art of oratory. The Greeks emphasized this art because Greece was a democracy. All male citizens were required to participate in public forums where they debated public policy. Moreover, when a citizen was accused of a crime, he had to defend himself by giving a speech in court. In short, if a person could not speak clearly and persuasively, he could not function as a responsible citizen. Christians later developed this art even further by tying the study of rhetoric to the proclamation of the gospel. If God commands us to spread the gospel through preaching, then we must learn how to speak. Confucius, however, was very skeptical of oratory. "The virtuous will be sure to speak correctly, but those whose speech is good may not always be virtuous."[12] He recognized that men who speak well are often the most corrupt. "Crafty speech disrupts virtue."[13] "Those of crafty words and ingratiating expression are rarely *ren.*"[14] In this regard, Confucius is much like Socrates, who opposed rhetoric on similar grounds. Confucius's skepticism of rhetoric and China's traditionally autocratic form of government prevented oratory from developing in China. Buddhist priests revived the art during the Period of Disunity, but this revival was short-lived.

Even though the Chinese classical tradition did not emphasize spoken rhetoric, it did emphasize written rhetoric. The primary goal of government schools was to prepare students for the imperial examinations (*keju*), which took the form of a written essay. These essays increased in complexity over time, culminating in the eight-legged essay (*baguwen* 八股文) during the Ming and Qing dynasties. The government valued an applicant's ability to communicate winsomely more than almost any other skill. In fact, this was one of the main critiques of the Neo-Confucians, who criticized government schools for "setting store in turning a nice literary phrase rather than seeking an all-round ability in the six arts."[15]

On the one hand, Chinese Christians should heed the warnings of Confucius, for the Bible says the same thing: "When words are many, transgression is not lacking, but whoever restrains his lips is prudent" (Prv. 10:19). The Apostle Paul intentionally avoided using "lofty speech" in his preaching, for he did not want to manipulate his audience into believing in Jesus through mere rhetorical display (1 Cor. 2:1–5). On the other hand, the Bible also tells us that well-crafted words can give life. "The lips of the righteous feed many" (Prv. 10:21). "A word fitly spoken is like apples of gold in a setting of silver" (Prv. 25:11). The church fathers recognized the dangers of rhetoric, but they also recognized its potential. Rhetoric in itself is neither good nor bad. It is simply a tool which can be used for good or for evil. Because our faith is spread through the spoken word, and because so much of our daily lives depends on speech, I think Chinese Christians would do well to imitate the Western church by expanding their long tradition of written rhetoric to include oratory. We want our students not only to write well but to speak well.

Some ancient schools of thought in China like the Mohists (*mojia* 墨家) and especially the school of the Logicians (*mingjia* 名家) emphasized that because language is intrinsically tied to thought, proper language education cannot neglect formal logic. Unfortunately, these schools were quickly snuffed out by the Legalists and Confucians. Only fragments of their writings on logic still exist today. Western educators, on the other hand, made logic a pillar of the classical curriculum, elevating it to one of the three arts of the Trivium. I believe Chinese classical Christian schools should recover the lost work of the Mohists and Logicians and restore logic to the language curriculum. Anyone who doubts the value of studying formal logic need only examine the abundant fruit it has born in the West.

In the Chinese classical tradition, script was primarily taught through literature. Both the Greeks and the Chinese believed that language is built on the authority of those who came before us. Therefore, in order to learn how to write properly we must study their works. But what books should Chinese children study?

First, we must emphasize again that no book warrants more time and attention than the Bible. Martin Luther warns us:

> I would advise no one to send his child where the Holy Scriptures are not supreme. Every institution that does not unceasingly pursue the study of God's word becomes corrupt ... I greatly fear that the universities, unless they teach the Holy Scriptures diligently and impress them on the young students, are wide gates to hell.[16]

As discussed previously, Christians "stand in awe of the words of the sages," which for us especially means the words of the saints. In addition to Scripture, classical Christian schools should also teach Christian classics, including famous Christian creeds and confessions, theological writings, and Christian literature. At the same time, we still must honor our pagan ancestors, to whom God also gave much wisdom. The most revered books of the Chinese classical tradition are the Confucian classics, namely the Four Books and the Five Classics. Liu Xie explains why the Chinese valued these books so highly:

The Classics are the perfection of the *Dao*, permanent and enduring, the grandest form of instruction and one that is never eradicated. They are works that take their image from Heaven and Earth, investigate the [realm of] the spirits and gods, give consideration to the order of things, determine the standards for human beings, penetrate the secret recesses of the soul, and reach all the way to the bone and marrow of literary works.[17]

Christian children should study the classics diligently, not only because of the wisdom contained inside but also because of their unparalleled influence on the Chinese language. Christians cannot master the Chinese language without studying the Chinese classics. Protestant missionaries in the nineteenth century greatly emphasized this point:

The Chinese classics must, therefore, not only have a place but a very important place in our Christian schools and colleges ... The very warp and woof of the Chinese language is derived from the classics. The great bulk of the quotations and illustrations in common use among writers; their poetical and historical allusions; the pronunciation and definition of the characters; in a word, the very essence and spirit of the language are produced, moulded and fashioned by the classics; and all the vast tomes of Chinese literature, history and philosophy are permeated and controlled by the literary style, as well as the moral principles, of the classics. No one can read or write a book in the Chinese language without having studied the classics. Nor can any one carry on a correspondence, commercial or diplomatic, without a knowledge of the classics."[18]

Even while advocating this, missionaries acknowledged the difficulty of teaching the Chinese classics in a Christian school:

What proportion of the pupil's time should be given to their study? Should the whole of the Four Books and Five Classics be studied? And if not, what portions should be omitted or only partially studied? How are they to be taught? By committing to memory verbatim, or is there a better way? How are heathenism and false science in them to be counteracted? How are the other faculties of the mind of the pupil, besides the memory, to be stimulated and developed in spite of the crampings and deadening influence of the study of the classics? ... These and kindred questions have perplexed every one of us who have had charge of mission schools, and it seems impossible to decide them satisfactorily, even after more than fifty years of experiment and observation by missionary educators in China.[19]

Chinese Christians are in a better position to answer these questions than foreign missionaries. Still, these questions will take many years to answer. A. P. Parker recommends writing a set of Christian commentaries on the classics as a resource for Christian teachers and students. Because we do not yet know the best method for teaching the Chinese classics, Parker recommends imitating the classical Chinese tradition:

For learning the Chinese books and for the purpose
for which those books are learned, there is no better
way than that which is followed by the Chinese themselves and which has stood the test of centuries of
experience.[20]

In traditional Chinese schools, the youngest students
memorized and recited both prose and poetry. As they
progressed, they began to compose their own prose and
poetry and to study history. The oldest students practiced
analyzing literature, while continuing memorization and
composition.

Although traditional Chinese schools revered the Four
Books and Five Classics more than any other, they did not
begin with them, nor did they limit their curriculum to only
these nine books. They recognized that some books are
easier to understand than others. In fact, the reason Zhu
Xi promoted the Four Books was because the Five Classics
were too obscure for the average reader. Classical Christian schools should imitate traditional Chinese schools in
this regard, selecting books that suit the abilities of their
students. The most popular classical texts in traditional primary schools were the *Classic of Filial Piety* (*Xiaojing* 孝经)
and the *Analects*. Although the *Classic of Filial Piety* and the
Analects are difficult reading for young children and contain
some teachings that are at odds with the Bible, teachers may
adapt acceptable portions for memorization and recitation.

The ancients especially favored rhymed primers for
teaching young children. The natural rhyme and rhythm
of the text turned what might otherwise be boring facts
into enjoyable, catchy chants. These primers were used in

teaching script, calculation, and even archery. Incidentally, elementary education in the West traditionally relied on similar mnemonic devices. Contemporary Chinese classical schools should adopt this same approach. Although they have no obligation to use the same primers that traditional schools used, some of these, like the *Sanzi Jing* (三字经), are still very effective today. In 1823, Walter Henry Medhurst (麦都思) published a Christian tract in imitation of the *Sanzi Jing* called by the same name. It underwent various revisions and became the most influential missionary tract in China during the nineteenth century. Christian teachers would do well to recover this short book, as well as to write their own primers.

As students mature, they may begin studying more difficult classics. In addition to the Confucian classics, students may study authors representing other schools of thought like Daoism, Legalism, and Mohism—authors such as Loazi, Zhuangzi, Han Feizi, and Mozi. Students may study famous poetry and prose writings from Xiao Tong's (萧统) sixth-century anthology *Selections of Refined Literature* or *Wen Xuan* (文选), which was one of the most popular textbooks in traditional Chinese schools. Students should also study famous works by later poets and prose writers, including the Four Classic Novels (*si da ming zhu* 四大名著), namely *Dream of the Red Chamber* (*honglou meng* 红楼梦), *Romance of the Three Kingdoms* (*sangguo yanyi* 三国演义), *Water Margin* (*shuihu zhuan* 水浒传), and *Journey to the West* (*xiyou ji* 西游记).

For the ancients, the study of literature also included the study of history, which was recorded not only in the

Five Classics but in other classics like the *Twenty-Four Histories* (*Ershisi shi* 二十四史), which collectively detail the history of each dynasty beginning in 2550 BC and ending in 1644 AD. The *Twenty-Four Histories* include such classics as Sima Qian's *Historical Records* (*Shiji* 史记) and the *Book of Han* (*Hanshu* 汉书). Christian teachers should resist the temptation to teach only history books composed in modern times. On the one hand, students should recognize that modern historians base their narratives primarily on the testimony of the ancients. By studying classical history books, students can access this testimony directly themselves without having to blindly accept the authority of modern historians. On the other hand, students also learn critical thinking skills by sifting through primary sources themselves. By comparing one dynasty's account of an event with another dynasty's account, students learn to critically analyze history through multiple perspectives. They discover how personal bias and political motivation influence one's interpretation of history. Students who only learn history through one modern textbook come to see the modern historian as omniscient. To them, studying history simply becomes a matter of blindly accepting the statements of men with PhDs rather than critically analyzing historical sources themselves. This is not to say that modern textbooks should be entirely avoided. They can be very helpful. But they should only serve as supplements to primary sources.

The study of literature in ancient China was primarily the study of ideas, that is *philosophy*. In fact, Matteo Ricci criticized the upper schools in China in his day for focusing on nothing but "philosophy."[21] As we teach the classics, we must focus not only on helping students to understand the content of these books but on bringing them into conversation with each other and with contemporary society. Students should recognize that each book is not an isolated collection of ideas but is rather one voice in a larger conversation. We want our students to draw connections between the books they read, identifying how each relates to the other. They should recognize that the ideas in these books are not only relevant to the past but have significantly influenced the present. They should "study the past in order to understand the present."[22] Most importantly, of course, students should recognize how these stories and ideas relate to Christ. Teachers should constantly bring the classics into conversation with Christianity and the Bible.

Chinese classical Christian schools must also include some study of Western literature and history. Even though the Confucian tradition emphasized the study of Chinese culture, it also encouraged the study of other cultures. "A *junzi* broadly studies all *wen*."[23] "Of the books under heaven, there is none not to be 'broadly studied' (*boxue*)."[24] Chinese children cannot understand the history of the church without understanding the history of the West. In fact, they cannot even understand some passages of Scripture without understanding Western history. The history of China—especially modern China—is also closely tied to the history of the West. Western history provides students with a backdrop by which they can better understand both their Christian heritage and their cultural heritage. Nevertheless, Chinese classical Christian schools should still prioritize

Chinese history. On the one hand, Chinese students live in China, not in the West. Chinese history is an essential aspect of their identity. From a more practical perspective, Chinese children will naturally be more interested in Chinese history than Western history. Children are naturally more curious about things that stand in closest relation to themselves. They will be more interested in the cat they see outside the classroom window than they will the lion in Africa that they cannot see. They will want to know more about their grandparents' experience as Red Guards in the Cultural Revolution than they will the feats of Julius Caesar in the Gallic Wars. Children need a reference point by which they can interpret the world. Only after carefully studying the cat in the window can they begin to understand what a lion is. In the same way, children need to understand the history of their own home before they can understand the history of somebody else's. If history class begins with ancient Egypt, students will feel both disoriented and disinterested. Teaching Chinese children history by beginning with Egypt is like teaching geography by beginning with the topography of Mars.

Students should also study Western literature, but for the most part it should be limited to Christian literature. When protestant missionaries convened at the second General Conference of the Protestant Missionaries of China in 1890, one of the main topics they discussed was Chinese Christian education. Nineteen different missionaries voiced their opinions regarding the content of the Chinese Christian curriculum. Not one of them suggested teaching Western classical literature.[25] The three main subjects they proposed were "Christian books (i.e. the Bible and theology books), the Chinese classics, and Western science."[26] Most of these men had received a classical Western education, and yet none of them believed that Chinese Christians needed to study the Western classics in order to receive a thorough Christian education. In fact, they believed that in many regards the Chinese classics were superior to the Western classics:

> The heathenism and immorality and false science of the Chinese classics are certainly no worse than those of the Greek and Latin classics that are taught in the Christian schools and colleges of Europe and America. In fact, as to moral purity the Chinese classics are far superior to those of Greece and Rome...there is little, if anything, to be found anywhere in the Chinese classics that can be objected to on the score of moral impurity.[27]

Those Christians who object on moral grounds to teaching the Chinese classics in Christian schools must object even more strongly to teaching the Western classics. For example, Plato is often held up as one of the bright lights of Western civilization. Augustine, who is very critical of most classical literature, nevertheless praises him. And yet, in his most famous work, the *Republic*, Plato advocates for destroying the family. He says that children should belong to the state and should not know who their real parents are. The institution of marriage should be destroyed. Men and women past their prime should be forbidden from having children, and children with disabilities should be killed. This stands in stark contrast to the *Analects*, which passionately defends the dignity of the family and the importance of the parent-child relationship. If we compare other classics from the Western tradition, such as Homer or Ovid, with those of the Chinese tradition, the moral contrast is even more striking.

Some may argue that Chinese children need to study Western classical literature in order to properly understand Christian literature, for the church fathers occasionally reference classical literature. If Chinese children are not familiar with this literature, how can they understand the church fathers? In his essay "The Idea of an 'English School,'" C. S. Lewis considers whether the Greco-Roman classics should be taught in English schools. He argues that classical literature influenced English literature only insofar as it provided "matter" to write about—"theories, histories, facts, myths, anecdotes, people."[28] But the Greco-Roman classics did not influence the "spirit" and "form" of English literature.** Lewis, therefore, does not believe that students must thoroughly study the Greco-Roman classics in order to properly understand English literature. When they come across a reference to classical texts, they can understand the reference with the aid of "classical dictionaries, historical textbooks, and translations."[29] They do not need to study the classics themselves.

Similarly, the "matter" of Christian literature sometimes came from Western classical literature, but its "spirit" is derived from the Word of God. For example, in the *Confessions*, Augustine laments that he wept over Dido's death

---

** These influences came, he says, from Anglo-Saxon, Old French, and Medieval Latin.

but not his own. Chinese students who have never read the *Aeneid* will not know who Dido is, but they do not need to read the *Aeneid* in order to understand Augustine. They can know who Dido is with the aid of a simple footnote. What they really need in order to understand Augustine's lament is a knowledge of the *Book of Psalms* or the *Book of Romans*. For these are the real source of his lament. The reference to Dido is peripheral. Chinese Christians simply do not need a thorough knowledge of Western classical literature in order to understand Christianity or the writings of the church fathers.

This does not mean that Chinese Christians should never study Western classical literature. Just as we would prefer a Chinese student who speaks both Chinese and Latin to one who speaks only Chinese, we would prefer a Chinese student who knows both Western and Chinese classical literature to one who only knows Chinese literature. But the problem we face with literature is the same problem we face with language—time is limited. Students who study the Western classics must study fewer of the Chinese classics. For the reasons outlined above, therefore, I believe primary and secondary schools should primarily teach the Chinese classics and the Christian classics. Students may begin studying the Greco-Roman classics at the end of high school and into college.

Chinese classical Christian schools must resist the temptation to simply copy the reading lists of American classical Christian schools. This temptation can be strong. After all, some American classical Christian schools have been around for decades. One might reasonably assume that these schools know what books to teach better than classical Christian schools in China that have little to no experience. Chinese teachers might feel as if they are trying to bake a cake, and if they simply follow the same recipe that the experienced chefs in America use they can make just as good of a cake. But reading lists are not like recipes. They are like maps. An American school with decades of experience might be able to produce a more elaborate and detailed map than a newly-established Chinese school, but it will be of little help to a student living in China if it is a map of America. The student needs a map of *China*. The question we should ask, then, is not "Which map is better?" but rather "Which place does the map depict?" and "Who intends to use it?" For a Chinese student, a hastily-drawn map of the Sichuan Basin will be of more use than a brilliantly-drawn map of the Florida Everglades. If we have to decide between adding Shakespeare or Du Fu (杜甫) to our reading list, we should not ask whose poetry is better but rather who will be reading them. Shakespeare will be more helpful to an American student, and Du Fu will be more helpful to a Chinese student. This is because the meaning of poetry is derived from the culture in which it is written and exerts a greater influence on that culture. This is also true of other subjects like history, language, music, and art.

Of course, if we are comparing two different maps of China, then we can ask which map is better. One will be more accurate than the other. One will display more information than the other. One will come in brighter colors than the other. If Chinese educators are comparing *Chi-*

nese poets to be taught to *Chinese* children, then they must evaluate the merits of the poetry itself. Some Chinese poets really are better than others. But they must ensure that they are evaluating curricula designed for Chinese children. They should not adopt the third-grade reading list of an American classical Christian school just because it proved effective in that school, for neither those authors nor those students are Chinese.

Some subjects, however, are less dependent on cultural context. American history is not as relevant to Chinese children as it is to American children, but mathematics is. Not all children need to know the details of the Boston Tea Party, but they do all need to know how much two cups of tea cost at one dollar per cup. The same is true for other subjects like biology, chemistry, physics, and logic. When dealing with these kinds of subjects, we can more easily compare curricula across cultures because the meaning of their content is shared between cultures. Christians in China can reject a story about a dragon from their curriculum because it was written by a European, for a dragon means something very different in a Western context than it does in a Chinese context. But they cannot reject a book on physics simply because it was written by a European. Dragons are different in China than they are in Europe, but the principles of flight are the same. In the one instance, the author's cultural background is important, for the story derives meaning from that culture. But in the other instance, it is irrelevant. The only criterion that matters with the physics book is whether it teaches physics well. If Chinese teachers discover that the European book teaches physics better than the Chinese book, then they should use it.

The upper school of ancient China culminated in the imperial exam. This was a written exam that consisted of argumentative essays on policy and classical literature in which students brought classical texts into conversation with modern politics. These exams were the primary target of criticism throughout most of Chinese history. Critics argued that they distracted from the original Confucian intent of education, namely moral cultivation. Others said that the exams discouraged students from studying other subjects that were not on the exam. Song Yingxing (宋应星, 1587–1666), the author of a famous Ming handbook on technology, writes in the preface of his book, "An ambitious scholar will undoubtedly toss this book onto his desk and give it no further thought: it is a work that is in no way concerned with the art of advancement in officialdom."[30]

On the one hand, Chinese Christian schools should avoid turning education into mere test preparation. They must stress that the goal of education is not just to obtain a degree or a job but to "grow up into Christ" (Eph. 4:15). Schools should reward students for exemplary Christian living and not only intellectual accomplishments. On the other hand, schools must also evaluate students' intellectual abilities, and I think some form of a policy debate essay is fitting as a capstone examination. The merit of such an essay is that it is comprehensive in nature. It requires students to analyze many different texts and apply them to contemporary needs in a winsome manner. It need not only concern literature and politics but may also address other subjects. This final essay may take the place of the "thesis" typically used as a capstone exercise in Western high schools.

Calculation or *shu* (数) is sometimes translated into English as mathematics, but this is misleading. In the classical tradition, *shu* did not only include subjects that we typically associate with mathematics, such as arithmetic and geometry, but also subjects that we generally associate with natural science, such as astronomy, geography, and surveying. It is better understood as "calculation" or "measurement." The *Guangya* (广雅), the oldest Chinese encyclopedia, defines *shu* in even broader terms. "*Shu*: method (*shu* 术)."[31] In short, calculation is the art of methodically quantifying the natural world.

From a practical perspective, calculation is essential because without it we cannot complete even the most basic daily tasks. Without a knowledge of calculation, we cannot know how far we have to travel to get to the market, what time we will arrive there, or how much we will have to pay for a dozen eggs. Calculation sharpens our analytical thinking skills, increasing our ability to solve problems. From a Christian perspective, calculation is essential because without it we cannot take dominion of the earth. Without it we cannot love our neighbor well. Without it we cannot even understand the Bible. We cannot know what the Bible means when it says that Jesus fed "five thousand" people with "five" loaves and "two" fish, or how big a temple is that is "sixty cubits long, twenty cubits wide, and thirty cubits high." Knowledge of calculation also inspires worship. Abraham discovers the wealth of God's blessings through arithmetic.†† David deduces God's kindness through astronomy.‡‡ Calculation helps us to better grasp the grandeur of God's creation, which consequently increases our joy in God. "Great are the works of the LORD, studied by all who delight in them" (Ps. 111:2). If we wanted to know what kind of person Leonardo da Vinci was, we would not only study the words he wrote. We would also study the things he made. In the same way, if we want to know who God is, we cannot only study the words he wrote. We must also study the world he made. Calculation gives us the tools to do this.

The sophistication of ancient Chinese science and mathematics is often overshadowed by the development of modern science in the West. When we compare Chinese science and Western science, we typically compare them as they existed after the sixteenth century. When we set Qing dynasty China next to nineteenth-century Europe, the differences are striking indeed. The Western world was far more advanced in science at the time than China. But if we compare the two cultures before the sixteenth century, the Chinese were in many respects ahead of the West. In his *Novum Organum*, famous Renaissance scientist and philosopher Francis Bacon considers the three inventions most responsible for the advancement of civilization in the world: "Printing, gunpowder, and the [magnetic] compass . . . these

---

†† "'Number the stars, if you are able to number them.' Then he said to him, 'So shall your offspring be'" (Gen. 15:5).

‡‡ "When I look at your heavens, the work of your fingers, the moon and the stars, which you have set in place, what is man that you are mindful of him, and the son of man that you care for him?" (Ps. 8:3–4)

three have changed the appearance and state of the whole world . . . no empire, sect, or star, appears to have exercised a greater power and influence on human affairs than these mechanical discoveries."[32] Bacon fails to point out, however, that these three technologies were all invented by the Chinese.

In 1954, British scientist and historian Joseph Needham undertook a monumental project of writing a detailed history of science and technology in China. *Science and Civilisation in China* now contains twenty-seven books in seven volumes. It has significantly influenced the attitudes and ideas of the scientific community about Chinese math and science and has received great acclaim worldwide. In the book, Needham demonstrates that before the scientific revolution in the West, China was "in many ways ahead of Europe for some previous fourteen centuries."[33] While the Greeks were especially adept at the pure sciences (abstract number, formal logic, etc.), the Chinese excelled in the applied sciences. "Between the first century BC and the fifteenth century AD, Chinese civilization was much more efficient than occidental in applying human natural knowledge to practical human needs."[34] In addition to the "Four Great Inventions" of China (the magnetic compass, gunpowder, papermaking, and printing), Needham lists hundreds of other ideas and technologies invented by the ancient Chinese.

One question, however, greatly perplexed Needham, and it was one of the primary questions that inspired his research in the first place. If ancient China was so scientifically and technologically advanced, why did modern science never develop there? Needham credits the rise of modern science in the West primarily to the Western concept of the "laws" of Nature, which provided a philosophical foundation on which the scientific method could stand. The Chinese never developed modern science because it had no such concept. Needham gives three reasons for this. The first reason concerns the negative associations most Chinese people at the time drew between "law" (*fa* 法) and the "Legalist" school of thought (*fajia* 法家), which competed with the Confucian school. The second reason concerns the Confucian preference for rites (*li* 礼) over law (*fa* 法) as the organizing principle of society. Although *li* was a form of natural law, it was not expressed in legal terms and was generally only applicable to human society. Needham's third and final reason is as follows:

> The autochthonous ideas of a supreme being, though certainly present from the earliest times, soon lost the qualities of personality and creativity. The development of the concept of precisely formulated abstract laws capable, because of the rationality of an Author of Nature, of being deciphered and re-stated, did not therefore occur.[35]

The great scientists of the West like Kepler, Descartes, Boyle, and Newton all rooted their science in the Christian idea of an omnipotent God that created the universe *ex nihilo* and governed it according to "laws." Without this Creator or these laws, they could not justify the scientific method. It is impossible to perform a reliable experiment in a world where the speed of light might suddenly change on a whim. It is also impossible to perform a reliable experiment in a world where human reason and sense perception are mere illusions or products of mere chance. Western scientists believed nature could be understood rationally because it (and they) were created by a rational God. The Chinese came close to a concept of natural law in the Neo-Confucian concept of *li* (理), which encompassed the entirety of the material world, but *li* only describes patterns inherent in nature. These patterns are not intentionally put there by a personal God for us to decipher but are "just there." In the Chinese view, the laws of nature were like ink marks on paper that just happen to form word-like images. In the Western view, however, the laws of nature were like words written by a living author meant for us to read. Needham says that the earlier Chinese conception of God had personal and creative qualities similar to the Christian God, but over time these qualities slowly vanished, and consequently so did the possibility of a divine Lawgiver. Without a Lawgiver there could be no philosophical foundation for the scientific method. Christianity also provides the only philosophical foundation by which we can justify the basic principles of mathematics, but I will not elaborate on them here. Scholars have addressed this topic elsewhere.[36]

If we want to redeem the Chinese art of calculation, therefore, we must begin by rooting it in the Christian God. Our schools cannot raise up the next Pascal or Newton unless our students share the same Christian worldview these men had. Teachers should strive to use math and science textbooks in which these Christian foundations are plainly stated. If they cannot find such textbooks, then they should regularly supplement secular textbooks with Christian content.

Even though Christianity was one of the primary catalysts that drove the scientific revolution, the great scientists at the time still relied heavily on the insights of their pagan ancestors. As mentioned earlier, Newton once commented in a letter to Robert Hooke, "If I have seen further it is by standing on the shoulders of giants."[37] Newton here is quoting from the twelfth-century Christian philosopher Bernard of Chartres, who was referring to the gigantic intellectual stature of the ancient Greeks and Romans. The great Christian mathematicians and scientists in history did not dismiss the learning of the ancients either because their ideas were "outdated" or because they were pagan. They recognized their wisdom and believed we should eagerly learn from them. For Chinese classical Christian schools, this does not only mean studying the math and science of the Greeks, Romans, and Arabs. It also means studying the math and science of the ancient Chinese.

CHAPTER 9

Archery and Charioteering (射御)

Of the six arts, the final two are likely to raise the most questions. Am I actually suggesting that contemporary Chinese classical Christian schools should teach archery and charioteering? Yes.

At the most basic level, archery and charioteering are physical education. If we want to cultivate the entire man, we cannot neglect the body. Unfortunately, Christians often do. As we've already discussed previously, the church has been greatly influenced by Platonic philosophy. Not a few Christians view the human body with indifference, if not disdain. Like Plato, they emphasize the importance of the immaterial soul and deemphasize the importance of the material body. For them, the body is not a garden to cultivate but a prison to escape from.

The Bible, however, stresses that humans are not only souls. We are souls united to bodies. A human without a body is incomplete. He is lacking an essential aspect of his humanity. We see this in God's creation of man in Genesis, but we see it even more clearly in the incarnation of Jesus. If humans were essentially only souls, then Jesus could save us without taking on a body. But the Scriptures teach otherwise. "Since therefore the children share in flesh and blood, he himself likewise partook of the same things . . . Therefore he had to be made like his brothers in every respect" (Heb. 2:14, 17). If we want to educate the whole person, therefore, we must cultivate the body.

Another doctrine of Christianity demonstrates the importance of the human body even more clearly than the incarnation. The Bible tells us that when we die and go to Heaven, our souls will be separated from our bodies. But the Bible does not locate our final hope in Heaven. It locates our final hope in the resurrection of the body. Eternal life does not entail our souls floating around an immaterial Heaven forever. As long as our souls remain in Heaven, we are incomplete. We are only fully restored when our souls are reunited with our bodies in the resurrection. Why did the Apostle Paul renounce all he had? What was his final hope? "That by all means possible I may attain the resurrection of the dead" (Phil. 3:11).

The Apostle Paul did not view his body as something to escape from. "For while we are still in this tent, we groan, being burdened—*not that we would be unclothed*, but that we would be further clothed, so that what is mortal may be swallowed up by life" (2 Cor. 5:4). Paul does not want to cast off his current body, nor does he simply want to exchange it with a new one. He wants his current body to be "further clothed"—that is, he wants his body to be glorified.

Elsewhere, Paul describes the difference between our current bodies and our resurrection bodies as the difference between a seed and a fully-grown plant (1 Cor. 15:35–54). Our current bodies are like acorns. They are sown into the ground through death, and at the resurrection they come up as oak trees. Paul's metaphor here is helpful in understanding how to think about physical education. When we exercise, we are not cultivating a body that we will one day throw away forever. We are cultivating a seed that will one day grow into an oak tree. An oak tree has very different properties from an acorn, just as our resurrection bodies will have very different properties from our current bodies. But there is still *continuity* between the two. An oak tree may not look much like the acorn it once was, but in some sense the two are still the same "thing." The tree is just a mature acorn, or, in Christian terms, it is a *glorified* acorn. In the same way, there is continuity between our current bodies and our resurrection bodies. The fact that God promises us an oak tree in the resurrection does not mean that the acorn is unimportant. On the contrary, it means that the acorn is extremely important, for that is what he is going to make the oak tree out of. The truth of the resurrection does not mean that physical education is a waste of time. It means that physical education is essential, for the body we are cultivating now is the same body that will one day be glorified forever. This does not mean that we exercise because only a fit body can rise from the dead. Even the fittest bodies will eventually deteriorate in the ground. Rather, we train our bodies as a confession of faith. Each time we run a lap or lift a barbell, we are confessing to the world, "I believe in the resurrection of the body."

C. S. Lewis makes another helpful point:

Who will trust me with a spiritual body if I cannot control even an earthly body? These small and perishable bodies we now have were given to us as ponies are given to schoolboys. We must learn to manage: not that we may some day be free of horses altogether but that some day we may ride bare-back, confident and rejoicing, those greater mounts, those winged, shining and world-shaking horses which perhaps even now expect us with impatience, pawing and snorting in the King's stables.[1]

Physical education, therefore, is not only a means of confessing the resurrection but of preparing for it. We value the bodies God has given us now because we value the bodies he will give us in the future. At the same time, we must be careful not to obsess over our bodies. The Bible says we should still prioritize spiritual growth over physical growth. "For while bodily training is of some value, godliness is of value in every way" (1 Tim. 4:8). It is possible to exercise too much, but this is not the temptation of most in the classical Christian education movement. Most students of the classics pay too little attention to physical education. This is not only true in the Western classical tradition but also in the Chinese classical tradition.

Before the time of Confucius, archery and charioteering were valued even more than script and calculation. But after Confucius introduced the study of the classics to the six arts curriculum, archery and charioteering fell to the wayside. The government promoted the policy of "emphasizing literature over military arts" (*zhongwen qingwu*). The emperor sometimes even completely banned civilians from practicing martial arts for fear of an uprising. With a few exceptions, the imperial exams were entirely literature-based.

The martial arts were only emphasized in military schools. Zhu Yuanzhang (朱元璋) of the Ming dynasty attempted to reintroduce martial arts to the imperial examination, requiring all university students to study archery, but his efforts were short-lived. I believe contemporary Christian educators should pick up this baton and reintroduce martial arts to the Chinese curriculum.

Some Christians may agree about the importance of physical education but disagree about teaching archery and charioteering in particular. After all, these are *martial* arts. They are arts of war. Why should Christian schools be training children for war?

In the *Republic*, Plato promotes the study of martial arts in primary school not for their military benefits and not even for their physical benefits. The main objective of military training, he says, is to cultivate the "soul."[2] For Plato, the soul is made up of three parts: the reason, the spirit, and the appetite. Each part corresponds to a specific virtue: the rational part corresponds to wisdom, the spirited part to courage, and the appetitive to temperance. This threefold division is very similar to Confucius's threefold "way" of the *junzi*—*ren*, wisdom, courage.[3] For Plato, martial arts cultivate the spirited aspect of the soul by instilling courage. "This, not developing physical strength, will be the goal of his efforts, as distinct from all other athletes, who diet and train for the sake of physical fitness."[4] Plato recognized what most of us have recognized about those who have seriously studied martial arts—martial arts cultivate a man's emotional and mental fortitude. Army boot camp is more of a psychological challenge than a physical challenge. Although Plato identifies courage as the primary virtue of martial arts, martial arts instill more than courage—they also instill discipline, responsibility, focus, hard work, and endurance.

The ancient Chinese promoted archery and charioteering for similar reasons. Archery and charioteering were not just arts of warfare. They were forms of *li* that cultivated virtue and discipline. "In archery we have something like the way of the superior man. When the archer misses the center of the target, he turns around and seeks for the cause of his failure in himself."[5] "As a father, being a good father should be your target; as a son, being a good son should be your target. As a lord, being a good lord should be your target; as an official, being a good official should be your target. So each archer shoots at his own target."[6] Archery trains a man in virtue by allowing him to practice acting out in ritual form disciplines and attitudes that he ought to be living out day to day. Even though sports like basketball or tennis can also instill virtue, they generally are not as effective as martial arts, which are more rigorous.

Plato warns us of focusing only on book learning and neglecting physical education. "People who engage exclusively in cultural studies end up shamefully soft."[7] The ancients, both in China and in the West, considered softness to be a vice in men—and this is not just a pagan sentiment. The Bible directly denounces softness as a sin. "Know ye not that the unrighteous shall not inherit the kingdom of God? Be not deceived: neither . . . effeminate, nor abusers of themselves with mankind shall inherit the kingdom of God" (1 Cor. 6:9–10 KJV). The Greek word for "effeminate" here is the exact same word Plato uses to describe a "soft" (*malakías*) man. It literally means a man who displays the qualities of a woman. Most modern translations of the Bible translate "effeminate" and "abusers of themselves with mankind" as one phrase—"men who practice homosexuality," but this is much too narrow. The Bible denounces not just homosexual activity but all forms of effeminacy in men. In modern times, however, softness is often considered a virtue. Soft men are praised as "kind," "warm," and "caring"—even "cool." I once saw a large propaganda poster on the wall of a Chinese subway advertising the local fire department. It was a giant photo of five pencil-thin Chinese firefighters dressed in shimmering-blue silk suits with pop-star hair and faces covered in make-up. They stared seductively into the camera, one holding a fire hose and another a fire extinguisher. A fire truck sat in the background. The moment I saw it I whispered to myself, "Rites and music are in ruins." Few jobs embody masculinity more than firefighting. A man whose job it is to rescue people from burning buildings ought to display characteristics like strength, responsibility, bravery, and an ability to endure hardship. These men, however, looked like they would be afraid to step outside the fire station for fear that the wind would mess up their hair.

This effeminization of society is not just a result of pop culture. It is a result of poor education. Boys do not know how to act like men because they've been told all their lives that the measure of a man is how many books he has read. This was the message sent by the imperial examination (*keju*), on which the ancient government education system was built, and it is the message sent by the current college entrance exam (*gaokao*), on which the modern public education system is built. Thus, we find men like Yan Zhitui (颜之推, 531–591) mocking well-respected "scholars" in his day who "cannot even reach the target" in archery.[8] In modern day China, we find "uncultured" day laborers outside our classrooms carrying 50-pound bundles of rebar across 300-foot-high scaffolding without safety equipment, while inside our classrooms we find "cultured" graduate students majoring in eighteenth-century literature who complain about having to walk up four flights of stairs to get to their air-conditioned classroom. If classical Christian schools want to raise up young men who "act like men" (1 Cor. 16:13), then they must redeem martial arts. God calls men to be protectors, to defend their wives and children, to rescue the weak and the needy. When a Christian man sees another man attacking a woman or a child, he should not stand by and watch. He should confront the man, and if need be, fight him. Martial arts equip him to do this. Martial arts do not only raise up good soldiers—they raise up good husbands, good fathers, and good citizens.

The modern Chinese public school system requires all middle school, high school, and college students to undergo "military training" (*junxun* 军训), but for all intents and purposes this training is a joke. Military training generally takes place for no more than one week out of the year. It consists primarily of learning to stand and move in formation according to the orders of the drill instructor. There is very little physical training besides running. The real motive for this training is to teach students to obey authority—a motive that in itself is commendable, but not when the obedience is blind obedience and the authority absolute.

One other shameful aspect of modern "military training" is that girls are required to participate in it. They must wear the same camouflage uniforms as the boys and partake in most of the same exercises. The Bible strictly prohibits this. "The woman shall not wear that which pertaineth unto a man" (Deut. 22:5 KJV). In the Hebrew, "that which pertaineth unto a man" refers especially to the armor worn by soldiers. It is a disgrace for a woman to imitate a male soldier, for it violates the God-ordained distinctions between men and women. In Confucian terms, it violates *li*. Classical Christian schools must affirm and respect the differences between the sexes, especially in regards to physical education.

Martial arts are generally aimed at cultivating masculine qualities, for they are arts of war. For the most part, therefore, girls should not study them. But this does not mean that girls should not study physical education. Schools should still provide physical training for girls but only in forms that respect their femininity. Dance, for example, provides physical exercise while simultaneously cultivating feminine virtues like elegance, gracefulness, modesty, flexibility, submissiveness, and so forth.

Because archery is much less aggressive compared to other martial arts, I think girls may also study it. There is a certain elegance involved with shooting a bow and arrow that is befitting to a woman, especially in the context of shooting a fixed target rather than a person in battle. The ancient archery competitions were more akin to dance recitals than sparring matches, for they were a form of *li*. The movements of the archers were even choreographed to music. What was important in these competitions was not so much the strength of the archer as the elegance in which the archer performed the required movements. At the same time, just as there is a feminine way to dance and a masculine way to dance, there is a feminine way to perform archery and a masculine way to perform archery. Boys and girls may both practice archery, but they must practice it in different ways. For girls, this means focusing primarily on elegance in form. For boys, this means focusing primarily on strength. The archery portion of the traditional military service exam (*wuju* 武举) tested students not only on accuracy and proper technique but also on strength. They were required to lift a heavy stone in a test called *duoshi* (掇石), which is equivalent to modern-day weightlifting. Archery education, therefore, should include weightlifting for boys. In addition, targets should be placed farther away and bows adjusted to a heavier draw weight than those used by girls.

The ancient Chinese began teaching archery when a student was in his early teens. Christian schools should do the same. Children who are not yet old enough to study archery may focus on strength and endurance exercises, as these are still technically part of archery education. In addition to the benefits discussed above, archery also requires less physical space than many other school sports. This is especially helpful for Christian schools that don't have the benefit of a large school building.

The history of charioteering is not as robust as that of archery. This is due largely to technological advancements.

By the end of the Han dynasty chariots were no longer used in warfare and were rarely used in ceremonial rites. They were replaced by cavalry. The military service exam, therefore, tested students not in archery and charioteering but in archery and equestrianism, which was simply an evolution of charioteering.

One of the most important aspects of charioteering is the horse. Broadly speaking, charioteering is animal training. While archery is concerned with mastering an inanimate object, charioteering is concerned with mastering an animate object—an animal. In this way, the arts of archery and charioteering together embody the "dominion mandate" given by God to man to exercise dominion over the earth and over the animals. Even in ancient China the bow and arrow represented man's dominion over the earth. The *Record of Rites* describes the first rite that a boy is to perform when he receives his first bow. He is required to shoot one arrow down into the earth, one into the sky, and one in each of the four directions, because "these are where a man's business lies."[9] In Chinese mythology, the famous archer Hou Yi (后羿) saves the earth from being scorched by shooting down nine of the ten suns with his bow, leaving us with the one we see today. In the same way that mastery of the bow represented man's dominion over the earth, so mastery of the horse represents man's dominion over animals. C. S. Lewis reflects on the dignity of this task:

> The 'real' or 'natural' animal [to an atheist] is the wild one, and the tame animal is an artificial or unnatural thing. But a Christian must not think so. Man was appointed by God to have dominion over the beasts . . .

The tame animal is therefore, in the deepest sense, the only 'natural' animal—the only one we see occupying the place it was made to occupy.[10]

Charioteering is the art of taming animals, of bringing them under the complete dominion of man and consequently dignifying them. Of all the animals, none is more clearly designed for man's use than a horse. The ancients often marveled at the perfect proportions of a horse compared to that of man. It is just begging to be tamed and ridden. If schools have access to horses, then they should make every effort to teach horseback riding. But because most schools do not have access to horses, they may substitute other animals. The main goal is to teach children not only how to care for animals but how to tame and train them. Lewis describes this mysterious process as one of uniting the animal with ourselves. The Bible says that we are "in" our master Christ. In a similar (but not identical) way, Lewis says that the tamed animal is "in" his master, so that the animal in some way shares in the personality of its master. Anyone who has trained an animal knows this mysterious and profound experience.

Of course, charioteering also concerns the technical skill and coordination involved with maneuvering a chariot. The traditional word used to describe charioteering in the six arts curriculum was *yu* (御), literally "driving" or "controlling." This aspect of charioteering is at least partially recreated in our use of modern transportation. A car is essentially a chariot pulled by a mechanical horse instead of a living one, and it, too, requires a driver. Even though much of the difficulty (and glory) of maneuvering a live horse is significantly diminished by modern transportation, a modern-day "driver's education" course is at least partially in keeping with the traditional charioteering curriculum. Bicycling, especially across difficult terrain, also utilizes some of the same skills involved with charioteering and equestrianism, such as agility, control, and coordination.

Of the six arts, charioteering is the most difficult to contextualize to modern-day China. I have provided a few principles and suggestions above, but I confess that my contributions here are limited. I leave the task of further developing and contextualizing this art to the ingenuity of Chinese classical educators.

Because archery and charioteering are less confrontational and less physically demanding than most martial arts, I recommend supplementing these with other martial arts, especially the traditional Chinese martial art of kungfu. One of the great benefits of kungfu is that it requires a boy to physically confront another boy whom he knows wants to attack him. This trial instills in him courage, which Plato and Confucius both identify as one of the primary virtues of the *junzi*. It also instills many of the other masculine qualities mentioned above. The Bible contains many examples of godly warriors and praises their heroic feats, so it is appropriate for Christian teachers to do the same. Kungfu is sometimes taught merely as a performance art, focusing only on proper form. While this provides some benefits, it does not instill important virtues like courage as well as full-contact sparring does. Therefore, I suggest that schools teach full-contact kungfu and not merely the performative kind. For the reasons discussed earlier, schools should restrict kungfu to only boys. The popular "*wuxia*" or "martial heroes" genre of Chinese literature frequently depicts female martial arts masters engaging in physical combat, but this runs contrary to their God-given natures. In the words of Confucius, it violates *li*.

The six arts did not include all realms of knowledge. Rather, they laid the foundations on which students could pursue more advanced studies in medicine, law, ethics, "mysterious learning" (*xuanxue* 玄学), and so forth. The Western medievals categorized these advanced studies in terms of three kinds of "philosophy"—natural philosophy (i.e. natural science), moral philosophy, and divine philosophy (i.e. metaphysics). The pinnacle and "queen" of all studies was theology.[11] Retaining these helpful Western categories, we can finally summarize our Christian six arts curriculum in terms of the goal, attitude, content, and method of study:

A Christian "Six Arts" Schema

GOAL

Self-cultivation through the
pursuit of the *Dao* (Christ)

ATTITUDE

Joy   Reverence   Humility

- Toward God
- Toward great leaders
- Toward sages

CONTENT

Love	Wisdom	Courage
Rites & Music	Script & Calculation	Archery & Charioteering
Orders our loves by instilling proper values and sentiments toward God, nature, and man	Cultivates language and computational skills, enabling us to analyze and communicate thought and to quantify the natural world	Strengthens the body and cultivates emotional and mental fortitude

Natural Philosophy (Natural Science)
Moral Philosophy
Divine Philosophy (Metaphysics)
Theology

METHOD

Study it broadly,
question it meticulously,
reflect on it carefully,
distinguish it clearly,
practice it earnestly

I propose this schema for Chinese classical Christian schools not as a fully-furnished house into which they can immediately move but only as a frame around which Christian scholars and teachers more qualified than myself should continue to build. Moreover, this is not *my* frame. This is the frame handed down to the Chinese church by their ancestors. It has stood the test of time, but like the rest of the world, it still needs a Redeemer.

Jesus planted these pedagogical insights into the minds of the ancient Chinese, but these seeds have only just sprouted. The six arts are still seedlings. They have not yet grown up into their full potential. Some will insist on designing the Chinese Christian curriculum around the seven liberal arts instead of the six arts because the seven arts are more developed and robust than the six arts.[12] Men in the West produced many more writings about the liberal arts than did the Chinese about the six arts. Even though the Chinese have produced many books on each of the six arts, I can find no book, ancient or modern, that systematically addresses the six arts as a whole, or that uses the six arts as an organizational framework for understanding the history and development of Chinese classical education. This book is my attempt to spur Chinese Christians on to such analysis.

One reason for this lack of systematic treatises on the six arts is that Chinese philosophy by nature does not typically rely on formal systems of thought as does Western philosophy.[13] The fact that the Chinese did not produce any systematic treatises on the six arts does not mean that they gave little thought to them. We would not expect Chinese in the Middle Ages to produce anything like Martianus Capella's *The Marriage of Philology and Mercury* or Hugh of Saint Victor's *Didascalicon*. They simply did not think in Western categories.

But I believe the biggest factor that influenced the development of the liberal arts in the West was the same factor that influenced the rise of Western civilization: the men who developed them were Christians. When the church in the West first inherited the seven liberal arts from the Greeks and Romans, the arts were still in disarray. Many even disagreed about how many liberal arts there actually were. It was only through centuries of Christian research and experiment that the seven arts matured into their current form. When we look at the six arts as they now exist, we find them in similar disarray as the early church found the seven arts. But this is not a reason to abandon them. It is a reason to *redeem* them. There are many more resources now on the seven arts than on the six arts, but this is only because the church created them. The six arts have yet to be touched by Christians. They have been lying in a tomb for many years now. But what might happen if Christ looked upon them and shouted, "Come out!" What might happen if he took them by the hand and said, "Arise!"

I believe this is the best path for Chinese Christian education because it is the tradition of the church. What I am proposing here is the same approach promoted by the church fathers, who did not reject the wisdom handed down to them by their pagan fathers but rather sought how to redeem this wisdom to the glory of God. For them this meant recovering the seven liberal arts. For Christians in China, this means recovering the six arts.

Chinese Christians should not think that adopting the six arts schema means completely rejecting the seven arts schema. The two are complementary in many ways. In fact, when the Jesuits translated the *Analects* into Latin, they called the six arts "liberal arts" (*liberales artes*).[14] The Jesuits clearly saw many similarities between the Chinese classical tradition and the Western classical tradition. As the Chinese church redeems the Chinese classical tradition, it should diligently study the Western liberal arts tradition for wisdom and insight. The six arts curriculum I am proposing in this book draws from this tradition, especially the concept of the Trivium.

At the same time, I believe that the six arts schema is better suited as a general framework for education than the seven arts because it is more comprehensive. The seven liberal arts in themselves are too narrow for an education that seeks to cultivate the entire man. The seven arts only focus on language and mathematics. The six arts, however, cultivate the entire man—heart, mind, and body. Rites and music are primarily concerned with piety (i.e. the heart); script and calculation are primarily concerned with the humanities and sciences (i.e. the mind); archery and charioteering are primarily concerned with physical education (i.e. the body). And yet, we cannot compartmentalize the six arts. Archery also cultivates the heart and mind, rites also cultivate the mind and body. All six arts work together and are intricately connected. As the ancient Chinese classic *Huainanzi* says, "The six arts are of different categories, but all are connected."[15] In short, compared with the seven arts schema, this six arts schema is more holistic.

This is not to say that the Western classical tradition was only concerned with language and mathematics. In their book *The Liberal Arts Tradition*, Kevin Clark and Ravi Jain summarize the Western liberal arts tradition using the acronym PGMAPT—piety, gymnastic, music, liberal arts, philosophy, and theology.[16] Subjects other than the seven liberal arts were taught in Western classical Christian schools. However, the Western classical tradition contains no comprehensive schema by which to organize this curriculum. The acronym "PGMAPT" is not a formulation of the ancients but a formulation of Clark and Jain. The Chinese, however, had such a schema, and it seems aptly suited for Christian use.

The six arts have other advantages over the seven arts, as well. For example, the six arts schema views music primarily as an aspect of *li*, whereas the seven arts schema views it primarily as a mathematical art. Even though music is certainly related to mathematics, in practice we experience it more as a form of *li*. The medieval church developed a robust view of music that is much better understood in the context of "rites and music" than in the context of the Quadrivium. They divided music into three kinds: the "music of the cosmos" (*musica mundana*), the "music of the body and soul" (*musica humana*), and "audible music" (*musica instrumentalis*). The Chinese tradition of rites and music takes all of these aspects into account. Even Scripture itself speaks of music in terms of *li* rather than math.

What other treasures might be hiding in this long-forgotten tradition? Only inquiring minds who dare to descend these ancient mines will find out.

CHAPTER 10

Obstacles to Classical Christian Education in China: Pride, Paganism & Politics

C lassical Christian education is a rich tradition that promises great blessing to the Chinese church, but it does not come without obstacles. The obstacles are many, but here I want to consider three that I think pose the greatest challenge to classical Christian schools in China: pride, paganism, and politics. Let us begin with the problem of pride.

Pride

Classical Christian education is built on the premise that the ancients (or at least *some* of the ancients) were wise. But when many Chinese Christians hear the name "Confucius" or the words "ancient culture," they do not think of wisdom but of idolatry. They think of ancestor worship. They think of hypocrisy. They think of anti-intellectualism, anti-progressivism, and anti-science. They think of arrogance. They think of countless souls being shackled by the bonds of moralism. They think of oppressive governments restricting free thought and demanding blind allegiance. "Wisdom" is about the last thing that comes to mind.

I once sat in on a Western literature class at a Chinese Christian college. The professor began his introduction to the course by telling the story of the Macartney Embassy, an English diplomatic mission to China in 1793 led by George Macartney. Macartney presented a number of gifts to the Qianlong Emperor in hopes of establishing better diplomatic and trade relations. The gifts were meant to display the advancement of Western civilization—globes, clocks, oil paintings, guns, and so on—in hopes of showing the emperor that the West had something to offer China. The emperor responded with a letter:

> Our dynasty's majestic virtue has penetrated unto every country under Heaven, and kings of all nations have offered their costly tribute by land and sea. As your ambassador can see for himself, we possess all things. I set no value on objects strange or ingenious, and have no use for your country's manufactures.[1]

The professor then asked, "Was this attitude a fluke? Was it just one individual case of an overblown ego?" No, he said. This attitude was the natural product of thousands of years of Confucian culture. He then proceeded to compare the Qing dynasty with England, emphasizing how backward Qing society was compared with the developed West. Finally, he played a short video displaying pictures of ancient Greco-Roman temples and art. The final picture showed a hand, and next to the hand a short caption:

"What kind of hand created this great human civilization?" The answer, he said, was obvious: "God's hand."

This professor reflects the attitude of many Chinese Christians. When they survey the history of Chinese civilization, they see many cultural sins. And because this civilization was traditionally a *Confucian* civilization, they conclude that Confucianism must be the fountainhead of all these sins. Christians are right to acknowledge the sins of their fathers. The professor above was right to condemn the arrogance of the Qianlong Emperor. But we must not assume that Confucianism or Chinese classical learning was necessarily the source of these sins.

Those who suggest that Confucianism is the source of China's cultural sins assume that those who committed these sins were simply obeying the teachings of their master. In other words, they assume that if Confucius had taught true righteousness, Chinese culture would reflect it. Instead of pride, legalism, and secularism we would find humility, grace, and the worship of God. But consider the implications of this assumption. The Confucian classics are not entirely consistent with the Bible, but suppose for a moment that they were. Suppose that the moral teachings contained in the Four Books and Five Classics perfectly mirrored those in the Old Testament. Would this have changed the social and moral decay of Chinese culture? No. How do we know? Because a few thousand years ago God gave one nation such a set of books, and that nation fell into ruin. The classical literature of Israel perfectly mirrored that of the Old Testament—for it *was* the Old Testament. These books were written by true sages, and like the Chinese the Israelites committed themselves to the teachings of these books. They performed sacrifices year after year professing to follow these teachings. But in the end the nation collapsed. There arose kings far more arrogant and wicked than the Qianlong Emperor. Was this because there was something wrong with the teachings they professed to obey? No. The teachings were perfect. The problem was not with the teachings but with the people—they were sinners.

Therefore, we cannot assume that the sins of Chinese culture were necessarily conceived or nurtured by the Chinese classics. This is especially true if we find the classics condemning the very actions and attitudes of those who profess to honor them. For example, some Christians assert that Confucian morality is nothing more than a mere "performance." They insist that it is only concerned with *appearing* good and not actually being good. And yet, one of the primary teachings in the *Great Learning* concerns "making the intentions perfectly genuine":

> Making the intentions perfectly genuine means being without self-deceit ... For this reason, a *junzi* is inevitably cautious when he is alone. The small person will do bad things when he is alone; there is nothing he may not do. When he is observed by a *junzi*, however, he will cover up the bad things that he has done and exhibit any good ones ... For this reason, a *junzi* is inevitably cautious when he is alone.[2]

We may be able to find many examples in Chinese history of self-professed Confucians treating morality as a mere performance, but this is not because the Confucian classics promote this. They directly condemn it. According to orthodox Confucianism, a true *junzi* does good even when he is alone. It is a "small man" who only cares about doing good when others are watching.

As we survey the history of Chinese education, we do not find a long tradition of Confucians faithfully applying the teachings of the Four Books and Five Classics. On the contrary, we find self-professed Confucians constantly twisting the teachings of the sages and appropriating them to accomplish their own agendas. When Zhu Xi surveyed the history of Chinese civilization up to his own day, he did not see a civilization led by Confucians. He saw only "pseudo-Confucians" (*suru* 俗儒).[3] According to Zhu, the Chinese had never truly implemented Confucianism. They honored Confucius with their mouths, but their hearts were far from him. Matteo Ricci similarly distinguished the "former Confucians" (*xianru* 先儒) from the "latter Confucians" (*houru* 后儒). The former Confucians were the authors of the Confucian classics and their early adherents, who faithfully promoted their teachings. The latter Confucians were those scholars, especially from the Han Dynasty onward, who strayed from these teachings. Ricci was especially concerned about how the latter Confucians had stripped Heaven of personhood and turned Him into an impersonal force, largely due to the influence of Daoism and Buddhism, but he also criticized them for failing to model the teachings on virtue in the Confucian classics.[4]

When the Qianlong Emperor expressed no interest in learning from Westerners, he was not acting in accord with

the teachings of Confucius. Confucius stressed the importance of studying broadly. "To study broadly and deepen
one's resolve, to question closely and reflect on things at
hand, *ren* lies therein."[5] This conviction led Zhu Xi to insist
that "all books under heaven" ought to be studied.[6] Confucius was not intellectually proud. He did not believe he
knew all things. "The Master said, 'Do I have knowledge?
No, I do not.'"[7] When he entered the temple he "asked
about everything."[8] The Qianlong Emperor considered
it a shameful thing to learn from what he believed to be
an inferior kingdom, but Confucius praises the man who
"loves learning and is not ashamed to ask and learn of his
inferiors."[9] We slander Confucius when we suggest that
the attitude of the Qianlong Emperor reflects the attitude
of Confucius.

The Bible says, "Fathers shall not be put to death because of their children" (Deut. 24:16). God does not pun-
ish fathers for the sins of their children, and yet that is
exactly what we do when we blame Confucius for the sins
of Confucians. The revolutionary Hong Xiuquan (洪秀全,
1814–1864) claimed to follow the God of Christianity, and
in the name of that God he massacred millions. But we
would rightly object to someone calling Jesus a bloodthirsty
tyrant on the basis of Hong's actions, for Hong's actions are
inconsistent with the teachings of Jesus. Before we blame
Confucius for the sins of self-professed Confucians, we
ought to first consider whether their actions are consistent
with the teachings of Confucius. If they are consistent with
those teachings, then we have reason to find fault with the
teachings. But if we find Confucius himself condemning

these actions, then we have no right to blame him for them. I have primarily used Confucius as an example here, but this principle applies to all of classical Chinese literature.

If Confucius does not promote intellectual pride, then why are so many Confucian scholars proud? Is it because Confucius secretly *does* promote intellectual pride? No. It is because it is easier to pretend that you know something than to admit that you are ignorant.[10] If Confucius does not believe that living a moral life means merely observing rituals, then why did so many of his followers? Is it because Confucius actually *does* believe that morality is simply observing rituals? No. It is because it is easier to perform a few rituals than to truly be a man of *ren*.[11] If Confucius believes that Heaven is supreme, then why is the largest atheistic state in the world promoting his teachings? Is it because Confucius really *is* an atheist? No. It is because the government would rather be God than submit to Him.[12] In short, the primary reason for the decay of Chinese civilization is not Confucianism but indwelling sin. The problem is not that Confucians are Confucians but that Confucians are sinners.

Most of the ideals of Confucianism are noble and lofty, and that is precisely the problem. Confucianism sets an impossible standard for sinners to obey. It is the same problem the Apostle Paul faced looking at God's law. "The very commandment that promised life proved to be death to me" (Rom. 7:10). But we should not therefore find fault with the commandment, for "the commandment is holy and righteous and good" (Rom. 7:12). The fault lies with us. When a sinner sees a moral standard he knows he cannot obey, he has only two options: reject the standard or pretend to obey it. The Chinese generally chose the latter. Chinese Christians are right to point out and confess this sin, but they should not despise the standard in the process.

I will emphasize again that I am not equating Confucianism with Christianity. Although Confucianism contains much that is complementary to Christianity, it is nevertheless a *pagan* philosophy. Some Confucian teachings are either incompatible with Christianity or incomplete. The followers of Confucius were sinners, but so was Confucius. The sages were not holy. Their hearts and minds were influenced by sin, and therefore their philosophies are sure to contain errors. As classical Christian educators, we must be diligent to point out these errors. Many Christians are suspicious of and even hostile to classical education because they mistakenly believe that it entails a sweeping approval of all things ancient. It does not. It entails praising wisdom where wisdom is found and exposing folly where folly is found. But I do not believe the majority of China's cultural sins can be traced to the philosophies of the sages. For the most part, we find the sages themselves condemning these sins.

As Christians, we must recognize the pervasive influence of sin in our ancestors, but even more importantly we must recognize it in ourselves. The ancient Chinese were prone to pride, but so are we. One way this pride manifests itself in classical Christian schools is in the same kind of hypocritical, pompous attitude that characterized many Confucian scholars. Students and teachers may become puffed up with pride by the fact that they are studying ancient philosophy and poetry while "those" students in the government schools are just mindlessly taking exams. We can become more concerned with appearing "cultured" rather than truly being righteous and wise. Mencius rebukes such pride. "With grand ambitions they say, 'Ah, the ancients! The ancients!' But when their conduct is scrutinized it does not match their words . . . And how snooty they are as they strut about!"[13] Hugh of Saint Victor issues an even more piercing rebuke:

> Many are deceived by the desire to appear wise before their time. They therefore break out in a certain swollen importance and begin to simulate what they are not and to be ashamed of what they are; and they slip all the farther from wisdom in proportion as they think, not of being wise, but of being thought so. I have known many of this sort who, although they still lacked the very rudiments of learning, yet deigned to concern themselves only with the highest problems, and they supposed that they themselves were well on the road to greatness simply because they had read the writings or heard the words of great men. "We," they say, "have seen them. We have studied under them. They often used to talk to us. Those great ones, those famous men, they know us." Ah, would that no one knew me and that I but knew all things![14]

Another way this pride manifests itself in Christian schools is in our attitude toward non-Christians. "This author is not a Christian," we think to ourselves, "so he doesn't know what he's talking about." If we are not careful, this kind of haughty spirit can overtake our classrooms.

Instead of studying the classics in order to learn wisdom, we can end up studying them only to criticize our ancestors.

As Christians we believe that God bestows wisdom not only on Christians but also on non-Christians. When we reject on principle the teachings of our pagan ancestors, we do not only sin against our ancestors. More importantly, we sin against God. Calvin reminds us again:

> If we reflect that the Spirit of God is the only fountain of truth, we will be careful, as we would avoid offering insult to him, not to reject or condemn truth wherever it appears. In despising the gifts, we insult the Giver ... We cannot read the writings of the ancients ... without the highest admiration.[15]

Do we, like Calvin, *admire* the teachings of the ancients? Or do we only criticize and ridicule them? When we read the classics, do we expect to find the wisdom of God, or do we only expect to find folly? Do we believe that God would only bestow his grace on us Christians, or do we believe that his grace is so abundant that it falls even on those who do not worship him?

Consider, for example, how Cassiodorus speaks of his pagan ancestors in his influential sixth-century work on classical Christian education, *Institutions of Divine and Secular Learning*. Cassiodorus has a very high view of Scripture and church tradition. He does not put them on the same level as classical, secular authors, and yet he still praises a number of his pagan ancestors and recommends their works for study in Christian schools. The following is just a small sample. "Although Cicero, the chief light of Latin eloquence, set these matters out fully and carefully in various books ... nevertheless Quintilian, an outstanding teacher after the flood of eloquence of Cicero, very ably expanded his teaching."[16] "Plato and Aristotle [were] worthy teachers of secular letters."[17] "Among the Greeks Nicomachus diligently explained this subject ... anyone who uses these works often will most certainly be filled with the light of reason."[18] "Alypius, Euclid, and Ptolemy among the Greeks as well as others have produced laudable instruction on this subject."[19] "There are fine Greek writers on this subject, including Euclid, Apollonius, Archimedes, and others."[20]

Listen to how Martin Luther speaks of his pagan ancestors:

> We are excelled and put to shame by the pagans of old, especially the Romans and Greeks. Although they had no idea of whether this estate were pleasing to God or not, they were so earnest and diligent in educating and training their young boys and girls to fit them for the task, that when I call it to mind I am forced to blush for us Christians, and especially for us Germans.[21]

Luther had such a high view of God's grace that he was even willing to admit that pagan knowledge sometimes *exceeds* that of Christians. He believed that his non-Christian neighbor might be smarter and more capable than he was. This is true humility.

Humility affects how we read the writings of non-Christians. If we would teach and study humbly, then we must read others' words with a charitable spirit. This means not assuming the worst of our neighbor, even if he is our enemy. This is very hard for us. We like to think the worst of our enemies. If we do not like Confucius, we will tend to impose the worst possible meaning on his words. This is unbecoming to a Christian. Suppose that a non-Christian man tells us, "I love my children." We do not have the right to respond, "No you don't. You may *say* that you love them, but you don't really love them. You can only truly love them if you believe in Jesus. Everything you do for them is actually only out of selfish motives." This kind of response masquerades as a Christian response. It pretends to be theologically accurate, but it actually violates the law of love. The Bible tells us that love "believes all things" and "hopes all things" (1 Cor. 13:7). This means that when our non-Christian neighbor tells us that he loves his children, we should not immediately question the intentions of his heart. We should believe him. We believe him not because we have an overly-optimistic view of human nature. We know that he has a sinful nature. But we believe him because we know that God bestows common grace on all men. This man's love for his children is certainly not perfect. It is tainted by sin. But by the grace of God it is still love.

In the same way, when we come across admirable teachings in classical literature we do not have the right to immediately question the motives of the authors. We cannot accuse them of being disingenuous just because they are not Christians. Our default response should be to assume that they mean what they say. Of course, if we have strong evidence that suggests otherwise, we should follow the evidence. If the man above says that he loves his children immediately after we watch him physically and verbally abuse them, then we have good reason to question his claims. But most of the Christian skepticism toward Chinese classical literature that I have seen is not based on direct evidence but only on a general propensity for human sinfulness or on the actions of other people but not on those of the authors themselves. By doing this, Christians essentially reject all of classical literature. The teachings that directly contradict the Bible they dismiss as sinful, and the teachings that are in accordance with the Bible they dismiss as the empty words of hypocrites who do not actually believe what they say. This is not only unloving. It is academically lazy. It amounts to slandering our ancestors in order to avoid honestly engaging with their arguments.

Reading humbly does not mean reading uncritically. On the contrary, humility is the only path toward true critical thinking. If we want to honestly engage with the arguments of an author, we must first understand what he actually thinks. But we cannot do this if we insist that he see the world through *our* eyes. We must see the world through *his*. We must make an honest effort to understand what he is actually trying to say rather than imposing our own definitions on his words. C. S. Lewis calls this the difference between "using" a book and "receiving" it.[22] When a proud man enters the world of an author, he insists on going wherever he wants to go. He judges the author's world before he has even understood it. But a humble man knows how to die to himself. When he enters the author's world, he allows the author to show him around before he makes any judgments about it. He even hopes he might learn something new.

Paganism

The second main challenge that Chinese classical Christian educators face is that of paganism. God incessantly warns Israel of being enticed by the idols of the Gentiles. His admonitions are not unwarranted. Time and again, when the Jews mix with Gentiles, they begin worshiping their idols. This same danger exists in classical Christian schools, for classical education promotes the study of pagan culture. The more we immerse ourselves in pagan culture the greater danger we face of drifting away from God toward idols. Our students may enter our schools as Christians, but if we are not careful, they may graduate as pagans.

Many in the classical Christian movement quote Augustine's admonition to "plunder the Egyptians" as a justification for studying pagan culture, but they often fail to quote his warning that immediately follows. "Whatever may be the riches he brings with him out of Egypt, yet unless he has kept the Passover, he cannot be safe."[23] Classical education is rewarding but dangerous. The great danger of plundering the silver and gold of the Egyptians is that we accidentally take their idols, too. Sometimes they can be just as shiny. The only way to avoid this danger is to regularly feast on the Passover Lamb. His blood must cover the doorposts of our classrooms. The glory of Christ must shine so brightly in our schools that when our students see the twinkle of an Egyptian idol in their textbooks, it is to them like the flicker of a candle next to a pillar of fire.

The Chinese church is no stranger to the dangers of paganism, for it was saved out of it. Many Chinese Christians believe that the reason the Chinese church experienced great revival during the Cultural Revolution is because it was during this time when traditional culture was forcefully wiped out and the "Four Olds" destroyed—old customs, old culture, old habits, old ideas. The many idols that pervaded Buddhism and Confucianism were destroyed, leaving the Chinese with nowhere to turn but Christ. One reason many believe the church did not significantly grow before the Cultural Revolution is because missionaries were too tolerant of the idolatry that pervaded China at the time. Consider the following description of late nineteenth-century China by one missionary:

> You are free to expose the follies of modern Buddhism and ridicule the absurdities of Taoism ... But say a word against Confucius, even give an unconditional hint that his system is incomplete and ... you will hear murmurs rise instantly, and possibly angry words.[24]

Facing such a hostile environment, some missionaries became too accommodating of traditional Chinese culture.[25] As Chinese Christians study their pagan past, they must not make the same mistake. They must renounce the idols of their ancestors. But this process requires great caution. They must not swing their hammers indiscriminately. They must make sure that they are smashing the *idols* of their ancestors and not their ancestors.

When Christians tour the house of Confucianism, they will undoubtedly find idols inside. But the solution to the problem is not to burn down the house—it is to destroy the idols. Because many attribute the revival of Christianity in China to the "destruction of the Four Olds," some advocate for a similar approach today. They believe it is an effective means of destroying traditional idols. But that is like saying that burning down houses is a good way of destroying idols. Sure, if they burn down the house of Confucianism they will destroy their ancestors' idols, but they will also destroy their books and their paintings, their maps and their genealogies, their musical instruments and their furniture. Worst of all, they will destroy their ancestors! Christians should not try to solve the problem of ancestor worship by renouncing Confucianism, much less their ancestors. They should solve the problem of ancestor worship by *renouncing ancestor worship*. "Destroying the Four Olds" is inherently evil because it is a wholesale rejection of our ancestors and the inheritance they have given us. It is a direct violation of the Fifth Commandment. The Bible warns us, "Do not despise your mother when she is old" (Prv. 23:22).

God revived the Chinese church through the Cultural Revolution, but this does not mean that the Cultural Revolution itself was a good thing. God greatly blessed and multiplied Israel as a result of Joseph's brothers selling him into slavery, but this does not mean that we should all go and betray our siblings. What Joseph's brothers did was a sin, even though God used it for good. The Cultural Revolution was also a sin, even though God used it for good. The fact that God blessed his church through the destruction of traditional culture does not mean that he desires us to continue destroying the Four Olds. His Word directly forbids it. We should be thankful for the way God turned this evil for good in the past, but we should not commit the same evils in hopes that God will bring about the same results as before. We should not sin that grace may abound.

When Daniel was taken to Babylon, he refused to defile himself with the king's food. Hananiah, Mishael, and Azariah refused to bow down to the golden image of Nebuchadnezzar. These men rejected the idols of Babylon, but they did not use the idolatry of the Babylonians as an excuse for rejecting their culture altogether. They studied "the literature and language of the Chaldeans" (Dan. 1:4). They obtained "learning and skill in all literature and wisdom"—so much so that their knowledge and wisdom was "ten times better" than even the best Babylonian scholars (Dan. 1:17–20). Moses was no different. He refused to worship the idols of Egypt, but he nevertheless studied "all the wisdom of the Egyptians" and was therefore "mighty in his words and deeds" (Acts 7:22). We must denounce the idolatry of our pagan ancestors, but at the same time we should affirm the wisdom found in their writings. Basil describes classical Christian education as a process of carefully discriminating between pagan literature like bees discriminating between flowers in order to make honey:

> Now, then, altogether after the manner of bees must we use these writings, for the bees do not visit all the flowers without discrimination, nor indeed do they seek to carry away entire those upon which they light, but rather, having taken so much as is adapted to their needs, they let the rest go. So we, if wise, shall take from heathen books whatever befits us and is allied to the truth, and shall pass over the rest.[26]

Listen again to the exhortation of Augustine:

> All branches of heathen learning have not only false
> and superstitious fancies and heavy burdens of un-
> necessary toil, which every one of us, when going out
> under the leadership of Christ from the fellowship of
> the heathen, ought to abhor and avoid; but they con-
> tain also liberal instruction which is better adapted to
> the use of the truth, and some most excellent precepts
> of morality; and some truths in regard even to the
> worship of the One God are found among them.[27]

Many Christians may agree with Augustine that we can
receive "liberal instruction" (i.e. knowledge of the liberal
arts) from our pagan ancestors, but far fewer will agree
that we can find "most excellent precepts of morality" in
their writings, much less "truths in regard to the worship
of the One God." After all, pagans are *pagan*. They are not
born again. How can they teach Christians anything about
morality or God if they do not know Christ? Some of the
most fervent opposition to Chinese classical learning rests
on this point. Christians argue that because the authors of
the classics were not born again and had no saving knowledge of God, all of their teachings on morality are funda-
mentally flawed.

How we answer this question depends on our view
of the grace of God. How extensive is it? Does common
grace extend only to the realm of the arts and sciences? Or
does it also extend to the realm of morality and theology?
A pagan man can understand rhetoric and geometry, but
can he understand what is *right* and *good*? A pagan man can
know history, but can he know *God*?

The church fathers wrote much about these questions. On the one hand, they affirm that any action is only truly and wholly virtuous if its final aim is the glory of God. Any moral action that does not have as its end the glory of God is ultimately sin. "For whatever does not proceed from faith is sin" (Rom. 14:23). Nevertheless, certain actions may *approximate* virtue, even if they are not perfectly virtuous. Consider Augustine's praise of the Roman senator Cato in the *City of God*:

> For there is no true virtue except that which is directed towards that end in which is the highest and ultimate good of man. Wherefore even the honors which Cato sought he ought not to have sought, but the state ought to have conferred them on him unsolicited, on account of his virtues. But, of the two great Romans of that time, Cato was he whose virtue was by far the nearest to the true idea of virtue.[28]

In the Parable of the Good Samaritan, Jesus praises the love that the Samaritan man showed to his neighbor, even though the Samaritan's theology was heretical. Caring for the sick and clothing the naked are virtuous actions, even if they are performed by unregenerate men. They may be tainted by sin, but they are not therefore entirely void of virtue. For they still reflect the nature of God, however imperfectly. In the words of Augustine, they are "near" to virtue. See how John Calvin explains this:

> In every age there have been some who, under the guidance of nature, were all their lives devoted to virtue. It is of no consequence, that many blots may

be detected in their conduct; by the mere study of virtue, they evinced that there was somewhat of purity in their nature ... Such examples, then, seem to warn us against supposing that the nature of man is utterly vicious, since, under its guidance, some have not only excelled in illustrious deeds, but conducted themselves most honorably through the whole course of their lives. But we ought to consider, that, notwithstanding of the corruption of our nature, there is some room for divine grace, such grace as, without purifying it, may lay it under internal restraint. For, did the Lord let every mind loose to wanton in its lusts, doubtless there is not a man who would not show that his nature is capable of all the crimes with which Paul charges it.[29]

Calvin has no problem admitting that some pagan men are "devoted to virtue," even though they are not believers in God. For Calvin, the truth of total depravity does not mean that men are incapable of performing any virtuous acts whatsoever. Rather, it means that men cannot *of their own nature* perform virtue and that their virtue is always tainted in some measure by sin. If left to his own devices, a pagan man would be utterly evil. But God, in his grace, restrains this evil and gives the man the ability to perform virtuous deeds like loving his family or sacrificing for his country. See how Calvin praises the Roman soldier Camillus:

I admit that the specious qualities which Camillus possessed were divine gifts, and appear entitled to commendation when viewed in themselves. But in what way will they be proofs of a virtuous nature? ... Still, the surest and easiest answer to the objection is, that those are not common endowments of nature, but special gifts of God, which he distributes in divers forms, and, in a definite measure, to men otherwise profane. For which reason, we hesitate not, in common language, to say, that one is of a good, another of a vicious nature; though we cease not to hold that both are placed under the universal condition of human depravity. All we mean is that God has conferred on the one a special grace which he has not seen it meet to confer on the other.[30]

Christians who entirely dismiss the moral teachings found in the Chinese classics and who refuse to praise the moral virtue of their ancestors are not acting in accord with the church's historical teaching on the subject. Their pessimism exceeds that of the Bible. They are rightly pessimistic of human nature, but their pessimism extends even to the grace of God. They do not believe that God might have given the authors of the classics the grace to actually believe what they say, much less to live it.

Some Christians insist that of all pagan writings, those to be most avoided by Christians are those that teach on virtue. Saint Basil, however, says exactly the opposite:

Since we must needs attain to the life to come through virtue, our attention is to be chiefly fastened upon those many passages from the poets, from the historians, and especially from the philosophers, in which virtue itself is praised.[31]

Few if any Western scholars have surpassed the nineteenth-century missionary James Legge in their knowledge of the Chinese classics. In addition to his missionary efforts, Legge was the first Professor of Chinese at Oxford University from 1876 to 1897. His English translations of the classics have yet to be surpassed in number, and they are still the most widely cited. Legge found much to praise in the moral teachings of the Chinese classics:

> The teaching of Confucianism on human duty is wonderful and admirable. It is not perfect indeed. It does not start from the first and great commandment, "Thou shalt love the Lord thy god with all thy heart, and with all thy soul, and with all thy mind;" and in speaking of the relation of husband and wife, as the first of the human relations, it does not discountenance polygamy, a thing tolerated even in the Old Testament. But on the last three of the four things which Confucius delighted to teach—"letters, ethics, devotion of soul, and truthfulness"—his utterances are in harmony with both the Law and the Gospel. A world ordered by them would be a beautiful world. With the exception which I have mentioned, what can be more excellent than the doctrine of the five human relations, and the five virtues pertaining to them?—than the lessons of Mencius about benevolence and righteousness?—than the oft-repeated inculcation of the superiority of influence in leading men to the right course, over force?—than the exhibition of the power of example?[32]

By acknowledging the wisdom of the moral precepts in the classics we are not suggesting that they are just as good as those in the Bible. They are not. The Bible's teachings on morality are far superior to the teachings of our pagan ancestors, for they are perfect. But if that is the case, why would we ever study the classics? Why not just use the Bible for all of our moral instruction? Legge gives us one reason:

> The judgment of Paul about the law contained in the Old Testament was, that "it was a schoolmaster to lead us to Christ," and I think that much in Confucianism may be made to serve a similar purpose with the Chinese. Let the missionary therefore show a willing appreciation of what is good in the system; and where he can see defects in the character of the sage himself, and especially in his want of historical truth in the *Chunqiu*, let him lay bare his nakedness with a tender hand.[33]

Other missionaries offer similar sentiments.[34] At best, pagan literature can only give us moral standards to aspire to, but it cannot give us the ability to reach those standards. Even Confucius acknowledged that he could not attain to the standards he was promoting.[35] But this is why Christ came into the world. Jesus redeems pagan literature by providing a means to attain to the lofty goals it aspires to. As Christians, we study the moral teachings of our pagan ancestors in order to discover how Christ fulfills them. In the Gospel of Luke, Jesus says, "Many prophets and kings desired to see what you see, and did not see it, and to hear what you hear, and did not hear it" (Lk. 10:24). When we recognize that Jesus is the fulfillment not only of our own longings, but of the longings of our ancestors, we cherish Him even more. Suppose we could read the writings of the wise men from the East before they came to visit the newborn Christ. Would we not feel a deep gratitude and joy rise up within us as we recognize how He satisfies all of their greatest hopes and longings?

But the moral teachings in the classics provide us with more than this. They help us to think about Biblical morals in different terms. They formulate them in new ways that are striking and memorable in our native tongues. Moreover, the Bible is generally only concerned with moral principles. It only occasionally gives instruction on how to apply those principles to specific, everyday situations. The classics, however, stoke our imaginations to help us think of new ways to apply these principles. They give us more real-life examples of men and women to imitate. They also serve as a reminder for us. The Bible tells children to love their siblings, but children often forget. They are usually reminded of the Bible's teaching not through the Bible itself but through the mouths of their parents. The classics are like a father admonishing us to work hard in school or a mother reminding us to speak respectfully to our teacher.

But what about pagan teachings about God? How can pagan writings contain "truths in regard to the worship of the One God," as Augustine claims? After all, doesn't the Bible tell us that pagans are pagan precisely because they "do not know God?"*

The Apostle Paul answers this question for us in his epistle to the Romans:

> For the wrath of God is revealed from heaven against all ungodliness and unrighteousness of men, who by their unrighteousness suppress the truth. For what

---

* See Jn. 1:10, 17:25; 1 Cor. 1:21; 1 Jn. 3:1.

can be known about God is plain to them, because God has shown it to them. For his invisible attributes, namely, his eternal power and divine nature, have been clearly perceived, ever since the creation of the world, in the things that have been made. So they are without excuse. For although they knew God, they did not honor him as God or give thanks to him, but they became futile in their thinking, and their foolish hearts were darkened. Claiming to be wise, they became fools, and exchanged the glory of the immortal God for images resembling mortal man and birds and animals and creeping things (Rom. 1:18-23).

Paul tells us that the reason pagans are "without excuse" on Judgment Day is precisely because "they knew God." If pagans did not know God, then they would have a good excuse for not worshiping Him. How can they worship what they do not know? But Paul says that they do know Him because "God has shown" himself to them through creation. In the next chapter, Paul tells us that God's law is "written on their hearts" (Rom. 2:15). The problem is not that pagans do not know God but rather that they do not *worship* Him. "For although they knew God, they did not honor him as God." They worship idols instead.

When Paul preaches to the Athenians in Acts, he does not speak about God as though He is a foreign God that the Athenians have never heard of. Rather, he speaks about God as though the Athenians already know of Him:

So Paul, standing in the midst of the Areopagus, said: "Men of Athens, I perceive that in every way you are very religious. For as I passed along and observed the objects of your worship, I found also an altar with this inscription: 'To the unknown god.' What therefore you worship as unknown, this I proclaim to you. The God who made the world . . . made from one man every nation of mankind to live on all the face of the earth, having determined allotted periods and the boundaries of their dwelling place, that they should seek God, and perhaps feel their way toward him and find him. Yet he is actually not far from each one of us, for "In him we live and move and have our being;" as even some of your own poets have said, "For we are indeed his offspring" (Acts 17:22-31).

Paul says that the God he is speaking of is the very God that they worship. "What therefore you worship as unknown, this I proclaim to you." It is the same God to Whom they built an altar. He tells them that their pagan ancestors could not only "seek" this God but could "find" Him, for He revealed Himself to them. He then quotes from two Greek poets to prove that the ancient Greeks knew of this God. The line "In him we live and move and have our being" is a quote from the poem *Cretica* by Epimenides. The second quote is from the poem *Phainomena* by Aratus, an Athenian poet.

But if the Athenians already know of this God, then why does Paul need to preach to them? He must preach to them because, although they already worship Him, they worship Him as "unknown." They already know *of* Him, for they built an altar to Him, but they do not yet *know* Him. The Bible says we can know God in two ways, which we can distinguish in Chinese as the difference between "knowing of" (*zhidao* 知道) and "knowing" (*renshi* 认识). We can know of (*zhidao*) God, as one knows the name or face of a classmate, or we can know (*renshi*) God, as one knows a friend. The one kind of knowledge is superficial and external, the other is intimate and personal. The Apostle Paul says that pagans "know God" (*zhidao shen*) (Rom. 1:21) but "do not know" (*bu renshi*) Him (Acts 17:23). They know the most basic knowledge about Him—His "eternal power and divine nature (Rom. 1:20)"—but their knowledge of Him is vague and mixed with error. In his sermon, Paul has to correct many of the Athenians' misconceptions about Him. Most importantly, pagans have no *saving* knowledge of Him. They know Him as Creator but not as Savior. They know Him as Judge but not as Friend.

But if the Chinese of old had at least a general knowledge of God, then we should be able to find Him in their writings. And, in fact, we can. He is sometimes referred to as the Lord on High (*Shangdi*) but more often as Heaven (*Tian*). Many will object that some attributes of *Shangdi* and *Tian* are inconsistent with those of Yahweh, and of course they are right. Pagan knowledge of God is only vague and incomplete. In fact, the two poems that Paul quotes from in his sermon to the Athenians are poems about *Zeus*, whose attributes are quite different from Yahweh. But the fact that the ancients did not see God clearly does not mean that they did not see Him at all. They could still intuit many of His most basic attributes. Consider the attributes of Heaven in the following passages. "All things originate from Heaven."[36] "Is there yet any one more honorable and wise than Heaven? Heaven is really the most honorable and wise."[37] "If some conduct is observed to be in accordance with the will of Heaven, it is called good conduct; if it is in opposition to the will of Heaven it is called bad conduct . . . Obedience to the will of Heaven is the standard of righteousness."[38] "Whatever good was possessed by the son of Heaven, he humbly ascribed the merit of it to Heaven."[39] "Righteousness surely comes from Heaven."[40] "Alas! there is no one that knows me . . . But there is Heaven—that knows me!"[41] "How do we know that Heaven desires to have men love and benefit one another and abominates to have them hate and harm one another? Because it loves and benefits men universally."[42] "He who obeys the will of Heaven, loving universally and benefiting others, will obtain rewards. He who opposes the will of Heaven, by being partial and unfriendly and harming others, will incur punishment."[43] "He who offends against Heaven has none to whom he can pray."[44] According to these passages, Heaven has a will. It knows us. All things originate from it. It is all-righteous, all-wise, all-loving, and supreme. Those who do not obey it will be punished. In short, the ancient Chinese knew God, but their knowledge of Him was still very limited. They knew of (*zhidao*) Him, but they did not know (*renshi*) Him.

Therefore, we do not study pagan writings in order to learn new information about the nature of God Himself. Jesus sends us out into the pagan world not in order to learn about God from them but in order to *teach* them about God. There is no knowledge about God in pagan writings that is not already stated more clearly and fully in Scripture. But this does not mean that pagan theology is entirely useless to us. In another sermon, Paul describes God's revelation to our pagan ancestors as a "witness" (Acts 14:17). It is not just a witness to them but also to us. For every time we see God in ancient culture, it is a reminder of His faithfulness. "It is indeed a wonderful fact to think of," says Legge, "that a worship of the one God has been maintained in the vicinity of their capitals by the sovereigns of China almost continuously for more than four thousand years."[45] When Legge finally had the chance to visit the Temple of Heaven in Beijing, he took off his shoes next to the altar and sang the Doxology with his colleagues.

The theological musings of our ancestors also help us better appreciate the coming of Christ into the world. In his autobiography *Surprised by Joy*, C. S. Lewis describes how most of his Christian teachers failed to recognize this point when teaching pagan literature:

> Here, especially in Virgil, one was presented with a mass of religious ideas; and all teachers and editors took it for granted from the outset that these religious ideas were sheer illusion. No one ever attempted to show in what sense Christianity fulfilled Paganism or Paganism prefigured Christianity. The accepted position seemed to be that religions were normally a mere farrago of nonsense, though our own, by a fortunate exception, was exactly true.[46]

Pagan literature foreshadows the coming of Christ. For even though our ancestors were pagan, they were nevertheless created in the image of God. Their theology, though wrong, was not completely wrong. They knew certain truths about the God Whose image they bore. In many respects, their ideas about Him were not so much anti-Christian as they were *pre*-Christian. "The question was no longer to find the one simply true religion among a thousand religions simply false. It was rather, 'Where has religion reached its true maturity? Where, if anywhere, have the hints of all Paganism been fulfilled?'"[47] When we study the writings of our pagan ancestors, the gospel shines even brighter. For we see Christ's death and resurrection not as the beginning of a foreign tale but as the climax of a story that our ancestors have been telling for generations.

Even so, we must never underestimate the dangers of paganism. Our pagan fathers recognized their duty to worship God, but for the most part their worship of Him was overshadowed by their worship of idols. Paul found one altar in Athens dedicated to the worship of God, but he found hundreds more not dedicated to Him. As we seek to discover Christ in the writings of our fathers, we must diligently avoid the error of syncretism—of conflating paganism with Christianity. Our ancestors were not Christians. They were not born again. We may admire them. We may learn from them. But we may not baptize them. Legge presents us with a final admonition:

> Christianity cannot be tacked on to any heathen religion as its complement, nor can it absorb any into itself without great changes in it and additions to it. Missionaries have not merely to reform, though it will be well for them to reform where and what they can; they have to revolutionize; and as no revolution of a political kind can be effected without disturbance of existing conditions, so neither can a revolution of a people's religion be brought about without heat and excitement ... Though missionaries try to acknowl-

edge what is good in [Confucianism], and to use it as not abusing it, they cannot avoid sometimes seeming to pull down Confucius from his elevation. They cannot set forth the gospel as the wisdom of God and the power of God unto salvation, and exhort to the supreme love of God and of Christ, without deploring the want of any deep sense of sin, and of any glow of piety in the followers of the Chinese sage. Let them seek to go about their work everywhere . . . without striving or crying, with meekness and lowliness of heart. Let no one think any labour too great to make himself familiar with the Confucian books. So shall missionaries in China come fully to understand the work they have to do; and the more they avoid driving their carriages rudely over the Master's grave, the more likely are they soon to see Jesus enthroned in his room in the hearts of the people.[48]

Politics

The final challenge to classical Christian education that I want to discuss here is politics. The Communist Party is aggressively anti-Christian, and therefore any church that attempts to start a Christian school outside of the Party's jurisdiction is almost sure to meet with legal opposition, not to mention economic and social pressure. Private Neo-Confucian academies during the Ming Dynasty faced similar persecution for promoting free thought, criticizing government policies, and competing with government schools. But it is not my purpose here to discuss these issues. Instead, I want to discuss another aspect of politics that exerts a much subtler influence on Christian schools but which is nevertheless significant.

One reason classical education appeals to so many Christians in America is because it is so different from the kind of education offered in American public schools. Many Americans feel as though they have lost their cultural heritage. Although American public schools still teach portions of the Western classics, the education system for the most part has strayed from its classical roots. This is only a reflection of a greater cultural trend. American culture is a progressive culture that generally disdains old and "outdated" ideas in favor of new and innovative ones. It is a purveyor of what C. S. Lewis calls "chronological snobbery"—the idea that the thinking, art, or science of an earlier time is inherently inferior to that of the present. Classical education stands in stark contrast to this cultural drift. Even though it is built on ancient ideas, it comes across to many Christians as something fresh and counter-cultural.

But the story is very different in China. After attempting to systematically destroy traditional culture during the Cultural Revolution, the Communist Party has now ironically initiated a massive campaign in the twenty-first century to recover it. This campaign is evident in all aspects of modern political and social life. In the realm of religion, we see it in calls for the "sinicization of Christianity." In the realm of education, we see it in the promotion of Chinese classical studies (*guoxue* 国学) or in the rapid growth of the Confucius Institute worldwide. For this reason, classical Christian education does not have the same allure for Chinese Christians as it does for Christians in the West. A form of Christian education based on the Chinese classical tradition sounds too much like something the Chinese government would promote. It sounds like Christian education "with Chinese characteristics," another favorite slogan of the Communist Party. This is one reason why those who promote classical Christian education typically advocate for a form of it based on the Western classical tradition. Latin, Plato, and the Trivium sound novel and exciting. The fact that they are closely tied to the historic Christian church only adds to their intrigue. But classical Chinese, Confucius, and the six arts sound too much like the curriculum of a *guoxue* school.

I understand this concern, and to some degree there is no easy way to avoid this confusion. Chinese Christian schools who promote classical Christian education will probably be accused by some Christians of "sinicizing Christianity" or of propagating nationalistic ideology. The only way to quell these concerns is to carefully explain the differences between what the Communist Party is trying to do and what the church is trying to do, which will take much time and patience. I will not go into all of these differences here. I trust the reader has already recognized a number of them, but I will still point out a few.

The Communist Party's promotion of traditional Chinese culture is driven solely by political motives. A government that just a few decades ago attempted to systematically destroy its cultural heritage has no real respect for it. The only reason it has changed its position is because it is politically expedient. The Communist Party recognizes that if it paints itself as the rightful heir and guardian of this five-thousand-year heritage, and, more importantly, if the Chinese people are *proud* of this heritage, then the people will be more loyal to the Party. Moreover, this rich heritage shows the world that Chinese civilization is vibrant, powerful, and autonomous. It proves that China does not need the help of Western powers to flourish. Essentially, it is a way for the Party to flex its muscles on the world stage.

The kind of classical education promoted by the Communist Party is not rooted in the Fifth Commandment. The government is not promoting classical learning because it has a deep respect for its ancestors, much less God. It does not promote the study of the ancients because it wants to learn from them. Jesus aptly rebuked the Pharisees, "Woe to you, scribes and Pharisees, hypocrites! For you build the tombs of the prophets and decorate the monuments of the righteous, saying, 'If we had lived in the days of our fathers, we would not have taken part with them in shedding the blood of the prophets" (Matt. 23:29–30). The Communist Party destroys a Confucian temple and then a few years later rebuilds it and christens it an "important cultural heritage site under national preservation." It builds monuments to Confucius, but if Confucius came back from the dead under a different name it would arrest him and charge him with "inciting social disorder" and "carrying out counter-revolutionary propaganda."

Classical Christian education is miles apart from the *guoxue* promoted by the Communist Party. The most glaring difference is that it is rooted in Christ. Classical Christian education affirms the lordship of Christ over all things, while *guoxue* affirms the lordship of the Communist Party over all things. Classical Christian education is concerned with raising up men and women who are loyal to Jesus. *Guoxue* is concerned with raising up men and women who are loyal to the Communist Party. Classical Christian education seeks the wisdom of God in the teachings of the ancients. *Guoxue* only seeks to prove that China is superior to all other nations.

Classical Christian education is not an affirmation of the government's project to recover Chinese classical learning. It is a rebuke. Augustine describes classical Christian education as taking back wisdom "from those who have unlawful possession of it."[49] The Chinese government has unlawful possession of the Chinese classical tradition, and it is the job of the Chinese church to take it back. Like so many emperors before it, the government has tried to make itself the sole arbiter and interpreter of the classics. It twists the teachings of the ancients to accomplish its own agenda. The wisdom of the ancients was a gift of God. The Chinese classical tradition does not belong to the Communist Party. It belongs to Christ. As Chinese Christians diligently study and teach the works of their fathers under the blessing of God, they participate in the work that Jesus began two thousand years ago to "reconcile to himself all things" (Col. 1:20).

In the Book of Isaiah, God describes the conversion of the Gentiles. "The coastlands shall hope for me, the ships of Tarshish first, to bring your children from afar, their silver and gold with them" (Is. 60:9). The Gentiles will not come to Zion empty-handed. They will bring "their silver and gold with them." God does not only want Chinese *people* in His kingdom. He wants their riches. God has blessed China with many cultural riches, and the church should be eager to mine these riches to the glory of God. This is not a matter of nationalism. Nationalism promotes culture-building simply for the sake of one's own country, not for the sake of God's Kingdom. It is not a coincidence that the Party's term for classical education is *guoxue*—literally, "national studies." What I am promoting, and what I think the Bible promotes, is not a self-centered pursuit of national glory but a selfless, God-centered pursuit of excellence. C. S. Lewis describes this well in *The Screwtape Letters*:

> [God] wants to bring the man to a state of mind in which he could design the best cathedral in the world, and know it to be the best, and rejoice in the fact, without being any more (or less) or otherwise glad at having done it than he would be if it had been done by another. [God] wants him, in the end, to be so free from any bias in his own favour that he can rejoice in his own talents as frankly and gratefully as in his neighbour's talents—or in a sunrise, an elephant, or a waterfall. He wants each man, in the long run, to be able to recognise all creatures (even himself) as glorious and excellent things. He wants to kill their animal self-love as soon as possible; but it is His long-term policy . . . to restore to them a new kind of self-love—a charity and gratitude for all selves, including their own; when they have really learned to love their neighbours as themselves, they will be allowed to love themselves as their neighbours.[50]

My hope is that the Chinese church can bring their cultural riches into the Kingdom of God and rejoice in them honestly and selflessly, just as they rejoice in the riches of Western civilization. But the majority of these riches have yet to be mined or made. The church in China is still young. The rain of the gospel has fallen on the leaves and branches of Chinese civilization, but it has yet to sink to the roots. Only God knows what glories await when it does.

CHAPTER 11

Conclusion

I alluded earlier to a college professor who tried to show the superiority of Western culture over Chinese culture by comparing China and England during the nineteenth century. It is easy for Chinese Christians to see the stark differences between the two and become enchanted with Western culture and disenchanted with their own. The professor was trying to encourage Chinese students to study Western literature over Chinese literature, but he could have just as easily been promoting Western classical education over Chinese classical education.

I agree with the professor that England was in many ways superior to China in the nineteenth century, but what made the English so great? Was it the fact that they were Western? No. It was the fact that they were *Christian*. The professor actually acknowledged this point, but the conclusion he wanted the students to draw was not that Christianity is better than paganism but that Western culture is better than Chinese culture. We can easily make the same mistake. We can compare a garden full of vibrant roses in England to a garden full of withering peonies in China and then conclude that roses must be better than peonies. The problem with China during the Qing dynasty was not that it was full of peonies instead of roses but that the peonies were dead. When we look at these two gardens, the question we should ask is not whether roses are better than peonies but whether watered flowers are better than un-watered ones. When Chinese Christians see the effects of Christianity on Western civilization compared to the effects of paganism on Chinese civilization, they should not conclude that China should be more Western but rather that China should be more Christian. What Qing China needed was not roses. It needed *life*.

The Chinese church can learn much from the West, but it will learn little if it only studies the differences between the Christian West and pagan China. A much better lesson can be drawn from comparing the Christian West and the pagan West. At one point, the flowers in the West were even more withered than the peonies in China. The Western classical tradition was riddled with idolatry and superstition. Some church fathers like Tertullian even wanted to reject it completely. It was only after centuries of carefully cultivating this garden that Christians brought it back to life. If Chinese Christians study how the church fathers did this, then they will be inspired to bring their own garden back to life. But if all they ever see are healthy roses, they will be tempted to simply dig up their peonies and plant roses instead. If they do this, not only will they lose the opportunity to see a peony in full glory—the roses they plant will wither, too.

The Kingdom of God is a vast garden with many kinds of flowers. "After this I looked, and behold, a great multitude that no one could number, from every nation, from all tribes and peoples and languages, standing before the throne and before the Lamb (Rev. 7:9)." Just as Christ bestows diverse gifts on each member of His Body, so He bestows diverse glories on each culture in His Kingdom. In England, He plants roses. In China, He plants peonies. In Greece, He plants poppies. In France, He plants irises. Just as "star differs from star in glory" (1 Cor. 15:41), so culture differs from culture in glory. All cultures are not "equal." Poppies are brighter than peonies, irises are taller than roses. But we would be foolish to embark on a mission to determine which flower is the "best." Is Latin better than Chinese? Some might say Latin is better because it is an inflected language. But we could just as easily say that Chinese is better because it is *not* inflected. We must ask, "Better at *what?*" If we want a tall flower, then an iris is better than a rose. If we want a flower with many petals, then a rose is better than an iris. Latin is better in some respects, and Chinese is better in others. But Christ is praised in both.

As Christians in the West and in the East attempt to recover our cultural heritages, we must not let cultural differences overshadow our unity in Christ. God has planted many different flowers in His garden, but the same sun shines on all of them. No Christian school, Chinese or American, can thrive unless it basks in that light. Moreover, we should often take our students strolling through God's vast garden. Chinese students should have the opportunity to admire an iris and to smell a rose. But these are not the flowers God has put under their care. The six arts schema I propose above incorporates aspects of the Western classical tradition, such as the Trivium, Western languages, and Western science. Nevertheless, Chinese Christians should take special care to tend the flowers which God has planted in their native soil.

In the end, classical Christian education exists to answer the question *Who am I?* In some sense, asking why Chinese Christian schools should emphasize the Chinese classical tradition over the Western classical tradition is like asking why a peony cannot look like a rose. This is who they *are*. This is their heritage. These are their parents. This is their *glory*. "The glory of children is their fathers" (Prv. 17:6). The Book of Revelation tells us that when the nations enter the New Jerusalem, "the kings of the earth will bring their glory into it . . . the glory and honor of the nations" (Rev. 21:24–26). God wants China to bring its glory into the New Jerusalem. In this book, I have commended the six arts tradition because I believe this tradition is one aspect of China's glory, but at present the six arts are not fully developed. In many ways, they are in the same condition as the seven arts when the church in the West first inherited them. But if the Chinese church takes up the responsibility of redeeming them, of cultivating them under the blessing of God, they are sure to flourish. The six arts sprouted under the care of pagans, but they will blossom in the hands of Christians.

Glossary

Boshi (博士)—erudite, broadly-learned official-scholar; the highest scholarly office in government, the holder of which was entrusted with providing council to the emperor and especially with teaching the Five Classics at the Imperial University. In modern Chinese, *boshi* means a doctor of philosophy (PhD).

Boxue (博学)—broad learning; an important Confucian ideal that emphasizes studying a broad range of knowledge as opposed to a specialist approach, which emphasizes studying a narrow range of knowledge deeply.

Calculation (*shu* 数)—the art of quantifying and measuring the natural world. Includes subjects such as mathematics, surveying, geography, and astronomy. One of the six arts.

Dao (道)—Way, Truth; a fundamental concept in Chinese philosophy with a broad range of meanings. Most commonly, the *Dao* refers to the basic order or principle underlying and animating the entire cosmos. Wisdom entails seeking to understand and submit to the *Dao*.

Eight-legged essay (*baguwen* 八股文)—a complex essay introduced to the imperial examinations during the

Ming dynasty. The essay was an evolution of the previous "[exposition on] the meaning of the classics" essay introduced during the Song dynasty and required candidates to expound on a Confucian concept by citing multiple quotes from the Classics and weaving them together in eight different "legs," each of which contained different requirements regarding length, format, style, rhyme, symmetry, tone, and so forth. Originally heralded as a brilliant display of scholarship and literary prowess, the essay was later blamed for the decline in education during the Ming and Qing dynasties due to its impractical and overly-complex nature.

Five Classics (*wujing* 五经)—the five foundational texts of Confucianism and Chinese classical education. In their earliest form, they included the *Book of Poetry* (*shijing* 诗经), the *Book of Documents* (*shangshu* 尚书), the *Book of Changes* (*zhouyi* 周易), the *Book of Rites* (*yili* 仪礼), and the *Spring and Autumn Annals* (*chunqiu* 春秋). The *Record of Rites* (*liji* 礼记) later replaced the *Book of Rites* as the primary rites text, although these two along with the *Rites of Zhou* (*zhouli* 周礼) were often studied together as the "Three Rites" (*sanli* 三礼) and were all considered to be included in the Five Classics. Records suggest that the Five Classics were originally the Six Classics, which included the now-lost *Book of Music* (*yuejing* 乐经). After Confucius's time, the "six arts" (*liuyi* 六艺) sometimes referred to the Six Classics or Five Classics.

Four Books (*sishu* 四书)—four foundational Confucian texts promoted by Zhu Xi during the Song Dynasty for being easier to understand than the Five Classics.

The Four Books surpassed the Five Classics in importance and influence and became the primary subject matter of the civil service exam during the Ming and Qing dynasties. The Four Books are the *Analects* (*lunyu* 论语), the *Mencius* (*mengzi* 孟子), the *Doctrine of the Mean* (*zhongyong* 中庸), and the *Great Learning* (*daxue* 大学). The latter two are chapters out of the *Record of Rites* (*liji* 礼记), one of the Five Classics.

Gewu (格物)—the investigation of things; an important Confucian concept promoted in the *Great Learning* which stresses that one obtains knowledge by observing and contemplating the natural world. The Neo-Confucian Zhu Xi stressed that *gewu* specifically entails fathoming an object's *li* (理).

Heaven (*tian* 天)—the supreme, all-righteous deity that governs all things and from which proceeds all virtue. Heaven is equated with the other traditional name of God, Supreme Emperor (*shangdi* 上帝).

Heavenly nature (*tianxing* 天性)—human nature; the nature given man by Heaven at birth. Many ancient Chinese educators describe education as a process of restoring or cultivating or understanding one's heavenly nature.

Imperial examination (*keju* 科举)—a civil-service examination used by the government to select candidates for bureaucracy. The imperial examination consisted of a written essay that tested candidates in knowledge of the Five Classics and literary prowess. The exam had precursors in the Han dynasty but did not come to prominence until the Tang dynasty. The imperial exam greatly influenced the nature of education in government schools, which sought to prepare students for the exam. Critics routinely blamed the exam for corrupting Chinese education.

Imperial University (*taixue* 太学, *guozijian* 国子监) —the highest institution of learning in ancient China, founded in the Han dynasty and abolished in the Qing dynasty.

Jixia Academy (稷下)—a famous academy established by the state of Qi around 360 BC but which had a strong private character. The academy hosted some of the most famous scholars in Chinese history, including Mencius and Xunzi, and produced some of the most famous texts, including the *Record of Rites*.

Junzi (君子)—superior man, gentleman, exemplary person; originally referred to the ideal aristocrat but was later co-opted by Confucius to refer to the ideal man. According to Confucianism, the purpose of education is to transform oneself into a *junzi*. The only level higher than a *junzi* is a sage (*shengren* 圣人), which few can attain.

Li (理)—principle, pattern, coherence; understood by Neo-Confucians as a rational principle inherent in all things and uniting all things. In order to fully understand a thing, one must grasp its *li* (*qiongli* 穷理) through careful observation and meditation.

Li (礼)—rite, ritual, rules of propriety, etiquette; a formal pattern of human conduct used to establish order in society and viewed as a kind of participation in the cosmic order. In earliest times, *li* were religious ceremonies; later, they came to include all forms of social etiquette. One of the six arts.

Liangzhi (良知)—innate knowing; a Neo-Confucian concept promoted by Wang Yangming during the Ming dynasty which stressed that one obtains knowledge not by examining the outside world but by examining one's own mind-heart (*xin* 心), which possesses innate knowledge about the world and especially about morality. Wang's philosophy of *liangzhi* arose as a reaction against Zhu Xi, who emphasized that one obtains knowledge through the "investigation of things" (*gewu* 格物), that is by observing and contemplating the outside world. The concept of *liangzhi* sparked a rise in populist education, but was also blamed for promoting anti-intellectualism.

Lower school (*xiaoxue* 小学)—traditional lower-level school where Chinese children studied before progressing on to the upper school. Children generally entered the lower school between 6–8 years old and studied there until they reached 15 years old.

Ren (仁)—humaneness, benevolence, love; the all-encompassing ethical ideal that includes all desirable qualities in a man, especially qualities such as kindness, trustworthiness, and respectfulness. The highest ethical ideal in Confucianism.

Ru (儒)—scholar; originally lower-class *shi*, *ru* were private teachers and scholars who provided instruction to interested disciples. The most famous *ru* was Confucius, from whom we get the term "Confucianism." But "Confucianism" in Chinese is literally the "school of *ru*" (*rujia* 儒家). Because this tradition predates Confucius and contains thinkers whose ideas sometimes differ with those of Confucius, most modern scholars prefer the term "Ruism" to "Confucianism."

Script (*shu* 书)—the art of reading and writing. One of the six arts, *shu* literally refers to the six types of written Chinese characters. The art of script, therefore, entailed studying the "six scripts" (*liushu* 六书).

Shengren (圣人)—sage; one who embodies wisdom and virtue to the highest degree, superior even to a *junzi* and unattainable to most men.

Shi (士)—scholar-official; member of the military class, the lowest level of the aristocracy. In earliest times, six arts education only extended down from the emperor to the *shi* class.

Shuyuan (书院)—academy; first established during the Tang dynasty as an alternative to government schools, the *shuyuan* was a popular type of private school that preserved and promoted learning, often at a level far exceeding government schools. These academies were frequently persecuted for spreading anti-government propaganda and were finally abolished during the Qing dynasty.

Taiji (太极)—the ultimate principle uniting all things and giving existence to all things, the sum of all *li* (理).

Temple school (*miaoxue* 庙学)—a term used beginning in the Yuan dynasty to refer to Confucian schools, which typically contained Confucian temples. This ritualization of schools was largely influenced by the rise of Buddhism.

Upper school (*dauxe* 大学)—the traditional upper-level school where Chinese children studied after completing lower school and before beginning college. Children generally entered the upper school at 15 years old and studied there until their early 20s.

Wen (文)—literature, culture, pattern; a broad term most often referring to literature or literary arts but also including other cultural refinements like rites and music. At its most basic level, *wen* is a unique pattern that distinguishes one thing from another. Thus, there is a *wen* of the heavens, a *wen* of earth, and a *wen* of man. The *wen* of man (*renwen*) is found primarily in man's unique language abilities, which he uses to elucidate the *Dao*.

Yi (义)—righteousness, justice; an important aspect of *ren*.

Notes

Foreword

1   Augustine, *De Doctrina Christiana (On Christian Teaching)* 2.40.

Introduction

1   Tertullian, *Prescriptions Against Heretics*, 7.

2   "One goes to the Philistines to sharpen one's plow, because secular learning is needed as a training for Christian preaching." The quote is found in Gregory's commentary on 1 Kings in *Patrologia Latina* vol. 79 col.356, compiled by Jacques Paul Migne. English translation by Henry Osborn Taylor, *Medieval Series*, vol. 1, *The Medieval Mind* (Revelation Insight Publishing Co., 2016), 429.

3   "But they gave their gold and silver and their garments to the people of God as they were going out of Egypt, not knowing how the things they gave would be turned to the service of Christ. For what was done at the time of the exodus was no doubt a type prefiguring what happens now." Augustine, *De Doctrina Christiana (On Christian Teaching)*, 2.40.

4   C. S. Lewis, "Christianity and Culture" in *Christian Reflections*, ed. Walter Hooper, (Grand Rapids, MI: William B. Eerdmans Publishing Company, 1995), 24.

5   For examples of Paul's interest in and use of Greek philosophy, see Acts 17:28, 1 Cor. 13:12, 1 Cor 15:33, Titus 1:12, Acts 17:23–25, 1 Cor. 9:16, Acts 14:15, Eph. 1:22–23, 1 Cor. 12:14–17. See also Acts 7:22, Dan. 1:17.

6   "What is Classical Education?" The CiRCE Institute, accessed May 2, 2017, https://www.circeinstitute.org/resources/what-classical-education.

7   "Understanding the Classical and Christian Difference: A Parent's Primer," The Ambrose School, accessed May 2, 2017, http://theambroseschool.org/about/the-classical-approach/.

8   "What is Classical Education?" Classical Academic Press, accessed May 2, 2017, https://classicalacademicpress.com/what-is-classical-education/.

9   "Classical Education Movement," *Wikipedia*, last modified February 28, 2017, accessed May 2, 2017, https://en.wikipedia.org/wiki/Classical_education_movement.

10   Rev. 7:9

11   Matt. 15:4–7

Notes

Part One

Chapter 1: Shang Dynasty to Eastern Zhou Dynasty

1 Some records suggest six.

2 There has never existed anything equivalent to a "middle/high school" (*zhongxue* 中学) in China until modern times. For this reason, it is important not to equivocate the ancient *xiaoxue* and *daxue* with the modern *xiaoxue* (elementary school) and *daxue* (college). Students left ancient *xiaoxue* at a later age than modern *xiaoxue* and began *daxue* at an earlier age than modern *daxue*.

3 Sun Peiqing 孙培青, *Zhongguo jiaoyushi* 中国教育史 [A History of Chinese Education], 3rd ed. (Shanghai: Huadong shifan daxue chubanshe 华东师范大学出版社, 2008), 16; Thomas H. C. Lee, *Education in Traditional China: A History* (Boston: Brill, 2000), 172.

4 "保氏, 掌谏王恶。而养国子以道, 乃教之六艺: 一曰五礼, 二曰六乐, 三曰五射, 四曰五驭, 五曰六书, 六曰九数。" *Zhouli* 周礼 [Rites of Zhou] 14.113.352, author's translation. For classical Chinese texts cited in this book, I have used the following method: When three numbers are cited, the first refers to the *juan* (scroll) of the original text; the second refers to the chapter/verse/passage number as found in Donald Sturgeon, ed., Chinese Text Project, 2017, http://ctext.org; and the third refers to the page number of the published version of the Chinese text I'm quoting from (found in the bibliography). So 14.113.352 means *juan* 14 of the *Zhouli*, passage 113 in the *Zhouli* manuscript found on ctext.org, and page 352 of the *Zhouli zhushu* [Rites of Zhou annotated] in *Shisanjing zhushu* 十三经注疏

275

[The Thirteen Classics annotated], ed. Li Xueqin 李学勤 (Beijing: Beijing daxue chubanshe 北京大学出版社, 1999). If only two numbers are cited, then the ctext.org reference has been omitted.

5   This is overlooked by most scholars, who claim that six arts education was exclusively for children of aristocrats. For an excellent explanation of this topic, see Wu Longhui 吴龙辉, "Liuyi de bianqian ji qi yu liujing zhi guanxi" 六艺的变迁及其与六经之关系 [The evolution of the six arts and its relationship to the Six Classics], Zhongguo Zhexueshi 中国哲学史 2 (2005): 42–43.

6   Zhu Yongxin, *Works by Zhu Yongxin on Education: History of Chinese Ancient Educational Thought* (McGraw-Hill, 2015), 18.

7   Chung-ying Cheng, "*Dao (Tao)*: The Way," in *Encyclopedia of Chinese Philosophy*, ed. Antonio S. Cua (New York: Routledge, 2003), 203.

8   Most of my information on archery in this book comes from Stephen Selby, *Chinese Archery* (Hong Kong: Hong Kong University Press, 2000).

9   "故古者教士以射御为急……人之生有疾则已，苟无疾，未有去射而不学者也。在庠序之间，固当从事于射也。有宾客之事则以射，有祭祀之事则以射，别士之行同能偶则以射，于礼乐之事，未尝不寓以射，而射亦未尝不在于礼乐祭祀之间也……居则以是习礼乐，出则以是从战伐。士既朝夕从事于此，而能者众。" Wang Anshi 王安石, *Shangrenzonghuangdiyanshishu*上仁宗皇帝言事书临川先生文集 [A letter to Emperor Renzong] 39.7.415, trans. Selby, 52–53.

Note that Selby mistakenly attributes this quote to Zhou Kong-jiao 周孔教 of the Ming dynasty.

10   For a summary of the most common views, see Zhang Qiwei 张奇伟, "Li de qiyuan zhi lishi sikao" 礼的起源之历史思考 [A historical reflection on the origins of *li*], *Shanxi shifan daxue jixu jiaoyu xuebao* 陕西师范大学继续教育学报 18, no. 3 (2001): 32–34.

11   In ancient Chinese thought, the supernatural realm consisted of a hierarchical pantheon of higher powers, with the "High God" (上帝) at the top, lower nature deities below him, and ancestors below them. For an explanation of this pantheon see David N. Keightley, "The High God (*Di*) and Other Powers," in *Sources of Chinese Tradition*, 2nd ed., vol. 1, *From Earliest Times to 1600*, ed. William Theodore de Bary and Irene Bloom (New York: Columbia University Press, 1999).

12   "夫唯禽兽无礼, 故父子聚麀。是故圣人作为礼以教人, 使人以有礼, 知自别于禽兽。" *Quli shang* 曲礼上 [Summary of the Rules of Propriety Part 1] in *Liji* 礼记 [Record of Rites] 1.9.15, trans. James Legge.

13   "Filial piety is (or was) the beginning of *li*." (孝, 礼之始也) *Zuozhuan* 左传 [Zuo Tradition] 8.2.345, author's translation.

14   "礼, 履也, 所以事神致福也。" Xu Shen 许慎, *Shuowen Jiezi* 说文解字 2.2.2, author's translation.

15   Yang Xiangdong 杨向东, "Liuyi zhong de yue, she, yu yu tiyu, meiyu" 六艺中的乐、射、御与体育、美育 [Music,

archery, and charioteering—physical and aesthetic education in the six arts], *Nankai xuebao: Zhexue shehui kexue ban* 南开学报：哲学社会科学版 6 (2002): 98.

16 "是故先王之制礼乐也，非以极口腹耳目之欲也，将以教民平好恶而反人道之正也。" *Yueji* 乐记 [Record of Music] in *Liji* 礼记 [Record of Rites] 37.6.1081, trans. James Legge.

17 "乐者，天地之和也；礼者，天地之序也。和故百物皆化；序故群物皆别。" *Yueji* 乐记 [Record of Music] in *Liji* 礼记 [Record of Rites] 37.14.1090, trans. James Legge. I have changed Legge's translation of *li* from "ceremonies" to "rites." This is generally the case throughout this book.

18 "使亲疏贵贱、长幼男女之理，皆形见于乐" *Yueji* 乐记 [Record of Music] in *Liji* 礼记 [Record of Rites] 38.28.1106, trans. James Legge.

19 "是故清明象天，广大象地，终始象四时，周还象风雨。五色成文而不乱，八风从律而不奸，百度得数而有常。小大相成，终始相生。倡和清浊，迭相为经。故乐行而伦清，耳目聪明，血气和平，移风易俗，天下皆宁。" *Yueji* 乐记 [Record of Music] in *Liji* 礼记 [Record of Rites] 38.31.1110, trans. James Legge.

20 Hoo Peih Seang 胡必相, *The Ceremonial Usages of the Chinese, B.C. 1121, as Prescribed in the "Institutes of the Chow Dynasty Strung as Pearls"* . . . , ed. and trans. William Raymond Gingell (London: Smith, Elder, & Co., 1852), 71.

21　Niu Mengqi 牛梦琪, "'Liu yi' jiaoyu de qiyuan yu fazhan" "六艺" 教育的起源与发展 [The origin and development of six arts education], *Dangdai jiaoyu luntan: xueke jiaoyu yanjiu* 当代教育论坛：学科教育研究 1 (2006): 44.

22　*Neize* 内则 [Pattern of the Family] in *Liji* 礼记 [Record of Rites] 28.77.869

23　See my quotations from Zhu Xi（朱熹, 1130–1200）and Zhu Yuanzhang（朱元璋, 1328–1398）in endnotes 11 and 35 of Chapter 3.

24　"君子曰德" *Wenwang Shizi* 文王世子[King Wen as son and heir] in *Liji* 礼记 [Record of Rites] 20.11.636, trans. James Legge.

25　"士制百姓于刑之中，以教祗德。穆穆在上，明明在下，灼于四方，罔不惟德之勤。故乃明于刑之中，率乂于民棐彝。" *Shangshu* 尚书 [Book of Documents] 19.3.540–541.

26　"仪刑文王，万邦作孚" *Shijing: Wen Wang* 诗经·文王 [Book of Poetry: Wen Wang], 292, author's translation.

27　"成王之孚，下土之式" *Shijing: Xia Wu* 诗经·下武 [Book of Poetry: Xia Wu], 308, trans. James Legge.

28　"乐，所以修内也，礼，所以修外也。礼乐交错于中，发形于外，是故其成也怿，恭敬而温文。" *Wenwang Shizi* 文王世子[King Wen as son and heir] in *Liji* 礼记 [Record of Rites] 20.10.634–5, author's translation.

29　"帝曰: '夔! 命汝典乐, 教胄子, 直而温, 宽而栗, 刚而无虐, 简而无傲。'" *Shangshu* 尚书 [Book of Documents] 3.16.78–9, author's translation.

30　Yang Xiangdong 杨向东, 99.

31　Chenyang Li, "*Li* as Cultural Grammar: On the Relation between *Li* and *Ren* in Confucius' 'Analects,'" *Philosophy East and West* 57, no. 3 (2007): 318, accessed May 3, 2017, http://www.jstor.org/stable/20109408.

32　James Legge, trans., *The Li Ki* [Record of Rites], in *The Chinese Classics: with a Translation, Critical and Exegetical Notes, Prolegomena, and Copious Indexes, 5 vols.* (Hong Kong: Legge; London: Trubner, 1861–1872).

33　G. K. Chesterton, *The Everlasting Man* (Sublime Books, 2012), 100, Kindle.

34　Thomas H. C. Lee, *Education in Traditional China: A History*, 205.

35　Chenyang Li, "*Li* as Cultural Grammar: On the Relation between *Li* and *Ren* in Confucius' 'Analects.'"

36　"射者, 所以观盛德也。是故古者天子以射选诸侯、卿、大夫、士。" *Sheyi* 射义 [The meaning of archery] in *Liji* 礼记 [Record of Rites] 62.3.1642–3, trans. Stephen Selby, 72.

37　Thomas H. C. Lee, *Education in Traditional China: A History*, 17.

38 "述而不作，信而好古" Confucius, *Lunyu* 论语 [Analects] 7.1.84, trans. James Legge.

39 "温故而知新" Ibid., 7.11.19, author's translation.

40 "学而时习之，不亦说乎？" Confucius, *Lunyu* 论语 [Analects] 1.1.1, trans. Robert Eno.

41 "知之者不如好之者，好之者不如乐之者。" Ibid., 6.20.78, trans. Robert Eno. I have slightly edited Eno's translation, replacing "it" with "something."

42 Yong Huang, *Confucius: A Guide for the Perplexed* (New York: Bloomsbury Academic, 2013), 4–5.

43 It is occasionally asserted that this belief did not extend to women, but there is no evidence to suggest that Confucius opposed women's education. The historical record is silent on the point. See Thomas H. C. Lee, *Education in Traditional China: A History*, 181.

44 "有教无类" Confucius, *Lunyu* 论语 [Analects] 15.39.218, trans. James Legge.

45 "性相近也，习相远也。" Ibid., 17.2.233, trans. James Legge.

46 "古之学者为己，今之学者为人。" Ibid., 14.24.195, trans. D. C. Lau.

47 "大学之道，在明明德，在亲民，在止于至善。" *Daxue* 大学 [The Great Learning] in *Liji* 礼记 [Record of Rites] 1.1.1592, trans. Robert Eno. I have slightly edited Eno's trans-

lation from "limit of the good" to "highest good," following Legge's translation of "highest excellence." *Shan* (善) is usually translated as "good" when used as a stand-alone virtue.

48 "古之欲明明德于天下者，先治其国。欲治其国者，先齐其家；欲齐其家者，先修其身。欲修其身者，先正其心。欲正其心者，先诚其意。欲诚其意者，先致其知。致知在格物。物格而后知至，知至而后意诚，意诚而后心正，心正而后身修，身修而后家齐，家齐而后国治，国治而后天下平。" *Daxue* 大学 [The Great Learning] in *Liji* 礼记 [Record of Rites] 42.2.1592, trans. James Legge.

49 "自天子以至于庶人，壹是皆以修身为本，其本乱而末治者否矣。" Ibid.

50 Weiming Tu, "The Sung Confucian Idea of Education: A Background Understanding," in *Neo-Confucian Education: The Formative Stage*, ed. William Theodore de Bary and John W. Chaffee (Berkeley: University of California Press, 1989), 139–140. For a more in-depth treatment on the subject see James Legge, *The religions of China: Confucianism and Taoism described and compared with Christianity* (London: Hodder and Stoughton, 1880).

51 "文王既没，文不在兹乎？……天之未丧斯文也，匡人其如予何？" Confucius, *Lunyu* 论语 [Analects] 9.5.113, trans. D. C. Lau.

52 "予所否者，天厌之！天厌之！" Ibid., 6.28.82, trans. James Legge.

53 "子曰：'莫我知也夫！……知我者，其天乎！'" Ibid., 14.35.199, trans. James Legge.

54 "天命之谓性，率性之谓道，修道之谓教。" *Zhongyong* 中庸 [Doctrine of the Mean] in *Liji* 礼记 [Record of Rites] 52.1.1422, author's translation.

55 "故君子不可以不修身；思修身，不可以不事亲；思事亲，不可以不知人；思知人，不可以不知天。" Ibid., 52.20.1446, trans. James Legge.

56 "君子有三畏：畏天命，畏大人，畏圣人之言" Confucius, *Lunyu* 论语 [Analects] 16.8.228, trans. James Legge. I have changed Legge's translation of 畏 from "stand in awe" to "revere." The Chinese is also sometimes translated as "fear."

57 Kwong-loi Shun, "Ren（仁）and Li（禮）in the Analects," in *Confucius and the Analects: New Essays*, ed. Bryan W. Van Norden (New York: Oxford University Press, 2002), 53. Chenyang Li, *The Tao Encounters the West: Explorations in Comparative Philosophy* (Albany: State University of New York Press, 1999), 96–97.

58 Weiming Tu, *Confucian Thought: Selfhood as Creative Transformation* (Albany: State University of New York Press, 1985), 87.

59 D. C. Lau, trans., *The Analects* (London: Penguin Group, 1979), 15. This explanation is given in Lau's introduction.

60 "Zi Zhang asked Confucius about *ren*. Confucius said, 'To be able to practice five things everywhere under heaven constitutes perfect virtue.' He begged to ask what they were, and was told, 'Gravity, generosity of soul, sincerity, earnestness, and kindness.'" （子张问仁于孔子。孔子曰："能行五者于天下，为仁矣。"请问之。曰："恭、宽、信、敏、惠。"）Confucius, *Lunyu* 论语 [Analects] 17.6.235, trans. James Legge.

61　"The man of *ren* finds pleasure in mountains." (仁者乐山) Ibid. 6.23.79

62　"贤贤易色，事父母能竭其力，事君能致其身，与朋友交言而有信。虽曰未学，吾必谓之学矣。"　Ibid., 1.7.8, trans. James Legge.

63　"不学礼，无以立。" Ibid., 16.13.230, trans. Chen-yang Li.

64　"恭而无礼则劳，慎而无礼则葸，勇而无礼则乱，直而无礼则绞。君子笃于亲则民兴于仁，故旧不遗则民不偷。" Ibid., 8.2.101, trans. Chenyang Li.

65　"人而不仁，如礼何？" Ibid., 3.3.30, author's translation.

66　Mencius, *Mengzi* 孟子 [Mencius] 7B.17.204.

67　"弟子入则孝，出则弟，谨而信，泛爱众，而亲仁。行有馀力，则以学文。" Confucius, *Lunyu* 论语 [Analects] 1.6.7, trans. Robert Eno. I've slightly altered Eno's translation, substituting "cleave to *ren*" for "cleave to those who are *ren*." I'm in agreement with Legge here that Confucius is speaking about cleaving to a specific virtue rather than a certain kind of person. I've also substituted "*wen*" for "the refinements of culture" so as not to confine the word to only one of many possible definitions.

68　Chen Xin 陈新, Shi Min 施敏, and Di Jinghua 翟敬华, "'Lunyu' lun 'wen'—'Lunyu' mantan zhi si" 《论语》论"文"——《论语》漫谈之四 [On wen in the Analects: part four of a discussion on the Analects], *Zhangjiakou zhiye jishu xueyuan xuebao* 张家口职业技术学院学报 26, no. 3 (2013): 48–50.

69   Confucius, *Lunyu* 论语 [Analects] 12.8.161.

70   "质胜文则野，文胜质则史。文质彬彬，然后君子。" Ibid., 6.18.78, translation James Legge.

71   Pang Yuyan 庞玉艳, "Lunyu 'wenmo' ju 'wen' yi zai kao" 《论语》"文莫"句"文"义再考 [A reflection on the meaning of *wen* in the *wenmo* sentence of the Analects], *Sichuan waiyu xueyuan xuebao: zhexue shehui kexue ban* 四川外语学院学报：哲学社会科学版 26, no. 3 (2010): 6–9.

72   Wu Longhui 吴龙辉, 3.

73   Zuo Qiuming 左丘明, *Guoyu* 国语 [Discourses of the States] 17.1.499. The books listed are the *Spring and Autumn Annals* (*Chunqiu* 春秋), *Shi* (世), the *Book of Poetry* (诗; i.e. 诗经), the *Book of Rites* (礼; i.e. 仪礼), the *Book of Music* (乐; i.e. 乐经), *Ling* (令), *Yu* (语), *Guzhi* (故志), and *Xundian* (训典).

74   Wu Longhui 吴龙辉, 3.

75   Endymion Wilkinson, *Chinese History: A New Manual*, 4th ed. (Harvard University Asia Center, 2015), 369.

76   Jiang Guobao 蒋国保, "Han ru cheng 'liujing' wei 'liuyi' kao" 汉儒称"六经"为"六艺"考 [A study on the Han Confucian designation of the "Six Classics" as the "six arts"], *Jiaoyu* 教育 12, no. 39 (2015): 34–40. I don't find Jiang's argument persuasive, as I don't think he accurately interprets the texts cited.

77 Wu Longhui 吴龙辉, 44.

78 Weiming Tu, "The Sung Confucian Idea of Education: A Background Understanding," 142.

79 "孔子曰："入其国，其教可知也。其为人也温柔敦厚，《诗》教也。疏通知远，《书》教也。广博易良，《乐》教也。洁静精微，《易》教也。恭俭庄敬，《礼》教也。属辞比事，《春秋》教也。" *Jingjie* 经解 [Exposition of the classics] in *Liji* 礼记 [Record of Rites] 50.26.1368, trans. James Legge. I have changed the names of the books from Legge's translation to conform to my own translation of them throughout this book.

80 "君子博学于文" Confucius, *Lunyu* 论语 [Analects] 6.27.81, author's translation.

81 Liu Zhiju 柳之榘, "Xizhou guanxue 'liuyi' zhi jiao de shuailuo he kongzi sixue de jiaoyu kecheng ji yingxiang" 西周官学"六艺"之教的衰落和孔子私学的教育课程及其影响 [The decline of six arts education in Western Zhou schools and the influence of Confucius's private curriculum], *Anwei shifan daxue xuebao: renwen shehui kexue ban* 安徽师范大学学报：人文社会科学版 1 (1985): 70.

82 "射不主皮" Confucius, *Lunyu* 论语 [Analects] 3.16.37, trans. Stephen Selby.

83 "故曰："为人父者以为父鹄，为人子者以为子鹄，为人君者以为君鹄，为人臣者以为臣鹄。"故射者，各射己之鹄。" *Sheyi* 射义 [The meaning of archery] in *Liji* 礼记 [Record of Rites] 62.8.1648, trans. Stephen Selby.

84 "子曰：'射有似乎君子，失诸正鹄，反求诸其身。'" *Zhongyong* 中庸 [Doctrine of the Mean] in *Liji* 礼记 [Record of Rites] 52.15.1433, trans. James Legge.

85 "志于道，据于德，依于仁，游于艺。" Confucius, *Lunyu* 论语 [Analects] 7.6.85, author's translation.

86 *Rujia* literally means the "school of *ru*," that is the "school of scholars." For this reason, Robert Eno has suggested replacing the term Confucianism with Ruism. Robert Eno, T*he Confucian Creation of Heaven: Philosophy and the Defense of Ritual Mastery* (Albany, NY: State University of New York Press, 1990), 7.

87 While most scholars take Mencius to mean that all men are essentially "good" in that their present moral natures are inherently upright, James Legge takes him to mean that being "good" is the proper end of man. To be human is to be "good." This does not mean that we are good presently but only that if we are "bad," it is because our natures are corrupt. We were not designed to be that way. James Legge, "Confucianism in Relation to Christianity" (paper presented at the Missionary Conference, Shanghai, May 11, 1877), accessed May 4, 2017, https://archive.org/details/confucianisminr01legggoog.

88 It should be noted that legalism was not the name of a particular school or movement during the period of the Hundred Schools of Thought but rather a term created by later Han thinkers who attempted to categorize various philosophies of the period into six major schools. Chris Fraser, "Major Rival Schools: Mohism and Legalism," in *The Oxford Handbook of World Philosophy*, ed. Jay L. Garfield and William Edelglass (New York: Oxford University Press, 2011), 59.

89   Yuri Pines, "Legalism in Chinese Philosophy," in *The Stanford Encyclopedia of Philosophy*, spring 2017 ed., ed. Edward N. Zalta, accessed May 4, 2017, https://plato.stanford.edu/archives/spr2017/entries/chinese-legalism/.

90   Chris Fraser, "Major Rival Schools: Mohism and Legalism," 59.

91   Mark Edward Lewis, "Scholars and the State," in T*he Cambridge History of Ancient China: From the Origins of Civilization to 221 B.C.*, ed. Michael Loewe and Edward L. Shaughnessy (Cambridge, U.K.: Cambridge University Press, 1999), 643.

92   Ibid.

93   Hu Meiqi 胡美琦, *Zhongguo jiaoyu shi* 中国教育史 [History of Chinese education] (Taiping: Sanmin shuju gufen youxian gongsi 三民书局股份有限公司, 1978), 139.

94   Thomas H. C. Lee, *Education in Traditional China: A History*, 44.

95   Ibid., 44–45.

96   Ibid., 44.

97   "大学之法，禁于未发之谓豫，当其可之谓时，不陵节而施之谓孙，相观而善之谓摩。此四者，教之所由兴也。发然后禁，则捍格而不胜；时过然后学，则勤苦而难成；杂施而不孙，则坏乱而不修；独学而无友，则孤陋而寡闻；燕朋逆其师；燕辟废其学。此六者，教之所由废也。" *Xue* 学记 [Record of Learning] in *Liji* 礼记 [Record of

Rites] 36.8.1061–2, trans. Xu Di, Yang Liuxin, Hunter McEwan, and Roger T. Ames.

98 "学者有四失，教者必知之。人之学也，或失则多，或失则寡，或失则易，或失则止。此四者，心之莫同也。知其心，然后能救其失也。" Ibid., 36.10.1064.

99 "记问之学，不足以为人师。必也听语乎，力不能问，然后语之；语之而不知，虽舍之可也。" Ibid., 36.14.1068.

100 "切问而近思，仁在其中矣。" Confucius, *Lunyu* 论语 [Analects] 19.6.256, trans. Robert Eno.

101 "子入大庙，每事问。或曰："孰谓鄹人之子知礼乎？入大庙，每事问。"子闻之曰："是礼也。" Ibid., 3.15.37, trans. James Legge.

102 Ibid.

103 "善问者，如攻坚木，先其易者，后其节目，及其久也，相说以解；不善问者反此。" *Xue* 学记 [Record of Learning] in *Liji* 礼记 [Record of Rites] 36.13.1067, trans. Xu Di, Yang Liuxin, Hunter McEwan, and Roger T. Ames.

104 "故君子之教喻也，道而弗牵，强而弗抑，开而弗达。" Ibid., 36.9.1063. I have slightly changed the original translation from "the role of exemplary persons as teachers" to "the role of a *junzi* as a teacher."

105 "博学之，审问之，谨思之，明辨之，笃行之。" *Zhongyong* 中庸 [Doctrine of the Mean] in *Liji* 礼记 [Record of Rites] 53.22.1447.

Chapter 2: Qin Dynasty to Tang Dynasty

1   For a summary of the reasons for this consensus, see Martin Kern, "Early Chinese Literature: Beginnings through Western Han," in *The Cambridge History of Chinese Literature*, vol. 1, ed. Stephen Owen (Cambridge: Cambridge University Press, 2010), 111–112.

2   Wang Bingzhao 王炳照, Guo Qijia 郭齐家, Liu Dehua 刘德花, He Xiaoxia 何晓夏, and Gao Qi 高奇, *Jianming zhongguo jiaoyu shi* 简明中国教育史 [Deciphering the history of Chinese education], rev. ed. (Beijing: Beijing shifan daxue. 北京师范大学出版社, 2001), 70.

3   "罢黜百家，独尊儒术"

4   Kirkland, Russell, "Tung Chung-shu," in *Great Thinkers of the Eastern World*, ed. Ian P. McGreal (New York: HarperCollins, 1995), 68.

5   Ibid., 68–70.

6   "于是后圣乃定五经，明六艺，承天统地，穷事察微……纂修篇章，垂诸来世……以节奢侈，正风俗，通文雅。" *Xinyu* 新语 [New Discourses] 1.14.2174, trans. D.W.Y. Kwok.

7   "表定六艺" Ibid., 10.1.2198.

8   Thomas H. C. Lee, *Education in Traditional China: A History*, 50.

9 Stephen Selby, *Chinese Archery*, 182.

10 The headmaster's title was later changed to *jijiu* (祭酒) or "libationer," reflecting the importance of rites. Sun Peiqing, 109.

11 Compare Thomas H. C. Lee, *Education in Traditional China: A History*, 42, and Sun Peiqing, 110.

12 An early Qing compilation by Juan Yuan (1764–1849) includes 243 biographies of famous astronomers and mathematicians. Of these, about 150 were from the early Han to the early Qing period. Only two of the 150 are known to have attended official schools of astronomy and mathematics. This suggests that the most accomplished mathematicians and astronomers were trained by their families or studied under technicians. Thomas H. C. Lee, *Education in Traditional China: A History*, 485–6.

13 Ibid., 49.

14 Ibid.

15 Thomas H. C. Lee, *Education in Traditional China: A History*, 51.

16 Lee, *Education in Traditional China*, 54.

17 "惟人参之，性灵所锺，是谓三才。为五行之秀，实天地之心，心生而言立，言立而文明，自然之道也。" Liu Xie 刘勰, *Wenxin diaolong* 文心雕龙 [The Literary Mind and the Carving of Dragons] 1.1.1.623, trans. Stephen Owen.

18 "鼓天下之动者存乎辞。" Liu is quoting here from the *Book of Changes*. Ibid., 1.1.5.624.

19 "人文之元，肇自太极" Ibid., 1.1.3.623.

20 "故知道沿圣以垂文，圣因文以明道" Ibid., 1.1.5.624.

21 Thomas H. C. Lee, *Education in Traditional China: A History*, 219.

22 Ibid., 220.

23 Ibid., 247.

24 Thomas H. C. Lee, "Sung Schools and Education Before Chu Hsi," in *Neo-confucian Education: The Formative Stage*, edited by William Theodore de Bary and John W. Chaffee (Berkeley and Los Angeles: University of California Press, 1989), 129.

25 Ibid.

26 "教授每日讲说经书三两纸，授诸生所诵经书文句音义，题所学书字样，出所课诗赋题目，撰所对属诗句，择所记故事。" Wang Chang 王昶, *Jinshi cuibian* 金石萃编 [A catalogue of finest bronze and stone ink imprints] (1805), accessed Jan. 22, 2018, http://www.guoxuedashi.com/guji/6864m/. 68.47–48, trans. Thomas H. C. Lee, *Education in Traditional China: A History*, 597.

27 "每日抽签，问所听经义三道，念书一二百字，学书十行，吟五七言古律诗一首，三日试赋一首（或四韵），看赋一道，看史传三五纸（内记故事三条）。"
Ibid., 68.48.

28 "每日念书约一百字，学书十行，吟诗一绝，对属一联，念赋二韵，记故事一件。" Ibid.

29 "每日念书五、七十字，学书十行，念诗一首。"
Ibid., 68.49.

30 "今首以乘除加减为法，称斗尺田为问，编诗括十三首，立图草六十六问" Quoted from Li Yan 李俨, *Shisan shisi shiji zhongguo minjian shuxue* 十三、十四世纪中国民间数学 [Popular Chinese mathematics in the thirteenth and fourteenth centuries] (Beijing: Beijing kexue chubanshe 科学出版社, 1957), 4, trans. Pei-yu Wu.

31 "今有钱六贯八百文，买物一斤，问一两直几何！答曰：四百二十五文" Quoted from Li Yan 李俨, *Zhong suanshi luncong* 中算史论丛 [Essays on the history of Chinese mathematics], vol. 2, in *Minguo congshu* 民国丛书 [The Republic of China Series], vol. 2, bk. 89 (Shanghai: Shanghai shudian 上海书店, 1997), 107, trans. Pei-yu Wu.

32 Ibid.

33 For a discussion of these military manuals as well as quoted portions, see Stephen Selby, *Chinese Archery*, 375–8.

Chapter 3: Song Dynasty to Qing Dynasty

1   Stephen Selby, *Chinese Archery*, 250.

2   Tzi-ki Hon, "Confucianism: Song (Sung)," in *Encyclopedia of Chinese Philosophy*, ed. Antonio S. Cua (New York: Routledge, 2003), 136.

3   "古之学者为己，今之学者为人。" Confucius, *Lunyu* 论语 [Analects] 14.24.195, trans. D. C. Lau.

4   William Theodore de Bary, "Chu Hsi's Aims as an Educator," in *Neo-confucian Education: The Formative Stage*, ed. William Theodore de Bary and John W. Chaffee (Berkeley and Los Angeles: University of California Press, 1989). Weiming Tu, "The Sung Confucian Idea of Education: A Background Understanding," in *Neo-confucian Education: The Formative Stage*, edited by William Theodore de Bary and John W. Chaffee (Berkeley and Los Angeles: University of California Press, 1989).

5   Peter Bol, *"This Culture of Ours": Intellectual Transitions in T'ang and Sung China* (Stanford, CA: Stanford University Press, 1992).

6   "It is said that the Way [*Dao*] has three aspects: substance [*ti*], function [*yong*], and literary expression [*wen*]. The bond between prince and minister and between father and son, humaneness, rightness, rites, and music—these are the things that do not change through the ages; they are its substance. The *Book of Poetry* and the *Book of Documents*, the dynastic histories, the writings of the philosophers—these perpetuate the right example down through the ages; they are its literary expression. To

activate this substance and put it into practice throughout the empire, enriching the life of the people and ordering all things to imperial perfection—this is its function." (臣闻圣人之道，有体、有用、有文。君臣父子，仁义礼乐，历世不可变者，其体也。《诗书》史传子集，垂法后世者，其文也。举而措之天下，能润泽斯民，归于皇极者，其用也。) Huang Zongxi 黄宗羲, *Songyuan xuean* 宋元学案 [Cases of Pedagogy in the Song and Yuan Dynasties] 1.82.25, trans. William Theodore de Bary. I've changed the names de Bary gives to the classics to conform to my translation of them in this book.

7 William Theodore de Bary, "Institutional, Educational, and Moral Reform in the Song," in *Sources of Chinese Tradition*, 2nd ed., vol. 1, *From Earliest Times to 1600*, ed. William Theodore de Bary and Irene Bloom (New York: Columbia University Press, 1999), 590.

8 William Theodore de Bary, "The Confucian Program of Reform," in *Sources of Chinese Tradition*, 2nd ed., vol. 1, *From Earliest Times to 1600*, ed. William Theodore de Bary and Irene Bloom (New York: Columbia University Press, 1999), 597.

9 See note on Zhu Xi in Appendix 2 of Edward Slingerland, trans., *The Essential Analects: Selected Passages with Traditional Commentary* (Hackett Publishing Company, 2006), 148.

10 "大学之书，古之大学所以教人之法也。盖自天降生民，则既莫不与之以仁义礼智之性矣。然其气质之禀或不能齐，是以不能皆有以知其性之所有而全之也。一有聪明睿智能尽其性者出于其闲，则天必命之以为亿兆之君师，使之治而教之，以复其性。" Zhu Xi 朱熹, *Daxue*

zhangju xu 大学章句序 [Preface to the interlinear analysis of the Great Learning]: 1.1.1, trans. Bryan W. Van Norden.

11 "三代之隆，其法寖备，然后王宫、国都以及闾巷，莫不有学。人生八岁，则自王公以下，至于庶人之子弟，皆入小学，而教之以洒扫、应对、进退之节，礼乐、射御、书数之文" Ibid., 1.2.1.

12 Zhu clarifies a bit later that these schools are administered by the government（"学校之政"）.

13 "及其十有五年，则自天子之元子、众子，以至公、卿、大夫、元士之适子，与凡民之俊秀，皆入大学，而教之以穷理、正心、修己、治人之道。" Ibid.

14 "自是以来，俗儒记诵词章之习，其功倍于小学而无用；异端虚无寂灭之教，其高过于大学而无实。" Ibid., 1.5.2.

15 Confucius, *Lunyu* 论语 [Analects] 1.6.7.

16 "诗书六艺" Zhu Xi 朱熹, *Lunyu jizhu* 论语集注 [Interlinear analysis of the Analects] 1.6.49.

17 "愚谓力行而不学文，则无以考圣贤之成法，识事理之当然" Ibid., trans. Bryan W. Van Norden. Quoted in Robin R. Wang, *Chinese Philosophy in an Era of Globalization* (Albany: State University of New York Press, 2004), 111.

18 致知 is most commonly translated as "extension of knowledge," but 知 can also be translated "knowing," and as de Bary demonstrates, Zhu Xi does not consider a man who has completed 致知 as someone who has acquired all knowledge

(which is impossible) but rather as someone who is able to locate the principle of anything through his intellectual faculties. It is not "knowledge" that is extended but the faculty of "knowing." William Theodore de Bary, "Chu Hsi's Aims as an Educator," 197.

19   "所谓致知在格物者，言欲致吾之知，在即物而穷其理也……至于用力之久，而一旦豁然贯通焉，则众物之表里精粗无不到……" Zhu Xi 朱熹, *Daxue zhangju* 大学章句 [Interlinear analysis of the Great Learning] 1.6.6–7, trans. William Theodore de Bary.

20   Zhu Xi 朱熹, *Zhuzi yulei* 朱子语类 [Classified conversations of Master Zhu] 94.2409.

21   "天下之事皆学者所当知……如礼乐制度、天文地理、兵谋刑法之属，亦皆当世所须而不可阙，皆不可以不之习也。" Zhu Xi 朱熹, *Huian xiansheng zhuwengong wenji* 晦庵先生朱文公文集 [Collected Works of Master Huian, Zhu Wengong] 69.3359, trans. Yung Sik Kim.

22   "天下之书无不博学审问" Ibid., 60.2891, trans. Yung Sik Kim.

23   Yung Sik Kim, 248. One example of such a passage comes from Confucius, *Lunyu* 论语 [Analects] 6.27.81: "A *junzi* studies broadly in *wen*" （君子博学于文）. Author's translation.

24   "虽未能洞究其精微，然也要识个规模大概" Zhu Xi 朱熹, *Zhuzi yulei* 朱子语类 [Classified conversations of Master Zhu] 117.2831, trans. Yung Sik Kim.

25   The *Doctrine of the Mean* and the *Great Learning* are both chapters out of the *Liji*.

26   Thomas H. C. Lee, *Education in Traditional China: A History*, 295.

27   Ibid., 383.

28   "父子有亲，君臣有义，夫妇有别，长幼有序，朋友有信。" Mencius, *Mengzi* 孟子 [Mencius] 5B.4.146, trans. Wing-tsit Chan.

29   "博学之，审问之，谨思之，明辨之，笃行之。" *Liji* 礼记 [Record of Rites] 53.22.1447, trans. Wing-tsit Chan.

30   Estimates range from 600 to 900 academies throughout China at the time. Thomas H. C. Lee, *Education in Traditional China: A History*, 93–94.

31   William Theodore de Bary, "Chu Hsi's Aims as an Educator," 213.

32   "则敬义立，而存养省察之功密，学者终身之大本植矣。" Cheng Duanli 程端礼, *Chengshi jiashu dushu fen nianri cheng* 程氏家塾读书分年日程 [Daily study of schedule for different classes in the Cheng family school] 1.44, trans. William Theodore de Bary.

33   Thomas H. C. Lee, *Education in Traditional China: A History*, 94.

34   "治国以教化为先，教化以学校为本" *Mingshi* 明史 [History of the Ming dynasty] 69.45.1686, author's translation.

35   "古者，人生八岁学礼、乐、射、御、书、数之文，十五学修身齐家治国平天下之道，是以周官选举之

298

制，曰六德，六行，六艺，文武兼用，贤能并举" Song Lian 宋濂, *Hongwu shengzheng ji* 洪武圣政记, 7.41.184, author's translation.

36 "汉、唐及宋，科举取士，各有定制，然但贵词章之学，而未求六艺之全。" Wang Shizhen 王世贞, *Yanshan tang bieji* 弇山堂别集 [Collected works of the yanshan hall] 81.5.1539, trans. Stephen Selby. This text is quoted from Wang Shizhen (1526-1590), a Ming dynasty statesman. The text varies slightly from the version quoted in the official Ming records (*Hongwu shengzheng ji*), from which the previous quote comes. The version in the official records has "virtuous arts" (*deyi* 德艺) here instead of "six arts" (*liuyi* 六艺). However, the "six arts" are explicitly mentioned in the preceding paragraph, demonstrating that the "virtuous arts" refers to the "six arts."

37 "务在经明行修，博古通今，文质得中，名实相称。" Ibid.

38 Ibid.

39 For an analysis of this decline, see Jiang Minglang 蒋明郎, "Cong liuyi dao bagu—dui zhongguo gudai tiyu jiaoyu shuailuo de sikao" 从六艺到八股——对中国古代体育教育衰落的思考 [From the six arts to the eight-legged essay: reflections on the decline of ancient Chinese physical education], *Xianyang shifan xueyuan xuebao* 咸阳师范学院学报 21, no. 6 (December 2006).

40 Thomas H. C. Lee, *Education in Traditional China: A History*, 167.

41   Thomas H. C. Lee, *Education in Traditional China: A History*, 392.

42   "知是心之本体。心自然会知。见父自然知孝，见兄自然知弟，见孺子入井，自然知恻隐。此便是良知。" Wang Yangming 王阳明, *Chuan xi lu* 传习录 [Instructions for practical living] 1.8.16, trans. Wing-tsit Chan.

43   For an excellent historical survey of the development of this concept, see William Theodore de Bary, *Learning for One's Self* (New York: Columbia University Press, 1991).

44   Thomas H. C. Lee, *Education in Traditional China: A History*, 348.

45   There were 1,239 known academies between 1522 and 1566. Ibid., 100.

46   "自世教衰，士子不通经术，但剽耳绘目，几幸弋获于有司……人材日下、吏治日偷，皆由于此……期与四方多士共兴复古学，将使异日者务为有用，因名曰复社。" Lu Shiyi 陆世仪, *Fushe jilue* 复社纪略 [Records of the Fushe] 1.9.181, trans. William S. Atwell.

47   William S. Atwell, "The Fu She," 346.

48   Ping Wen Kuo, *The Chinese System of Public Education*, 58.

Part Two

Chapter 4: Christian Foundations and the Western Tradition

1 Augustine, *De Doctrina Christiana (On Christian Teaching)*, 1.22.13.

2 One of the best defenses of Christian education I have read is Louis Berkhof and Cornelius Van Til, *Foundations of Christian Education: Addresses to Christian Teachers*, ed. Dennis E. Johnson (Phillipsburg, NJ: Presbyterian and Reformed Publishing Company, 1990).

3 Ibid., 2.18.37.

4 The authors suggest the acronym PGMAPT. Kevin Clark and Ravi Scott Jain, *The Liberal Arts Tradition: A Philosophy of Christian Classical Education* (Classical Academic Press, 2013). Kindle.

5 Ibid., 274.

6 "What is Classical Education?" The CiRCE Institute, accessed May 2, 2017, https://www.circeinstitute.org/resources/what-classical-education.

7 "Understanding the Classical and Christian Difference: A Parent's Primer," The Ambrose School, accessed May 2, 2017, http://theambroseschool.org/about/the-classical-approach/.

8 "What is Classical Education?" Classical Academic Press, accessed May 2, 2017, https://classicalacademicpress.com/what-is-classical-education/.

9 "Classical Education Movement," Wikipedia, last modified February 28, 2017, accessed May 2, 2017, https://en.wikipedia.org/wiki/Classical_education_movement.

10 Battista Guarino, "A Program of Teaching and Learning," in *Humanist Educational Treatises*, ed. and trans. Craig W. Kallendorf (Cambridge, MA: Harvard University Press, 2002), 307.

11 Battista Guarino, "A Program of Teaching and Learning," 307–309.

12 G. K. Chesterton, *Orthodoxy* (William Clowes and Sons, Limited, 1934), loc. 603–621, Kindle.

13 John of Salisbury, *Metalogicon*, 1.12.

14 Hugh of Saint Victor, *Didascalicon*, 3.3.

15 Martin Luther, "To the Councilmen of All Cities in Germany that they Establish and Maintain Christian Schools," in *The Annotated Luther,* vol. 5, *Christian Life in the World*, ed. Hans J. Hillerbrand (Minneapolis: Fortress Press, 2017), 270.

16 Theodore Arthur Buenger, "The Classics and the Protestant Reformation," *The Classical Weekly* 11, no. 28 (May 1918): 37.

17   *Letter from Sir Isaac Newton to Robert Hooke, February 5, 1675*, Historical Society of Pennsylvania, accessed February 4, 2018, https://digitallibrary.hsp.org/index.php/Detail/objects/9792.

18   C. S. Lewis, "On the Reading of Old Books," in *God in the Dock* (HarperOne, 2014), 201. Kindle.

19   Ibid., 202.

Chapter 5: The Necessity of Chinese Roots

1   John Calvin, *Institutes of the Christian Religion*, 2.2.15.

2   D. Z. Sheffield, "The Relation of Christian Education to the Present Condition and Needs of China," in *Records of the General Conference of the Protestant Missionaries of China, Held at Shanghai, May 7–20, 1890* (Shanghai: American Presbyterian Mission Press, 1890), 469–73.

3   Ibid., 473.

4   Augustine, *De Doctrina Christiana (On Christian Teaching)*, 1.28.17.

5   "樊迟问仁。子曰：'爱人。'问知。子曰：'知人。'" Confucius, *Lunyu* 论语 [Analects] 12.22.168, author's translation. In Chinese thought, *ren* is the sum and perfection of all moral virtues. It is the embodiment of the "superior man" or *junzi*. For classical Chinese texts cited in this book, I have used the following method: When three numbers are cited, the

first refers to the *juan* (scroll) of the original text; the second refers to the chapter/verse/passage number as found in Donald Sturgeon, ed., Chinese Text Project, 2017, http://ctext.org; the third refers to the page number of the published version of the Chinese text I'm quoting from (found in the bibliography). So 14.113.352 means *juan* 14 of the *Zhouli*, passage 113 in the *Zhouli* manuscript found on ctext.org, and page 352 of the *Zhouli zhushu* [Rites of Zhou annotated] in *Shisanjing zhushu* 十三经注疏 [The Thirteen Classics annotated], ed. Li Xueqin 李学勤 (Beijing: Beijing daxue chubanshe 北京大学出版社, 1999). If only two numbers are cited, then the ctext.org reference has been omitted.

6 Hugh of Saint Victor, *Didascalicon*, 1.1. Hugh identifies wisdom in the person of Christ (i.e. Wisdom).

7 John Calvin, *Institutes of the Christian Religion*, 1.1.1.

8 "知其性，则知天矣。存其心，养其性，所以事天也。" Mencius, *Mengzi* 孟子 [Mencius] 13A.1.350–1, trans. D. C. Lau.

9 Basil the Great, "Essay to Young Men on the Right Use of Greek Literature", 3.

Chapter 6: A Christian Approach to Chinese Classical Education

1 "仁之难成久矣！" *Biaoji* 表记 [Record on example] in *Liji* 礼记 [Rook of Rites] 54.19.1477, trans. James Legge.

2 "我未见好仁者，恶不仁者。" Confucius, *Lunyu* 论语 [Analects] 4.6.49, trans. Robert Eno.

3 "行义以达其道。吾闻其语矣，未见其人也。" Confucius, *Lunyu* 论语 [Analects] 16.11.229, author's translation.

4 "善人，吾不得而见之矣" Confucius, *Lunyu* 论语 [Analects] 7.26.93, trans. D. C. Lau.

5 "已矣乎！吾未见好德如好色者也。" Confucius, *Lunyu* 论语 [Analects] 15.13.212, trans. James Legge. I have replaced Legge's translation of "beauty" with Eno's translation of "sex."

6 "子曰：'君子道者三，我无能焉：仁者不忧，知者不惑，勇者不惧。'" Analects 14.28.197, trans. James Legge. I have slightly edited Legge's translation, replacing "am not equal to it" with "I cannot attain it." The original text literally means "I am not able." I have also replaced "superior man" with "*junzi.*"

7 "子曰：……君子之道四，丘未能一焉：所求乎子以事父，未能也；所求乎臣以事君，未能也；所求乎弟以事兄，未能也；所求乎朋友先施之，未能也。" *Zhongyong* 中庸 [Doctrine of the Mean] in *Liji* 礼记 [Record of Rites] 52.13.1431, trans. James Legge. I have slightly edited Legge's translation, replacing "not attained" with "not able," which better reflects the original text.

8 "今之教者，呻其占毕，多其讯，言及于数，进而不顾其安，使人不由其诚，教人不尽其材；其施之也悖，其求之也佛。夫然，故隐其学而疾其师，苦其难而不知其益也，虽终其业，其去之必速。教之不刑，其此之由乎！" *Xue* 学记 [Record of Learning] in *Liji* 礼记 [Record of Rites] 36.7.1060, trans. Xu Di, Yang Liuxin, Hunter McEwan, and Roger T. Ames.

9 "大德不官，大道不器" *Xue* 学记 [Record of Learning] in *Liji* 礼记 [Record of Rites] 36.17.1071, author's translation.

10 "国不以利为利，以义为利也" *Daxue* 大学 [The Great Learning] in *Liji* 礼记 [Record of Rites] 大学 1.16.1603, trans. James Legge.

11 "古之学者为己，今之学者为人。" Confucius, *Lunyu* 论语 [Analects] 14.24.195, trans. D. C. Lau.

12 "志于道，据于德，依于仁，游于艺。" Confucius, *Lunyu* 论语 [Analects] 7.6.85, author's translation.

13 Augustine, *De Doctrina Christiana (On Christian Teaching)*, 1.22.

14 "大学之道，在明明德，在亲民，在止于至善。" *Daxue* 大学 [The Great Learning] in *Liji* 礼记 [Record of Rites] 1.1.1592, trans. Robert Eno. I have slightly edited Eno's translation from "limit of the good" to "highest good," following Legge's translation of "highest excellence." *Shan* (善) is usually translated as "good" when used as a stand-alone virtue.

15   "自天子以至于庶人，壹是皆以修身为本，其本乱而末治者否矣。" *Daxue* 大学 [The Great Learning] in *Liji* 礼记 [Record of Rites] 42.2.1592, trans. James Legge.

16   Weiming Tu, "The Sung Confucian Idea of Education: A Background Understanding," in *Neo-Confucian Education: The Formative Stage*, ed. William Theodore de Bary and John W. Chaffee (Berkeley: University of California Press, 1989), 139–140. For a more in-depth treatment on the subject see James Legge, *The religions of China: Confucianism and Taoism described and compared with Christianity* (London: Hodder and Stoughton, 1880).

17   "思知人，不可以不知天。" *Zhongyong* 中庸 [Doctrine of the Mean] in *Liji* 礼记 [Record of Rites] 52.20.1441, author's translation. Literally, "In order to know men, [a ruler] cannot not know Heaven."

18   "不能乐天，不能成其身。" *Aigong Wen* 哀公问 [Questions of Duke Ai] in *Liji* 礼记 [Record of Rites] 50.10.1379, author's translation.

19   "知其性，则知天矣。存其心，养其性，所以事天也。" Mencius, *Mengzi* 孟子 [Mencius] 13A.1.350–1, trans. D. C. Lau.

20   "获罪于天，无所祷也。" Confucius, *Lunyu* 论语 [Analects] 3.13.36, trans. James Legge.

21   "今天下之王公大人士君子，中实将欲遵道利民，本察仁义之本，天之意不可不顺也。顺天之意者，义之法也。" Mozi, *Tian zhi zhong* 天志中 [Will of Heaven II] in *Mozi* 墨子 [Mozi] 25.9.115, trans. W. P. Mei.

22 "天命之谓性，率性之谓道，修道之谓教。" *Zhongyong* 中庸 [Doctrine of the Mean] 52.1.1422, trans. James Legge.

23 "盖自天降生民，则既莫不与之以仁义礼智之性矣。然其气质之禀或不能齐，是以不能皆有以知其性之所有而全之也。一有聪明睿智能尽其性者出于其闲，则天必命之以为亿兆之君师，使之治而教之，以复其性。" Zhu Xi 朱熹, *Daxue zhangju xu* 大学章句序 [Preface to the interlinear analysis of the Great Learning] 1.1.1, trans. Bryan W. Van Norden.

24 Hugh of Saint Victor, *Didascalicon*, 1.1–2.1.

25 "思知人，不可以不知天。" *Zhongyong* 中庸 [Doctrine of the Mean] in *Liji* 礼记 [Record of Rites] 52.20.1441, author's translation.

26 "不能乐天，不能成其身。" *Aigong Wen* 哀公问 [Questions of Duke Ai] in *Liji* 礼记 [Record of Rites] 50.10.1379, author's translation.

27 "学而时习之，不亦说乎？" Confucius, *Lunyu* 论语 [Analects] 1.1.1, trans. Robert Eno.

28 "知之者不如好之者，好之者不如乐之者。" Ibid., 6.20.78. I have slightly edited Eno's translation, replacing "it" with "something."

29 "君子有三畏：畏天命，畏大人，畏圣人之言" Confucius, *Lunyu* 论语 [Analects] 16.8.228, trans. James Legge. I have changed Legge's translation of 畏 from "stand in awe" to "revere." The Chinese is also sometimes translated as "fear."

30 "天何言哉？" Ibid., 17.19.241, author's translation.

31 "子曰：'我非生而知之者，好古，敏以求之者也。'" Ibid., 7.20.92.

32 "述而不作，信而好古" Confucius, *Lunyu* 论语 [Analects] 7.1.84, trans. James Legge.

33 "子曰：'由！诲女知之乎？知之为知之，不知为不知，是知也。'" Confucius, *Lunyu* 论语 [Analects] 2.17, trans. D. C. Lau.

34 "学然后知不足" *Xue* 学记 [Record of Learning] in *Liji* 礼记 [Record of Rites] 36.3, trans. James Legge.

35 "敏而好学，不耻下问" Confucius, *Lunyu* 论语 [Analects] 5.15.62, author's translation.

36 "弟子入则孝，出则弟，谨而信，泛爱众，而亲仁。行有馀力，则以学文。" Confucius, *Lunyu* 论语 [Analects] 1.6.7, trans. Robert Eno. I've slightly altered Eno's translation, substituting "cleave to *ren*" for "cleave to those who are *ren*." I'm in agreement with Legge here that Confucius is speaking about cleaving to a specific virtue rather than a certain kind of person. I've also substituted "*wen*" for "the refinements of culture" so as not to confine the word to only one of many possible definitions. *Wen* can also refer to literature, culture, and the institution of rites and music.

37 "盖有不知而作之者，我无是也。" Ibid., 7.28.94, trans. James Legge.

38 "学而不思则罔" Ibid., 2.15.20.

39 "博学之，审问之，谨思之，明辨之，笃行之。" *Zhongyong* 中庸 [Doctrine of the Mean] in *Liji* 礼记 [Record of Rites] 53.22.1447.

40 "所谓致知在格物者，言欲致吾之知，在即物而穷其理也……至于用力之久，而一旦豁然贯通焉，则众物之表里精粗无不到……" Zhu Xi 朱熹, *Daxue zhangju* 大学章句 [Interlinear analysis of the Great Learning] 1.6.6–7, trans. William Theodore de Bary.

41 "月映万川" Zhu Xi 朱熹, *Zhuzi yulei* 朱子语类 [Classified conversations of Master Zhu] 94.2409.

42 Hugh of Saint Victor, *Didascalicon*, 2.1.

43 "君子博学于文，约之以礼，亦可以弗畔矣夫！" Confucius, *Lunyu* 论语 [Analects] 12:15.165, trans. James Legge.

44 "天下之书无不博学审问" Zhu Xi 朱熹, *Huian xiansheng zhuwengong wenji* 晦庵先生朱文公文集 [Collected Works of Master Huian, Zhu Wengong] 60.2891, trans. Yung Sik Kim.

45 "天下之事皆学者所当知" Ibid., 69.3359, author's translation.

46 "虽未能洞究其精微，然也要识个规模大概" Zhu Xi 朱熹, *Zhuzi yulei* 朱子语类 [Classified conversations of Master Zhu] 117.2831, trans. Yung Sik Kim.

47 "大学之法，禁于未发之谓豫，当其可之谓时，不陵节而施之谓孙，相观而善之谓摩。此四者，教之所由兴也。发然后禁，则捍格而不胜；时过然后学，则勤苦而难成；杂施而不孙，则坏乱而不修；独学而无友，则孤陋而寡闻；燕朋逆其师；燕辟废其学。此六者，教之所由废也。" *Xue* 学记 [Record of Learning] in *Liji* 礼记 [Record of Rites] 36.8.1061–2, trans. Xu Di, Yang Liuxin, Hunter McEwan, and Roger T. Ames.

48 "学者有四失，教者必知之。人之学也，或失则多，或失则寡，或失则易，或失则止。此四者，心之莫同也。知其心，然后能救其失也。" Ibid., 36.10.1064.

49 "故君子之教喻也，道而弗牵，强而弗抑，开而弗达。" Ibid., 36.9.1063. I have slightly changed the original translation from "the role of exemplary persons as teachers" to "the role of a *junzi* as a teacher."

50 "记问之学，不足以为人师。必也听语乎，力不能问，然后语之；语之而不知，虽舍之可也。" Ibid., 36.14.1068.

51 "善问者，如攻坚木，先其易者，后其节目，及其久也，相说以解；不善问者反此。" Ibid., 36.13.1067.

52 *Xueji* 学记 [Record of Learning] in *Liji* 礼记 [Record of Rites] 36.8, trans. James Legge.

53 "保氏，掌谏王恶。而养国子以道，乃教之六艺：一曰五礼，二曰六乐，三曰五射，四曰五驭，五曰六书，六曰九数。" *Zhouli* 周礼 [Rites of Zhou] 14.113.352, author's translation.

Chapter 7: Rites and Music（礼乐）

1 "大乐与天地同和……以著万物之理" *Yueji* 乐记 [Record of Music] in *Liji* 礼记 [Record of Rites] 37.14.1087, author's translation.

2 "子曰：'君子道者三，我无能焉：仁者不忧，知者不惑，勇者不惧。'" Analects 14.28.197, trans. James Legge. I have slightly edited Legge's translation, replacing "am not equal to it" with "I cannot attain it." I have also replaced "superior man" with "*junzi*" and "bold" with "courageous."

3 "夫物之感人无穷，而人之好恶无节，则是物至而人化物也。人化物也者，灭天理而穷人欲者也。" *Yueji* 乐记 [Record of Music] in *Liji* 礼记 [Record of Rites] 37.8.1083–4, trans. James Legge.

4 "是故先王之制礼乐也，非以极口腹耳目之欲也，将以教民平好恶而反人道之正也。" Ibid., 37.6.1081.

5 Plato, *Republic*, 401e–402a. I have translated the word μουσική (mousikḗ) as "music."

6 Augustine, *De Doctrina Christiana (On Christian Teaching)*, 1.27.

7 "樊迟问仁。子曰：'爱人。'" Confucius, *Lunyu* 论语 [Analects] 12.22.168, author's translation.

8 "仁、爱也" Xunzi, *Xunzi* 荀子 [Xunzi] 27.21.435.

9   C. S. Lewis, *The Abolition of Man* (HarperCollins e-books, 2009), 15–16, Kindle.

10   "礼乐偵天地之情" *Yueji* 乐记 [Record of Music] in *Liji* 礼记 [Record of Rites] 乐记 38.39.1116, trans James Legge.

11   "人而不仁，如礼何？人而不仁，如乐何？" Confucius, *Lunyu* 论语 [Analects] 3.3.30, author's translation.

12   "By extensively studying all learning, and keeping himself under the restraint of the rules of propriety (*li*), one may thus likewise not err from what is right." (君子博学于文，约之以礼，亦可以弗畔矣夫！) Ibid., 12:15.165, trans. James Legge.

13   "乐，所以修内也，礼，所以修外也。礼乐交错于中，发形于外，是故其成也怿，恭敬而温文。" *Wenwang Shizi* 文王世子 [King Wen as son and heir] in *Liji* 礼记 [Record of Rites] 20.10.634–5, author's translation.

14   "夫民有血气心知之性，而无哀乐喜怒之常，应感起物而动，然后心术形焉。是故......宽裕肉好、顺成和动之音作，而民慈爱。流辟邪散、狄成涤滥之音作，而民淫乱。" *Yueji* 乐记 [Record of Music] in *Liji* 礼记 [Record of Rites] 38.27.1104, trans. James Legge.

15   "乐者，天地之和也；礼者，天地之序也。和故百物皆化；序故群物皆别。" Ibid., 37.14.1090, trans. James Legge.

16   "使亲疏贵贱、长幼男女之理，皆形见于乐" Ibid., 38.28.1106.

17 "是故清明象天，广大象地，终始象四时，周还象风雨。五色成文而不乱，八风从律而不奸，百度得数而有常。小大相成，终始相生。倡和清浊，迭相为经。故乐行而伦清，耳目聪明，血气和平，移风易俗，天下皆宁。" Ibid., 38.31.110.

18 "为礼不敬，临丧不哀，吾何以观之哉！" Confucius, *Lunyu* 论语 [Analects] 3.26.46, trans. Arthur Waley.

19 "礼云礼云，玉帛云乎哉？乐云乐云，钟鼓云乎哉？" Ibid., 17.11.238, trans. James Legge.

20 Hugh of Saint Victor, *De sacrementis legis naturalis et scripturae*, in *Patrologia Latina*, ed. J. P. Migne 175, 34B, quoted in Stephen C. Jaeger, *The Envy of Angels: Cathedral Schools and Social Ideals in Medieval Europe, 950–1200* (Philadelphia: University of Pennsylvania Press, 1994), 262.

21 Bernard of Clairvaux, *Vita Malachiae*, 19.43, Opera 3:348.18ff, quoted in Stephen C. Jaeger, *The Envy of Angels: Cathedral Schools and Social Ideals in Medieval Europe, 950–1200* (Philadelphia: University of Pennsylvania Press, 1994), 273.

22 Confucius, *Lunyu* 论语 [Analects], 10.

23 Hugh of Saint Victor, *De institutione novitiorum*, in *Patrologia Latina*, ed. J. P. Migne 10.935B, quoted in Stephen C. Jaeger, *The Envy of Angels: Cathedral Schools and Social Ideals in Medieval Europe, 950–1200* (Philadelphia: University of Pennsylvania Press, 1994), 260.

24   Ibid., 12.938A–B, quoted in Stephen C. Jaeger, *The Envy of Angels: Cathedral Schools and Social Ideals in Medieval Europe, 950–1200* (Philadelphia: University of Pennsylvania Press, 1994), 261.

25   For an excellent survey of the development of *mores* education during the Middle Ages, see Stephen C. Jaeger, *The Envy of Angels: Cathedral Schools and Social Ideals in Medieval Europe, 950–1200* (Philadelphia: University of Pennsylvania Press, 1994).

Chapter 8: Script and Calculation（书数）

1   "不知言，无以知人也。" Confucius, *Lunyu* 论语 [Analects] 20.3.270, trans. James Legge. I have slightly changed Legge's translation from "the force of words" to "language."

2   "惟人参之，性灵所锺，是谓三才。为五行之秀，实天地之心，心生而言立，言立而文明，自然之道也。" Liu Xie 刘勰, *Wenxin diaolong* 文心雕龙 [The Literary Mind and the Carving of Dragons] 1.1.1.623, trans. Stephen Owen.

3   "故知道沿圣以垂文，圣因文以明道" Ibid., 1.1.5.624.

4   "鼓天下之动者存乎辞。" Ibid., 1.1.5.624. Liu is quoting here from the *Book of Changes*.

5   "人文之元，肇自太极" Ibid., 1.1.3.623.

6   Augustine, *De Doctrina Christiana (On Christian Teaching)*, 2.42.

7   Martin Luther, "To the Councilmen of All Cities in Germany that they Establish and Maintain Christian Schools," in *The Annotated Luther*, vol. 5, *Christian Life in the World*, ed. Hans J. Hillerbrand (Minneapolis: Fortress Press, 2017), 258–9.

8   "道沿圣以垂文"Liu Xie 刘勰,*Wenxin diaolong*文心雕龙 [The Literary Mind and the Carving of Dragons] 1.1.5.624, trans. Stephen Owen.

9   Martin Luther, "To the Councilmen of All Cities in Germany that they Establish and Maintain Christian Schools," in *The Annotated Luther*, vol. 5, *Christian Life in the World*, ed. Hans J. Hillerbrand (Minneapolis: Fortress Press, 2017), 260.

10   Quintilian, *The Orator's Education*, 1.1.12.

11   Ibid., 1.1.20.

12   "有德者，必有言。有言者，不必有德。" Confucius, *Lunyu* 论语 [Analects] 14.4.183, trans. James Legge.

13   "巧言乱德" Ibid., 15.27.215, trans. Robert Eno.

14   "巧言令色，鲜矣仁。" Ibid., 17.17.240.

15   "汉、唐及宋，科举取士，各有定制，然但贵词章之学，而未求六艺之全。" Wang Shizhen 王世贞, *Yanshan tang bieji* 弇山堂别集 [Collected works of the yanshan hall] 81.5.1539, trans. Stephen Selby. This text is quoted from Wang Shizhen (1526–1590), a Ming dynasty statesman. The text varies slightly from the version quoted in the official Ming records (*Hongwu shengzheng ji*), from which the previous quote comes. The

version in the official records has "virtuous arts" (*deyi* 德艺) here instead of "six arts" (*liuyi* 六艺). However, the "six arts" are explicitly mentioned in the preceding paragraph, demonstrating that the "virtuous arts" refers to the "six arts."

16   Martin Luther, "To the Christian Nobility of the German Nation Concerning the Reform of the Christian Estate, 1520," trans. Charles M. Jacobs, rev. James Atkinson, in *Luther's Works*, vol. 44, *The Christian in Society*, ed. James Atkinson (Minneapolis: Fortress Press, 1966), 207.

17   "经也者，恒久之至道，不刊之鸿教也。故象天地，效鬼神，参物序，制人纪，洞性灵之奥区，极文章之骨髓者也。" Liu Xie 刘勰, *Wenxin diaolong* 文心雕龙 [The Literary Mind and the Carving of Dragons] 1.3.1.627, trans. Stephen Owen.

18   A. P. Parker, "The Place of the Chinese Classics in Christian Schools and Colleges," in *Records of the General Conference of the Protestant Missionaries of China, Held at Shanghai, May 7–20, 1890* (Shanghai: American Presbyterian Mission Press, 1890), 492.

19   Ibid., 492–3.

20   Ibid., 494.

21   "The result is that scarcely anyone devotes himself to these studies . . . because they are not fostered by honors as is the study of philosophy, to which students are attracted by the hope of glory and the rewards attached to it." Matteo Ricci, *Della entrata della Compagnia di Giesu e Christianita nella Cina*, ed. Madd-

alena del Gatto (Macerata: Quodlibet, 2000), quoted in Endymion Wilkinson, *Chinese History: A New Manual*, 4th ed. (Harvard University Asia Center, 2015), 469.

22　"温故而知新" Confucius, *Lunyu* 论语 [Analects] 7.11.19, author's translation.

23　"君子博学于文" Ibid., 6.27.81, author's translation.

24　"天下之书无不博学审问" Zhu Xi 朱熹, *Huian xiansheng zhuwengong wenji* 晦庵先生朱文公文集 [Collected Works of Master Huian, Zhu Wengong] 60.2891, trans. Yung Sik Kim.

25　See C. W. Mateer, "How May Educational Work be Made to Advance the Cause of Christianity in China," D. Z. Sheffield, "The Relation of Christian Education to the Present Condition and Needs of China," A. P. Parker, "The Place of the Chinese Classics in Christian Schools and Colleges," and the following discussion in *Records of the General Conference of the Protestant Missionaries of China, Held at Shanghai, May 7–20, 1890* (Shanghai: American Presbyterian Mission Press, 1890), 456–509.

26　A. P. Parker, 491.

27　Ibid., 495.

28　C. S. Lewis, "The Idea of an 'English School,'" in *Image and Imagination* (HarperOne, 2014), 280. Kindle.

29　Ibid., 305.

30　"丐大业文人弃掷案头此书与功名进取毫不相关也" Song Yingxing 宋应星, *Tiangong kaiwu* 天工开物 [Useful

things produced by the skill of man from the works of nature],
quoted in Endymion Wilkinson, *Chinese History: A New Manual*,
4th ed. (Harvard University Asia Center, 2015), 469.

31 "数，术也。"*Guangya*广雅[Guangya] 5.455. *Shu* (术)
can also be translated as "technique."

32 Francis Bacon, *Novum Organum*, ed. Joseph Devey
(New York: P.F. Collier & Son, 1902), 105.

33 Joseph Needham, *Science and Civilisation in China*, vol.
5, *Chemistry and Chemical Technology*, pt. 4, *Spagyrical Discovery and
Invention: Apparatus, Theories and Gifts* (Cambridge: Cambridge
University Press, 2000), xxxviii.

34 Joseph Needham, "Science and Society in East and
West," in *The Grand Titration: Science and Society in East and West*, by
Joseph Needham (London: Allen & Unwin, 1969), 190.

35 Joseph Needham, *Science and Civilisation in China*, vol.
2, *History of Scientific Thought* (Cambridge: Cambridge University
Press, 2005), 582.

36 For a good treatment of this topic, see Vern S. Poythress, *Redeeming Mathematics: A God-Centered Approach* (Wheaton,
IL: Crossway, 2015).

37 *Letter from Sir Isaac Newton to Robert Hooke, February
5, 1675*, Historical Society of Pennsylvania, accessed February
4, 2018, https://digitallibrary.hsp.org/index.php/Detail/ob-
jects/9792.

Chapter 9: Archery and Charioteering (射御)

1   C. S. Lewis, *Miracles* (HarperCollins e-books, 2009), 266. Kindle.

2   Plato, *Republic*, 410c.

3   "君子道者三，我无能焉：仁者不忧，知者不惑，勇者不惧。" Confucius, *Lunyu* 论语 [Analects] 14.28.197, trans. James Legge. I have slightly edited Legge's translation, replacing "am not equal to it" with "I cannot attain it." The original text literally means "I am not able." I have also replaced "superior man" with "*junzi*."

4   Plato, *Republic*, 410b.

5   "射有似乎君子，失诸正鹄，反求诸其身。" *Zhongyong* 中庸 [Doctrine of the Mean] in *Liji* 礼记 [Record of Rites] 52.15.1433, trans. James Legge.

6   "故曰：" 为人父者以为父鹄，为人子者以为子鹄，为人君者以为君鹄，为人臣者以为臣鹄。" 故射者，各射己之鹄。" *Sheyi* 射义 [The meaning of archery] in *Liji* 礼记 [Record of Rites] 62.8.1648, trans. Stephen Selby.

7   Plato, *Republic*, 410d.

8   "射既不能穿剳" Yan Zhitui 颜之推, *Yanshi jiaxun* 颜氏家训 3.8, quoted in Endymion Wilkinson, *Chinese History: A New Manual*, 4th ed. (Harvard University Asia Center, 2015), 469.

9 "故男子生，桑弧蓬矢六，以射天地四方。天地四方者，男子之所有事也。" *Sheyi* 射义 [The meaning of archery] in *Liji* 礼记 [Record of Rites] 62.10.1653, trans. James Legge.

10 C. S. Lewis, *The Problem of Pain* (HarperCollins e-books, 2009), 143–4. Kindle.

11 For a thorough explanation of each of these branches of study, see Kevin Clark and Ravi Jain, *The Liberal Arts Tradition: A Philosophy of Christian Classical Education* (Classical Academic Press, 2013).

12 Shang Guanjian 上官剑, "'Liu yi' yu 'qiyi': zhongxifang 'ziyou xueke' suyuan zhi bijiao" "'六艺'与'七艺'：中西方'自由学科'溯源之比较" [The "six arts" and the "seven arts": comparing the origins of the eastern and western "liberal arts"], *Gaojiao tansuo* 高教探索 4 (2010).

13 Bart Dessein, "Confucianized Rationality: Some Reflections on East Asia, Wisdom, and Science," in *Contemporary East Asia and the Confucian Revival*, ed. Jana S. Rosker and Natasa Visocnik (Cambridge Scholars Publishing, 2015), [xxxv].

14 Thierry Meynard, *The Jesuit Reading of Confucius: The First Complete Translation of the Lunyu (1687) Published in the West* (Leiden: Brill, 2015), 59.

15 "六艺异科而皆同道。" Liu An 刘安, *Taizuxun* 泰族训 [The exalted lineage] in *Huainanzi* 淮南子 [Huainanzi] 20.10, trans. John S. Major et al.

16   Kevin Clark and Ravi Scott Jain, *The Liberal Arts Tradition: A Philosophy of Christian Classical Education* (Classical Academic Press, 2013). Kindle.

Chapter 10: Obstacles to Classical Christian Education in China

1   "其实天朝德威远被，万国亲王，种种贵重之物，梯航毕集，无所不有。尔之正使等所亲见。然从不贵奇巧，并无更需尔国制办物件。" J. Mason Gentzler, *Changing China: Readings in the History of China from the Opium War to the Present* (New York: Praeger Publishers, 1977), 25.

2   "所谓诚其意者，毋自欺也......故君子必慎其独也！小人闲居为不善，无所不至，见君子而后厌然，掩其不善，而著其善......故君子必慎其独也。" *Daxue* 大学 [The Great Learning] in *Liji* 礼记 [Record of Rites] 1.3.1592, trans. Robert Eno. I have slightly edited Eno's translation, substituting "when he is alone" for "of his solitude" and "when he is at ease."

3   "自是以来，俗儒记诵词章之习，其功倍于小学而无用；异端虚无寂灭之教，其高过于大学而无实。" Zhu Xi 朱熹, *Daxue zhangju xu* 大学章句序 [Preface to the interlinear analysis of the Great Learning]: 1.5.2.

4   Matteo Ricci, *Tianzhu shiyi* 天主实义 [The True Meaning of the Lord of Heaven].

5   "博学而笃志，切问而近思，仁在其中矣。" Confucius, *Lunyu* 论语 [Analects] 19.6.256, trans. Robert Eno.

6 "天下之书无不博学审问" Zhu Xi 朱熹, *Huian xian-sheng zhuwengong wenji* 晦庵先生朱文公文集 [Collected Works of Master Huian, Zhu Wengong] 60.2891, trans. Yung Sik Kim.

7 "子曰：'吾有知乎哉？无知也。'" Confucius, *Lu-nyu* 论语 [Analects] 9.8.114, trans. Robert Eno.

8 "子入大庙，每事问。" Ibid., 3.15.37, trans. James Legge.

9 "敏而好学，不耻下问" Ibid., 5.15.62, author's translation.

10 "When a small man commits an error, he will always make excuses." （小人之过也必文。） Ibid., 19.8.257, trans. Robert Eno.

11 "'It is according to rites,' they say. 'It is according to rites,' they say. Are gems and silk all that is meant by rites?" （礼云礼云，玉帛云乎哉？） Ibid., 17.11.238, trans. James Legge.

12 "The emperor may not make the standard at will. There is Heaven to give him the standard. That the emperor gives the standard to the high dukes, to the feudal lords, to the scholars, and to the common people, the gentlemen in the world clearly understand. But that Heaven gives the standard to the emperor, the people do not know well." （天子未得次己而为政，有天政之。天子为政于三公、诸侯、士、庶人，天下之士君子固明知，天之为政于天子，天下百姓未得之明知也。） Mozi, *Tian zhi shang* 天志上 [Will of Heaven I] in *Mozi* 墨子 [Mozi] 23.3.104, trans. W.P. Mei.

13 "其志嘐嘐然，曰古之人，古之人。夷考其行而不掩焉者也……行何为踽踽凉凉?" Mencius, *Mengzi* 孟子 [Mencius] 14B.83.405, trans. Robert Eno. I have slightly edited Eno's translation to reflect the present tense.

14 John of Salisbury, *Metalogicon*, 3.13.

15 John Calvin, *Institutes of the Christian Religion*, 2.2.15.

16 Cassiodorus, *Institutions of Divine and Secular Learning*, in *Institutions of Divine and Secular Learning and On the Soul*, trans. James W. Halporn, intr. Mark Vessey (Liverpool: Liverpool University Press, 2004), 183–4.

17 Ibid., 208.

18 Ibid., 215.

19 Ibid., 222.

20 Ibid., 224.

21 Martin Luther, "To the Councilmen of All Cities in Germany that they Establish and Maintain Christian Schools," in *The Annotated Luther*, vol. 5, *Christian Life in the World*, ed. Hans J. Hillerbrand (Minneapolis: Fortress Press, 2017), 268.

22 "A work of (whatever) art can be either 'received' or 'used'. When we 'receive' it we exert our senses and imagination and various other powers according to a pattern invented by the artist. When we 'use' it we treat it as assistance for our own activities. The one, to use an old-fashioned image, is like being taken for a bicycle ride by a man who may know roads we have never

yet explored. The other is like adding one of those little motor attachments to our own bicycle and then going for one of our familiar rides." C. S. Lewis, *An Experiment in Criticism* (London and New York: Cambridge University Press, 1961). Kindle.

23   Augustine, *De Doctrina Christiana (On Christian Teaching)*, 2.41.

24   John Ross 罗约翰, "Our Attitude towards Confucianism," *The Chinese Recorder and Missionary Journal*, vol. 18 (January–February, 1887), 3.

25   One of the primary debates at the first General Conference of the Protestant Missionaries of China in 1877 concerned the relationship between Confucianism and Christianity. Those who argued that Confucianism is complementary to Christianity did so under the banner of "Confucius plus Christ" (孔子加基督). Those who opposed them were represented by the slogan "Confucius or Christ" (孔子或基督). For an overview of this debate, see Hu Wei Qing 胡卫清, "Missionaries in Modern China and their Perceptions of Confucianism (近代来华传教士的儒学观)," in *Christianity*, ed. Zhuo Xinping 卓新平, trans. Chi Zhen and Caroline Mason (Ledien and Boston: Brill, 2013).

26   Basil the Great, "Essay to Young Men on the Right Use of Greek Literature," 4.

27   Augustine, *De Doctrina Christiana (On Christian Teaching)*, 2.40.

28   Augustine, *City of God*, 5.12.

29   John Calvin, *Institutes of the Christian Religion*, 2.3.3.

30   Ibid., 2.3.4.

31   Basil the Great, "Essay to Young Men on the Right Use of Greek Literature," 5.

32   James Legge, "Confucianism in Relation to Christianity" (paper presented at the Missionary Conference, Shanghai, May 11, 1877), accessed May 4, 2017, https://archive.org/details/confucianisminr01legggoog, 9.

33   Ibid., 11.

34   John Ross (罗约翰) calls Confucianism a "handmaid of Christianity." See John Ross 罗约翰, "Our Attitude towards Confucianism," *The Chinese Recorder and Missionary Journal*, vol. 18 (January–February, 1887), 10. W.A.P. Martin (丁韪良) likens Confucius to Moses. See *A Cycle of Cathay; or, China, South and North. With Personal Reminiscences*, 3rd ed. (New York: Fleming H. Revell, 1900), 288.

35   "The Master said, 'The way of the *junzi* is threefold, but I cannot attain it . . ." (子曰：'君子道者三，我无能焉……) Confucius, *Lunyu* [Analects] 14.28.197, trans. James Legge. "The Master said: ". . . In the *Dao* of the *junzi* there are four duties, not one of which I am yet able to perform . . ." (子曰：……君子之道四，丘未能一焉……) *Zhongyong* 中庸 [Doctrine of the Mean] in *Liji* 礼记 [Record of Rites] 52.13.1431, trans. James Legge.

36 "万物本乎天" *Jiao te sheng* 郊特牲 [The single victim at the border sacrifices] in *Liji* 礼记 [Record of Rites] 26.24.801, trans. James Legge.

37 "不知亦有贵知夫天者乎？曰：天为贵，天为知 而已矣。" Mozi, *Tian zhi zhong* 天志中 [Will of Heaven II] in *Mozi* 墨子 [Mozi] 24.2.108, trans. W. P. Mei.

38 "顺天之意，谓之善意行，反天之意，谓之不善 意行……顺天之意者，义之法也。" Ibid., 24.9.114.

39 "天子有善，让德于天" *Jiyi* 祭义 [The meaning of sacrifices] in *Liji* 礼记 [Record of Rites] 48.39.1342, trans. James Legge.

40 "义果自天出矣。" Mozi, *Tian zhi zhong* 天志中 [Will of Heaven II] in *Mozi* 墨子 [Mozi] 24.2.108, trans. W.P. Mei.

41 "莫我知也夫！……知我者，其天乎！" Confucius, *Lunyu* 论语 [Analects] 14.35.199, trans. James Legge.

42 "天必欲人之相爱相利……以其兼而爱之，兼而 利之也。" Mozi, *Fayi* 法仪 [On the necessity of standards] in *Mozi* 墨子 [Mozi] 4.3.10, trans. W. P. Mei.

43 "顺天意者，兼相爱，交相利，必得赏。反天意 者，别相恶，交相贼，必得罚。" Mozi, *Tian zhi shang* 天志 上 [Will of Heaven I] in *Mozi* 墨子 [Mozi] 23.4.104–5, trans. W.P. Mei.

44 "获罪于天，无所祷也。" Confucius, *Lunyu* 论语 [Analects] 3.13.36, trans. James Legge.

45   James Legge, *The religions of China: Confucianism and Taoism described and compared with Christianity* (London: Hodder and Stoughton, 1880), 251.

46   C. S. Lewis, *Surprised by Joy* (New York: Mariner Books, 2012), 62. Kindle.

47   Ibid., 235.

48   James Legge, "Confucianism in Relation to Christianity" (paper presented at the Missionary Conference, Shanghai, May 11, 1877), accessed May 4, 2017, https://archive.org/details/confucianisminr01legggoog, 12.

49   Augustine, *De Doctrina Christiana (On Christian Teaching)*, 2.40.

50   C. S Lewis, *The Screwtape Letters: Annotated Edition* (HarperOne, 2013), 1073. Kindle.

BIBLIOGRAPHY

Atwell, William S. "The Fu She." In *The Unfolding of Neo-Confucianism*, edited by William Theodore de Bary. Studies in Oriental Culture, vol. 10. New York: Columbia University Press, 1975.

Augustine. *City of God.* Veritatis Splendor Publications, 2012. Kindle.

———. *De Doctrina Christiana* (On Christian Teaching), translated by J. F. Shaw. Digireads.com Publishing, 2010. Kindle.

Bacon, Francis. *Novum Organum.* Edited by Joseph Devey. New York: P. F. Collier & Son, 1902.

Basil the Great. "Essay to Young Men on the Right Use of Greek Literature." In *Essays on the Study and Use of Poetry*, by Plutarch and Basil the Great, translated by Frederick Morgan Padelford. Yale Studies in English, vol. 15. New York: Henry Holt and Company, 1902.

Berkhof, Louis and Cornelius Van Til. *Foundations of Christian Education: Addresses to Christian Teachers.* Edited by Dennis E. Johnson. Phillipsburg, NJ: Presbyterian and Reformed Publishing Company, 1990.

Bol, Peter. *"This Culture of Ours": Intellectual Transitions in T'ang and Sung China*. Stanford, CA: Stanford University Press, 1992.

Buenger, Theodore Arthur. "The Classics and the Protestant Reformation." The Classical Weekly 11, no. 28 (May 1918): 34–37.

Calvin, John. *Institutes of the Christian Religion*. Acheron Press, 2012.

Cassiodorus. *Institutions of Divine and Secular Learning and On the Soul*. Translated by James W. Halporn. Introduction by Mark Vessey. Liverpool: Liverpool University Press, 2004.

Chan, Wing-tsit. "Chu Hsi and the Academies." In *Neo-confucian Education: The Formative Stage*, edited by William Theodore de Bary and John W. Chaffee, 389-413. Berkeley and Los Angeles: University of California Press, 1989.

Chen Xin 陈新, Shi Min 施敏, and Di Jinghua 翟敬华. "Lunyu lun 'wen'—Lunyu mantan zhi si" 《论语》论 "文"

—— 《论语》漫谈之四 [On *wen* in the Analects: part four of a discussion on the Analects]. *Zhangjiakou zhiye jishu xueyuan xuebao* 张家口职业技术学院学报 26, no. 3 (2013): 48–50.

Cheng, Chung-ying. "*Dao (Tao)*: The Way." In *Encyclopedia of Chinese Philosophy*, edited by Antonio S. Cua, 202-205. New York: Routledge, 2003.

Cheng Duanli 程端礼. *Chengshi jiashu dushu fen nianri cheng* 程氏家塾读书分年日程 [Daily study of schedule for different classes in the Cheng family school]. Hefei: Huangshan shushe 黄山书社, 1992.

Chesterton, G. K. *The Everlasting Man.* Sublime Books, 2012. Kindle.

―――. *Orthodoxy.* William Clowes and Sons, Limited, 1934. Kindle.

Clark, Kevin and Ravi Scott Jain. *The Liberal Arts Tradition: A Philosophy of Christian Classical Education.* Classical Academic Press, 2013. Kindle.

Confucius. *The Analects.* Translated by Arthur Waley. New York: Alfred A. Knopf, Inc., 2000.

―――. *The Analects.* Translated by D. C. Lau. London: Penguin Group, 1979.

―――. *The Analects of Confucius: An Online Teaching Translation.* Version 2.2. Translated by Robert Eno. Eno, 2015. Accessed May 3, 2017. http://www.indiana.edu/~p374/ Analects_of_Confucius_(Eno-2015).pdf.

―――. *Confucian Analects.* Translated by James Legge. In *The Chinese Classics: with a Translation, Critical and Exegetical Notes, Prolegomena, and Copious Indexes, 5 vols.* Hong Kong: Legge; London: Trubner, 1861–1872. I have substituted Legge's romanizations with pinyin.

―――. *The Essential Analects: Selected Passages with Traditional Commentary.* Translated by Edward Slingerland. Hackett Publishing Company, 2006.

―――. *Lunyu zhushu* 论语注疏 [The Analects annotated]. In *Shisanjing zhushu* 十三经注疏 [The Thirteen Classics annotated], edited by Li Xueqin 李学勤. Beijing: Beijing daxue chubanshe 北京大学出版社, 1999.

De Bary, William Theodore. "Chu Hsi's Aims as an Educator." In *Neo-confucian Education: The Formative Stage*, edited by William Theodore de Bary and John W. Chaffee, 186–218. Berkeley and Los Angeles: University of California Press, 1989.

———. "The Confucian Program of Reform." In *Sources of Chinese Tradition*. 2nd ed. Vol. 1, *From Earliest Times to 1600*, edited by William Theodore de Bary and Irene Bloom, 596–7. New York: Columbia University Press, 1999.

———. "Institutional, Educational, and Moral Reform in the Song." In *Sources of Chinese Tradition*. 2nd ed. Vol. 1, *From Earliest Times to 1600*, edited by William Theodore de Bary and Irene Bloom, 590. New York: Columbia University Press, 1999.

———. *Learning for One's Self*. New York: Columbia University Press, 1991.

Dessein, Bart. "Confucianized Rationality: Some Reflections on East Asia, Wisdom, and Science." In *Contemporary East Asia and the Confucian Revival*, edited by Jana S. Rosker and Natasa Visocnik, [xxv–xxxvii]. Cambridge Scholars Publishing, 2015.

Eno, Robert. *The Confucian Creation of Heaven: Philosophy and the Defense of Ritual Mastery*. Albany, NY: State University of New York Press, 1990.

Fraser, Chris. "Major Rival Schools: Mohism and Legalism." In *The Oxford Handbook of World Philosophy*, edited by Jay L. Garfield and William Edelglass, 58-67. New York: Oxford University Press, 2011.

Gentzler, J. Mason. *Changing China: Readings in the History of China from the Opium War to the Present.* New York: Praeger Publishers, 1977.

Guangya 广雅. In *Qinding siku quanshu* 钦定四库全书 [Complete library in four sections], compiled by Zhang Yi 张揖.

Guarino, Battista. "A Program of Teaching and Learning." In *Humanist Educational Treatises*, edited and translated by Craig W. Kallendorf, 261–309. Cambridge, MA: Harvard University Press, 2002.

Hon, Tzi-ki. "Confucianism: Song (Sung)." In *Encyclopedia of Chinese Philosophy*, edited by Antonio S. Cua, 135–139. New York: Routledge, 2003.

Hoo Peih Seang 胡必相. *The Ceremonial Usages of the Chinese, B.C. 1121, as Prescribed in the "Institutes of the Chow Dynasty Strung as Pearls"* . . . Edited and translated by William Raymond Gingell. London: Smith, Elder, & Co., 1852.

Hu Meiqi 胡美琦. *Zhongguo jiaoyu shi* 中国教育史 [History of Chinese education]. Taiping: Sanmin shuju gufen youxian gongsi 三民书局股份有限公司, 1978.

Hu Wei Qing 胡卫清. "Missionaries in Modern China and their Perceptions of Confucianism (近代来华传教士的儒学观)." In *Christianity*, edited by Zhuo Xinping 卓新平, translated by Chi Zhen and Caroline Mason, 135–192. Ledien and Boston: Brill, 2013.

Huang, Yong. *Confucius: A Guide for the Perplexed.* New York: Bloomsbury Academic, 2013.

Huang Zongxi 黄宗羲. *Songyuan xuean* 宋元学案 [Cases of Pedagogy in the Song and Yuan Dynasties]. Edited by Quan

Zuwang 全祖望. Vol. 1. Zhonghua shuju 中华书局, 1982.

Hugh of Saint Victor. *The Didascalicon of Hugh of Saint Victor*. Translated by Jerome Taylor. New York: Columbia University Press, 1991.

Jaeger, Stephen C. *The Envy of Angels: Cathedral Schools and Social Ideals in Medieval Europe, 950–1200*. Philadelphia: University of Pennsylvania Press, 1994.

Jiang Guobao 蒋国保. "Han ru cheng 'liujing' wei 'liuyi' kao" 汉儒称 "六经" 为 "六艺" 考 [A study on the Han Confucian designation of the "Six Classics" as the "six arts"]. *Jiaoyu* 教育 12, no. 39 (2015): 34–40.

Jiang Minglang 蒋明郎. "Cong liuyi dao bagu—dui zhongguo gudai tiyu jiaoyu shuailuo de sikao" 从六艺到八股——对中国古代体育教育衰落的思考 [From the six arts to the eight-legged essay: reflections on the decline of ancient Chinese physical education]. *Xianyang shifan xueyuan xuebao* 咸阳师范学院学报 21, no. 6 (December 2006): 75–77.

John of Salisbury. *The Metalogicon*. Translated by Daniel D. McGarry. Philadelphia: Paul Dry Books, 2009.

Keightley, David N. "The High God (*Di*) and Other Powers." In *Sources of Chinese Tradition*. 2nd ed. Vol. 1, *From Earliest Times to 1600*, edited by William Theodore de Bary and Irene Bloom, 10–13. New York: Columbia University Press, 1999.

Kern, Martin. "Early Chinese Literature: Beginnings through Western Han." In *The Cambridge History of Chinese Litera-

ture. Vol. 1, edited by Stephen Owen, 1–114. Cambridge: Cambridge University Press, 2010.

Kim, Yung Sik. *The Natural Philosophy of Chu Hsi (1130–1200)*. The American Philosophical society, 2000.

Kirkland, Russell. "Tung Chung-shu." In *Great Thinkers of the Eastern World*, edited by Ian P. McGreal, 67–70. New York: HarperCollins, 1995.

Kirkpatrick, Andy and Zhichang Xu. *Chinese Rhetoric and Writing: An Introduction for Language Teachers*. Fort Collins, Colorado: The WAC Clearinghouse and Parlor Press, 2012.

Kuo, Ping Wen. *The Chinese System of Public Education*. Teachers College, Columbia University Contributions to Education, vol. 64. New York City: Teachers College, Columbia University, 1915.

Kuyper, Abraham. "Calvinism a Life-System." In *Lectures on Calvinism*. Grand Rapids, MI: Wm. B. Eerdmans Publishing Company, 1943.

Kwok, D. W. Y. "Lu Jia: The Natural Order and the Human Order." In *Sources of Chinese Tradition*. 2nd ed. Vol. 1, *From Earliest Times to 1600*, edited by William Theodore de Bary and Irene Bloom, 285–289. New York: Columbia University Press, 1999.

Lee, Thomas H. C. *Education in Traditional China: A History*. Boston: Brill, 2000.

———. "Sung Schools and Education Before Chu Hsi." In *Neo-confucian Education: The Formative Stage*, edited by William Theodore de Bary and John W. Chaffee, 105–136.

Berkeley and Los Angeles: University of California Press, 1989.

Legge, James. "Confucianism in Relation to Christianity." Paper, Missionary Conference, Shanghai, May 11, 1877. Accessed May 4, 2017. https://archive.org/details/confucianisminr01legggoog.

———, trans. *The Li Ki* [Record of Rites]. In *The Chinese Classics: with a Translation, Critical and Exegetical Notes, Prolegomena, and Copious Indexes, 5 vols.* Hong Kong: Legge; London: Trubner, 1861–1872. I have substituted Legge's romanizations with pinyin.

———. *The religions of China: Confucianism and Taoism described and compared with Christianity.* London: Hodder and Stoughton, 1880.

———, trans. *The She King* [Book of Poetry]. In *The Chinese Classics: with a Translation, Critical and Exegetical Notes, Prolegomena, and Copious Indexes, 5 vols.* Hong Kong: Legge; London: Trubner, 1861–1872. I have substituted Legge's romanizations with pinyin.

Lewis, C. S. *The Abolition of Man.* HarperCollins e-books, 2009. Kindle.

———. "Christianity and Culture." In *Christian Reflections*, edited by Walter Hooper, 12–36. Grand Rapids, MI: William B. Eerdmans Publishing Company, 1995.

———. *An Experiment in Criticism.* London and New York: Cambridge University Press, 1961. Kindle.

———. "The Idea of an 'English School.'" In *Image and Imagination.* HarperOne, 2014. Kindle.

————. *Miracles*. HarperCollins e-books, 2009. Kindle.

————. "On the Reading of Old Books." In *God in the Dock*. HarperOne, 2014. Kindle.

————. *The Problem of Pain*. HarperCollins e-books, 2009. Kindle.

————. *The Screwtape Letters: Annotated Edition*. HarperOne, 2013. Kindle.

————. *Surprised by Joy*. New York: Mariner Books, 2012. Kindle.

Lewis, Mark Edward. "Scholars and the State." In *The Cambridge History of Ancient China: From the Origins of Civilization to 221 B.C.*, edited by Michael Loewe and Edward L. Shaughnessy, 641–644. Cambridge: Cambridge University Press, 1999.

Li, Chenyang. "*Li* as Cultural Grammar: On the Relation between *Li* and *Ren* in Confucius' 'Analects.'" *Philosophy East and West* 57, no. 3 (2007): 311-29. Accessed May 3, 2017. http://www.jstor.org/stable/20109408.

————. *The Tao Encounters the West: Explorations in Comparative Philosophy*. Albany: State University of New York Press, 1999.

Liji zhengyi 礼记正义 [Standard meaning of the *Record of Rites*]. In *Shisanjing zhushu* 十三经注疏 [The Thirteen Classics annotated], edited by Li Xueqin 李学勤. Beijing: Beijing daxue chubanshe 北京大学出版社, 1999.

Li Yan 李俨. *Shisan shisi shiji zhongguo minjian shuxue* 十三、十四世纪中国民间数学 [Popular Chinese mathematics in the thirteenth and fourteenth centuries]. Beijing: Beijing kexue chubanshe 科学出版社, 1957.

———. *Zhong suanshi luncong* 中算史论丛 [Essays on the history of Chinese mathematics], vol. 2, in *Minguo congshu* 民国丛书 [The Republic of China Series], vol. 2, bk. 89. Shanghai: Shanghai shudian 上海书店, 1997.

Liu An 刘安. *Huainanzi* 淮南子. Translated and annotated by Cheng Guangzhong 陈广忠. Beijing: Zhonghua shuju 中华书局, 2012.

———. *The Huainanzi: A Guide to the Theory and Practice of Government in Early Han China.* Translated and edited by John S. Major, Sarah A. Queen, Andrew Seth Meyer, and Harold D. Roth. New York: Columbia University Press, 2010.

Liu Gu 陆贾. *Xinyu* 心语 [New Discourses]. Zhongguo taolve dadian 中国韬略大典 [Chinese military classics collection], edited by Gao Chao 高潮 and 甘华鸣, vol. 8. Beijing: Zhongguo guoji guangbo chubanshe 中国国际广播出版社, 1997.

Liu Xie 刘勰. *Wenxin diaolong* 文心雕龙 [*The Literary Mind and the Carving of Dragons*]. In *Wenxin diaolong* cidian [Glossary of The Literary Mind and the Carving of Dragons], edited by Zhou Zhenfu 周振甫. Beijing: Zhonghua shuju 中华书局, 1996.

———. *Wen-hsin tiao-lung.* Translated by Stephen Owen. In *Harvard-Yenching Institute Monograph Series.* Vol. 30, *Readings in Chinese Literary Thought,* by Stephen Owen, 183–298. Cambridge, MA: Harvard University Asia Center, 1992.

Liu Zhiju 柳之榘. "Xizhou guanxue 'liuyi' zhi jiao de shuailuo he kongzi sixue de jiaoyu kecheng ji yingxiang" 西周官

学"六艺"之教的衰落和孔子私学的教育课程及其影响 [The decline of six arts education in Western Zhou schools and the influence of Confucius's private curriculum]. *Anwei shifan daxue xuebao: renwen shehui kexue ban* 安徽师范大学学报：人文社会科学版 1 (1985): 67–74.

Lu Shiyi 陆世仪. *Fushe jilue* 复社纪略 [Records of the Fushe]. In *Donglin shimo* 东林始末. Shanghai: Shanghai shudian 上海书店, 1982.

Luther, Martin. "To the Christian Nobility of the German Nation Concerning the Reform of the Christian Estate, 1520," trans. Charles M. Jacobs, rev. James Atkinson. In *Luther's Works*. Vol. 44, *The Christian in Society*, ed. James Atkinson. Minneapolis: Fortress Press, 1966.

———. "To the Councilmen of All Cities in Germany that they Establish and Maintain Christian Schools." In *The Annotated Luther*. Vol. 5, *Christian Life in the World*, edited by Hans J. Hillerbrand, 235-280. Minneapolis: Fortress Press, 2017.

Martin, W. A. P. 丁韪良, *A Cycle of Cathay; or, China, South and North. With Personal Reminiscences*. 3rd ed. New York: Fleming H. Revell, 1900.

Mateer, C. W. "How May Educational Work be Made to Advance the Cause of Christianity in China." In *Records of the General Conference of the Protestant Missionaries of China, Held at Shanghai, May 7–20, 1890*, 456–457. Shanghai: American Presbyterian Mission Press, 1890.

Mencius. *Mencius*. Translated by D. C. Lau. New York: Penguin Classics, 2004.

————. *Mencius: An Online Teaching Translation*. Version 1.0. Translated by Robert Eno. Eno, 2015. Accessed May 3, 2017. http://www.indiana.edu/~p374/Mengzi.pdf.

————. *Mengzi zhushu* 孟子注疏 [Mencius annotated]. In *Shisanjing zhushu* 十三经注疏 [The Thirteen Classics annotated], edited by Li Xueqin 李学勤. Beijing: Beijing daxue chubanshe 北京大学出版社, 1999.

Meynard, Thierry. *The Jesuit Reading of Confucius: The First Complete Translation of the Lunyu (1687) Published in the West*. Leiden: Brill, 2015.

Mingshi 明史 [History of the Ming dynasty]. Zhonghua shuju 中华书局, 1974.

Mozi 墨子. *Mozi* 墨子 [Mozi]. Translated by Sun Bo 孙波. Beijing: Huaxia chubanshe 华夏出版社, 2001.

————. *Mozi* 墨子 [Mozi]. Translated by W.P. Mei. Accessed February 5, 2018. http://ctext.org/mozi/ens.

Needham, Joseph. *Science and Civilisation in China*. Vol. 2, *History of Scientific Thought*. Cambridge: Cambridge University Press, 2005.

————. *Science and Civilisation in China*. Vol. 5, *Chemistry and Chemical Technology*. Part 4, *Spagyrical Discovery and Invention: Apparatus, Theories and Gifts*. Cambridge: Cambridge University Press, 2000.

————. "Science and Society in East and West." In *The Grand Titration: Science and Society in East and West*. By Joseph Needham, 190–217. London: Allen & Unwin, 1969.

Newton, Isaac, and Robert Hooke. *Letter from Sir Isaac Newton to Robert Hooke, February 5, 1675*. Historical Society of Pennsylvania. Accessed February 4, 2018. https://digitallibrary.hsp.org/index.php/Detail/objects/9792.

Niu Mengqi 牛梦琪. "'Liu yi' jiaoyu de qiyuan yu fazhan" "六艺"教育的起源与发展 [The origin and development of six arts education]. *Dangdai jiaoyu luntan: xueke jiaoyu yanjiu* 当代教育论坛：学科教育研究 1 (2006): 42-45.

Osborn, Henry Taylor. *Medieval Series*. Vol. 1, *The Medieval Mind*. Revelation Insight Publishing Co., 2016.

Pang Yuyan 庞玉艳. "Lunyu 'wenmo' ju 'wen' yi zai kao" 《论语》"文莫"句"文"义再考 [A reflection on the meaning of wen in the wenmo sentence of the Analects]. *Sichuan waiyu xueyuan xuebao: zhexue shehui kexue ban* 四川外语学院学报：哲学社会科学版 26, no. 3 (2010): 6–9.

Parker, A. P. "The Place of the Chinese Classics in Christian Schools and Colleges." In *Records of the General Conference of the Protestant Missionaries of China, Held at Shanghai, May 7–20, 1890*, 490–496. Shanghai: American Presbyterian Mission Press, 1890.

Pines, Yuri. "Legalism in Chinese Philosophy." In *The Stanford Encyclopedia of Philosophy*. Spring 2017 edition, edited by Edward N. Zalta. Accessed May 4, 2017. https://plato.stanford.edu/archives/spr2017/entries/chinese-legalism/.

Plato. *Republic*. Translated by Robin Waterfield. New York: Oxford University Press, 2008.

Poythress, Vern S. *Redeeming Mathematics: A God-Centered Approach*. Wheaton, IL: Crossway, 2015.

Quintilian. *The Orator's Education*. Edited by Donald A. Russell. Cambridge and London: Harvard University Press, 2001.

Records of the General Conference of the Protestant Missionaries of China, Held at Shanghai, May 7–20, 1890. Shanghai: American Presbyterian Mission Press, 1890.

Ross, John 罗约翰. "Our Attitude towards Confucianism." *The Chinese Recorder and Missionary Journal*. Vol. 18 (January–February, 1887), 1–11.

Selby, Stephen. *Chinese Archery*. Hong Kong: Hong Kong University Press, 2000.

Shang Guanjian 上官剑. "'Liu yi' yu 'qiyi': zhongxifang 'ziyou xueke' suyuan zhi bijiao" "六艺"与"七艺"：中西方"自由学科"溯源之比较 [The "six arts" and the "seven arts": comparing the origins of the eastern and Western "liberal arts"]. *Gaojiao tansuo* 高教探索 4 (2010): 43–47.

Shangshu zhengyi 尚书正义 [Standard meaning of the Book of Documents]. In *Shisanjing zhushu* 十三经注疏 [The Thirteen Classics annotated], edited by Li Xueqin 李学勤. Beijing: Beijing daxue chubanshe 北京大学出版社, 1999.

Sheffield, D. Z. "The Relation of Christian Education to the Present Condition and Needs of China." In *Records of the General Conference of the Protestant Missionaries of China, Held at Shanghai, May 7–20, 1890*, 467–475. Shanghai: American Presbyterian Mission Press, 1890.

Shijing 诗经 [Book of Poetry]. Edited by Tang Songbo 唐松波. Zhonghua chuantong wenhua jingpin wenku 中华传统文化精品文库, vol. 8. Beijing: Xinhua chubanshe, 2003.

Shun, Kwong-loi. "*Ren* (仁) and *Li* (禮) in the Analects." In *Confucius and the Analects: New Essays*, edited by Bryan W. Van Norden, pp. 53–72. New York: Oxford University Press, 2002.

Song Lian 宋濂. Hongwu shengzheng ji 洪武圣政记. In *Guochao diangu* 国朝典故, 176–191. Beijing: Beijing daxue chubanshe 北京大学出版社, 1993.

Sturgeon, Donald, ed. Chinese Text Project. 2017. http://ctext.org.

Sun Peiqing 孙培青. *Zhongguo jiaoyushi* 中国教育史 [A History of Chinese Education]. 3rd ed. Shanghai: Huadong shifan daxue chubanshe 华东师范大学出版社, 2008.

Tu, Weiming. *Confucian Thought: Selfhood as Creative Transformation.* Albany: State University of New York Press, 1985.

———. "The Sung Confucian Idea of Education: A Background Understanding." In *Neo-Confucian Education: The Formative Stage*, edited by William Theodore de Bary and John W. Chaffee, 139–150. Berkeley and Los Angeles: University of California Press, 1989.

Van Norden, Bryan W., trans. *The Great Learning.* Van Norden, 2006. Accessed May 4, 2017. http://faculty.vassar.edu/brvannor/Phil210/Translations/daxuejizhu.pdf.

Wang Anshi 王安石. *Shang renzong huangdi yanshi shu* 上仁宗皇帝言事书 [A letter to Emperor Renzong]. In *Linchuan xiansheng wenji* 临川先生文集 [The collected works of Mr. Lin Chuan], 410–423. Shanghai: Zhonghua shuju Shanghai bianji suo 中华书局上海编辑所, 1959.

Wang Bingzhao 王炳照, Guo Qijia 郭齐家, Liu Dehua 刘德花, He Xiaoxia 何晓夏, and Gao Qi 高奇. *Jieming zhongguo jiaoyu shi* 解明中国教育史 [Deciphering the history of Chinese education]. Rev. ed. Beijing: Beijing shifan daxue. 北京师法大学出版社, 2001.

Wang Chang 王昶. *Jinshi cuibian* 金石萃编 [A catalogue of finest bronze and stone ink imprints], 1805. Accessed January 22, 2018. http://www.guoxuedashi.com/guji/6864m/.

Wang, Robin R. *Chinese Philosophy in an Era of Globalization.* Albany: State University of New York Press, 2004.

Wang Shizhen 王世贞. *Yanshan tang bieji* 弇山堂别集 [Collected works of the yanshan hall]. Beijing: Zhonghua shuju 中华书局, 1985.

Wang Yangming 王阳明. *Chuan xi lu quanyi* 传习录全译 [Instructions for practical living]. Edited by Yu Minxiong 于民雄 and Gu Jiu 顾久. Guizhou: Guizhou renmin chubanshe 贵州人民出版社, 1996.

———. *Instructions for Practical Living and Other Neo-Confucian Writings.* Translated by Wing-tsit Chan. New York and London: Columbia University Press, 1963.

Wilkinson, Endymion. *Chinese History: A New Manual.* 4th ed. Harvard University Asia Center, 2015.

Wu Longhui 吴龙辉. "Liuyi de bianqian ji qi yu liujing zhi guanxi" 六艺的变迁及其与六经之关系 [The evolution of the six arts and its relation to the Six Classics]. *Zhongguo Zhexue shi* 中国哲学史 2 (2005): 42–47.

Wu, Pei-yu. "Education of Children in the Sung." In *Neo-confucian Education: The Formative Stage*, edited by William Theodore de Bary and John W. Chaffee, 307–324. Berkeley and Los Angeles: University of California Press, 1989.

Xu Shen 许慎. *Shuowen jiezi* 说文解字. Beijing: Jiuzhou chuban-she 九州出版社, 2001.

Xueji 学记 [Record of Learning]. Translated by Xu Di, Yang Liuxin, Hunter McEwan, and Roger T. Ames. In *Chinese Philosophy on Teaching and Learning: Xueji in the Twenty-First Century*. Edited by Xu Di and Hunter McEwan. Albany: State University of New York Press, 2006.

Xunzi 荀子. *Xunzi* 荀子. Beijing: Zhonghua shuju 中华书局, 2011.

Yang Xiangdong 杨向东. "Liuyi zhong de yue, she, yu yu tiyu, meiyu" 六艺中的乐、射、御与体育、美育 [Music, archery, and charioteering—physical and aesthetic education in the six arts]. *Nankai xuebao: Zhexue shehui kexue ban* 南开学报：哲学社会科学版 6 (2002): 98-102.

Zhang Qiwei 张奇伟. "Li de qiyuan zhi lishi sikao" 礼的起源之历史思考 [A historical reflection on the origins of *li*]. *Shanxi shifan daxue jixu jiaoyu xuebao* 陕西师范大学继续教育学报 18, no. 3 (2001): 32-34.

Zhu Xi 朱熹. *Daxue zhangju* 大学章句 [Interlinear analysis of the Great Learning]. In *Sishu zhangju jizhu* 四书章句集注 [Interlinear Analysis of and Collected Commentaries to the Four Books]. Xinbian zhuzi jicheng 新编诸子集成, vol. 1. Beijing: Zhonghua shuju 中华书局, 1983.

———. *Daxue zhangju xu* 大学章句序 [Preface to the interlinear analysis of the Great Learning]. In *Sishu zhangju jizhu* 四书章句集注 [Interlinear Analysis of and Collected Commentaries to the Four Books]. Xinbian zhuzi jicheng 新编诸子集成, vol. 1. Beijing: Zhonghua shuju 中华书局, 1983.

————. *Huian xiansheng zhuwengong wenji* 晦庵先生朱文公文集 [Collected Works of Master Huian, Zhu Wengong]. Bk. 4. Edited by Xu Deming 徐德明 and Wang Tie 王铁. Zhuzi quanshu 朱子全书 [The complete works of Master Zhu], vol. 23. Shanghai: Shanghai guji chubanshe 上海古籍出版社; Anhui jiaoyu chubanshe 安徽教育出版社, 2002.

————. *Lunyu jizhu* 论语集注 [Interlinear analysis of the Analects]. In *Sishu zhangju jizhu* 四书章句集注 [Interlinear Analysis of and Collected Commentaries to the Four Books]. Xinbian zhuzi jicheng 新编诸子集成, vol. 1. Beijing: Zhonghua shuju 中华书局, 1983.

————. *Zhuzi yulei* 朱子语类 [Classified conversations of Master Zhu]. Vol. 6–7. Beijing: Zhonghua shuju 中华书局, 1986.

Zhu, Yongxin. *Works by Zhu Yongxin on Education: History of Chinese Ancient Educational Thought.* McGraw-Hill, 2015.

Zhouli zhushu 周礼注疏 [Rites of Zhou annotated]. In *Shisanjing zhushu* 十三经注疏 [The Thirteen Classics annotated], edited by Li Xueqin 李学勤. Beijing: Beijing daxue chubanshe 北京大学出版社, 1999.

Zuo Qiuming 左丘明. *Guoyu yizhu* 国语译注 [Discourses of the States annotated], edited by Wu Guoyi 邬国义, Hu Guowen 胡果文, and Li Xiaolu 李晓路. Zhonghua guji yizhu congshu 中华古籍译注丛书 [Commentaries on Chinese ancient texts series]. Shanghai: Shanghai guji chubanshe 上海古籍出版社, 1994.

Zuozhuan yizhu 左传译注 [The *Zuo Tradition* annotated], edited by Li Mengsheng 李梦生. Zhonghua guji yizhu congshu 中华古籍译注丛书 [Commentaries on Chinese ancient texts series]. Shanghai: Shanghai guji chubanshe 上海古籍出版社, 1998.

Made in the USA
Las Vegas, NV
19 February 2023

67789657R00205